The Case for Bitcoin

By Andrew Barisser

The Case for Bitcoin

Preface

This book is less about Bitcoin the technology as it is about Bitcoin the driver of social and economic change. The public perception of Bitcoin is profoundly muddied by half-truths, ignorance, and general myopia. Authoritative sources of information that are not also intensely technical are scarce. Scarcer still are books considering its long-range societal implications.

What is most missing in the Bitcoin literature is a non-technical approach to the societal and economic consequences of the Blockchain paradigm. Trustlessness as it pertains to society: this is the all-important topic that has not received justice.

My first and most basic goal is to expose the reader to a fair defense of Bitcoin. This has been sorely lacking. While Bitcoin has its proponents, we often appear to outsiders more as zealots than as sober, rational individuals. Our well-founded excitement has been misinterpreted as the gesticulations of cultic worshippers. I will try to explain why Bitcoin is a beautiful technology and why it matters. I will make the case for Bitcoin.

I will start with an appreciation of the technical highlights before I move on to the broader social and economic implications of Bitcoin. I will distinguish Bitcoin, the product, from the underlying Blockchain technology, its central innovation. I will spend considerable time responding to the arguments used against Bitcoin which I have collected from around the web. I shall try to do them justice.

To make the case for Bitcoin, I will compare it against the current monetary and social order. In doing so, we shall trespass into diverse and complex topics ranging from economics, to politics, to discussions of human nature. If we are to properly discuss the paradigm of Bitcoin, which carries such broad implications, we must touch upon equally many different subject areas.

At no point will I try to give a comprehensive overview of Bitcoin, nor will I describe every technical detail. It is not a primer, an overview, or a technical resource. These topics are well-covered elsewhere. And while I have assumed no prior knowledge of Bitcoin, the book does not aim for newbie-friendly simplicity. This book is for well-informed, thinking folk who are willing to be convinced. And if you are already convinced, you may enjoy my responses to the skeptics, or my musings about what the future may hold.

My singular purpose is to express my thoughts as clearly as possible. My opinions appear to be in the extreme minority, so I felt it necessary to write a book dedicated towards defending them. I am not an inborn ideologue. I list potential pitfalls and weaknesses of Bitcoin alongside its triumphs.

I felt the need to write this book because, while other books describe the How and the What of Bitcoin, seemingly none describe the Why. Many books already will tell you that you can get-rich quick, or provide thorough technical analyses, or offer simplistic introductions for beginners. This book is none of these things. I want to trigger a sophisticated discussion on the ultimate promise of Bitcoin and the meaning of a Blockchain-based future.

I first considered writing this book two years ago except I thought it was already too late. I thought that the arguments I wanted to make were already too obvious. Bitcoin was too well-understood, its potential too apparent. The counter-arguments I had heard, such as that it was a Ponzi scheme, were already demonstrably false. I thought that my views on money, government, cryptography, and privacy were too widespread to bother explaining them to anyone.

But despite the impressive works of those who came before me, I have learned that the message still has not come across. Huge segments of the population, indeed quite often well-read, intelligent people, believe in blatant mischaracterizations of Bitcoin. Insulated by my own fascination with the subject, I had underestimated the widespread lack of understanding surrounding Bitcoin. Even with all the resources out there, myths and blatant mischaracterizations abound. I kept hearing the same counter-arguments, which I felt I could rebut, if only I had a platform. I resolved to log all those moments, and to write a book to finally answer them. This is that book.

If you are a Bitcoin skeptic, this book is written foremost for you. I will wrestle with your doubts head on. If you know little or nothing of Bitcoin, I will introduce you to an amazing new paradigm. For those that are excited by Bitcoin's potential, we will revel in the full glory of still untapped possibilities. For the cautious, we will soberly weigh the real challenges facing Bitcoin. And finally, for those who are knowledgeable, and for those who are certain already that Bitcoin is doomed, I mean to challenge you directly. This book is for you.

Introduction

Bitcoin is a revolutionary new system of currency invented in 2009 by the still-mysterious pseudonym: Satoshi Nakamoto. It was a creation of such staggering genius that, from its beginnings as an arcane computer science project, it exploded into a widely used, paradigm changing system used across the world: all in the space of 6 years. But while Bitcoin is, from a technical standpoint, a magnificent creation, commercially and in the public consciousness it is very much still in its infancy.

However new and small, the Bitcoin system matters a great deal. It is no longer merely a hacker's novelty. It is a system that is growing by leaps and bounds. It is a new kind of force on the world's stage. Though they do not know it yet, fiat currencies have been rendered obsolete by an upstart newcomer. While not nearly so venerable, at its core Bitcoin is better at being currency than traditional currency is. This and this alone is what has catapulted a hacker's creation into a valuation worth billions of dollars, on the tip of every geek's tongue, and drawing the attention of powerful and disparate governments.

Bitcoin is something you should know about. As it grows, it will play a larger role on the world's stage until, conceivably, it is a major fixture in finance. You do not want to be caught off-guard. You want to understand, if even cursorily, the nature of this impending force. Moreover, a savvy investor might position himself, in multitudinous ways, in anticipation of the new opportunities afforded by Bitcoin. Thus, from a purely self-interested point of view, you should read this book.

Bitcoin the technology is compelling, at the very least, on grounds of elegance. I want you to be in a position to admire the brilliance of its initial formulation, to realize the fundamental advantages of its design that make it both efficacious and distinctive. You ought to know about Bitcoin because it is so ingenious. Every Bitcoiner has had a special moment when it all suddenly clicks and the vast latent power of the Blockchain is made manifest. I want you to feel that same magic.

Above all, Bitcoin has been widely and unfairly disparaged in the media. As a parvenu in the old club of currencies, with no powerful allies and little punching weight, it is an easy target. Many criticisms levelled against Bitcoin are plainly false. Others are less obviously wrong and require more nuanced counter-arguments. For this reason, Bitcoin desperately needs a book where such arguments can be spelled out at greater length. This is that book. You need to read this book because you probably have never given Bitcoin its fighting chance; you need to hear its side of the story.

Currency as Anecdote

Currency has always been a bizarre thing. Its job is so abstract. Its physical embodiment is so seemingly arbitrary. And whereas now it may seem like an edifice of society, carefully shepherded by its own specialists, in our long and twisted history it has come in many disparate forms. Taking a quick glance at its spectacular history gives us perspective over the precarious nature of currency: the risks, the pitfalls, and the purpose.

Sound Wampum and Dutch Perfidy

Those of Indo-European heritage may be used to the value of shiny things; but this is a hopeless cultural quirk. In the 1600's the North Eastern Native Americans used wampum, black and white shells, as money. Wampum was labor intensive to produce and therefore scarce. As shells and thus coming from the sea, one might stop to wonder whether it was the coastal natives who first propounded such a system. In any case, when the Europeans arrived they found that the natives respected these shells as real money. Encountering the natives in the early 1600s, a Dutch missionary wrote that "Their money consists of certain little bones [wampum], mode of shells or cockles... They value these little bones as highly as many Christians do gold, silver, or pearls; but they do not like our money, and esteem it no better than iron"[i].

While European colonists had no intrinsic interest in wampum, they had an avaricious demand for fur pelts. These they could obtain from the Native Americans in exchange for wampum. Wampum was "*the magnet which drew the beaver out of the interior forests.*"[ii] Since the colonial economy in those early days centered around the fur trade, wampum became indispensable. It was actively used in early colonial New England. It was even formally declared a legitimate colonial currency with fixed exchange rates for European money based on color and quality. We may imagine our Pilgrim forefathers carefully managing their wampum assets with self-aware incredulity.

From the beginning there were challenges in standardization. Managing the heterogeneity of different wampum beads was an intractable problem; attaching prices in pounds and shillings to different colored beads was challenging enough. The problem posed by the diversity of wampum was an indicator, in hindsight, as to what would constitute effective money.

The old status quo of the Wampum supply was violently upset through contact with European technology. Metal drills from Europe greatly accelerated the production of wampum, which hitherto had been a highly labor intensive process. The Dutch even established specialized wampum factories where it could be mass produced. Instead of selling imported European goods in exchange for wampum, and hence furs, one could short circuit the entire process by simply producing wampum itself. What better way is there to make money than to fabricate it?

We can only empathize with thrifty Iroquois who, having fastidiously set aside his hard-earned wampum for so many years, found himself swamped by indistinguishable Dutch knock-offs. It was a cruel trick. The Dutch sent the real value of wampum plummeting. One can imagine the windfall of furs they achieved before the wampum market became saturated. In a sense they had stolen from those thrifty Iroquois who had saved. As wampum had little intrinsic value besides as currency, Dutch mass manufacture of it represented a total waste of resources: workshops devoted to making an excess of something no one really wanted, besides as money. And that final purpose they destroyed utterly. Soon wampum was no longer currency but merely a native novelty. Thank the Dutch.

The recalcitrant reader will dismiss the story of wampum as merely the downfall of a primitive currency: one not fit to complete on the world's stage. But the next story concerns the archetypal European favorite: gold. And it follows not the plight of the vanquished, but that of the conqueror.

When Money is Ruinous

The Spanish conquest of the New World is well known for its enormous historical significance. It made Spain a global empire. It fueled its war-machine. The trauma and genocide inflicted on the native civilizations were horrific, indeed, without comparison in modern history. And it is well-known that Spain acquired vast riches as a result of its conquests in gold and silver. These were, indeed, largely the motives for the rapine slaughter. Religious or territorial aggrandizement were very much secondary to the primary aim of acquiring wealth.

Vast quantities of gold and silver were taken with indiscriminate violence. When the Incan Emperor Atahualpa was taken prisoner in 1532 by Francisco Pizarro, an enormous ransom was demanded. Gold and silver were to fill an entire room from floor to ceiling. Treasures from all over the Incan Empire were sent to fill this room. It has been estimated that a staggering 13,000 pounds of gold were delivered there. Amazingly, soon the room was filled. Fearful of releasing him, the Spanish forcibly baptized and murdered Atahualpa. He was the last Incan Emperor.

Huge new sources of silver were found, in addition to those of gold. When an enormous silver vein was discovered in modern day Bolivia, an entire city sprouted up to feed off of it. Potosi became, in a very short time, one of the biggest cities in the world. Vast quantities of silver were produced. The Spanish royal treasury was greatly enriched. Spanish silver flowed throughout Europe, throughout the entire world. The influx of money was like a boulder dropped in a pond; the financial waves echoed and reflected in every distant nook.

So great was the Spanish influence on money that Spanish silver coins became de facto currency almost everywhere. In the English American colonies Spanish pieces of eight were widely used. They would be legal tender in the US as late as 1857. Indeed, the US dollar was inspired by the Spanish Dollar. Because it was standardized and so widespread as to be pervasive, the Spanish Dollar was the first globally recognized currency. By their control over mineral resources in the New World, the Spanish had their hand on the lever of the world's supply of currency. And they opened the spigot.

The sums of newfound silver and gold were so enormous as to dramatically increase the entire world's monetary supply [iii]. Prices rose dramatically. In Europe, consumer commodities such as wheat and textiles suddenly cost a lot more as denominated in silver. The effects were far-reaching. In faraway China, a nearly insatiable demand for silver drew currency ever eastward. Europeans finally had something with which to buy Chinese goods (the Chinese were little interested in European manufactures).

Spain used its new wealth to reach a pinnacle of power in Europe. They decisively defeated the French in Italy where they would dominate for centuries. In the Low Countries and in Germany, Habsburg power was supreme. Spain and Austria, in dynastic union, were the superpower of the Christian world. In practically every court, Spanish power had to be considered; in many, it was feared. It was all largely paid for in gold and silver from the New World[iv].

But in swallowing such vast lands, people, and wealth, the Spanish swallowed poison. And for all their misdeeds in the New World, all the stolen gold would only sap their strength at home. It did not appear obvious at first. The prevailing view at the time was that gold, symbol of wealth, quite simply represented the prosperity of the nation. The more a country had, the richer it was! Perfectly obvious, right? In fact it was disastrously wrong.

As treasure arrived in Spain, so too was it spent, and more so. Paradoxically for the country that largely controlled the world's monetary supply, the Spanish Crown was constantly going into debt. The influx of precious metals, however vast, was simply never enough. But the government could always issue more debt by promising later payment with future arrivals of the Treasure Fleet. Ill-advisedly, the monarchy over-reached itself, taking on too many foes in too many wars. The economic results were catastrophic. The Spanish Crown went bankrupt four times in the 16th century (1557, 1560, 1576, 1596). Many banking families were ruined: the Renaissance equivalent of modern bank failures. By the 17th century, despite its continued, unique access to large sums of precious metals, Spain was in an economic decline that would last for centuries. What had gone wrong?

The nature of Spain's acquisitions proved its undoing. Wealth, it turns out, cannot be taken so easily. As Spain acquired so much gold and silver, these commodities displaced conventional goods, such as wine, as exports. Making things and selling them to foreigners became unnecessary. Why bother when foreign goods could simply be purchased very cheaply with New World silver? Put another way, foreign goods became cheap and Spanish goods unattractive as exports. Instead, precious metals became the main export. Spain became an exporter, not of goods, but of money itself.

The Spanish economy suffered from what is today known as Dutch Disease, in which a country has an attractive natural resource that dominates that country's export market, driving up prices for other goods, thereby making all other goods unattractive to foreigners. In this way a single commodity, like oil, can suppress demand for other kinds of exports. For example, Saudi Arabia is in no hurry to establish textile mills, because they can buy enough foreign imports from their oil money. Turkey, by contrast, has no oil and is in a hurry to build textile mills, export shirts, and buy foreign goods with the proceeds. Spain in the 16th and 17th centuries suffered from crippling Dutch Disease. Traditional elements of the Spanish economy stagnated as gold and silver took central stage. As a visiting Frenchman put it in 1603, "Everything is dear in Spain except silver.'"

Uniquely, Spain's main export was money itself. This was the worst kind of Dutch Disease. While oil is burnt and more is always needed, silver continued to circulate. It served a purpose as currency, but more of it was not necessarily better. As Spain steadily pumped the world full of American silver, the real value of that silver declined significantly. It could buy less and less. Their main export was something that inherently devalued itself. In exporting so much precious metal, the Spanish were shooting themselves in the foot. At the same time, Dutch disease killed off other kinds of export by disincentivizing them at home. This was a vicious cycle that reduced Spain to penury. Soon American silver would not be enough. Over time Spain became a second-class power, then a third-rate power, and economically quite backwards.

The example of the Dutch, ever present in these stories, serves as a brilliant contrast. Once under Spanish rule, they rebelled and fought a war called the Eighty Years' War. This war more than any other broke Spanish power. The Netherlands, a small country, not only managed to stave off the entire might of the Spanish Empire, but they wrought havoc on Spanish possessions throughout the world. In 1621 a Dutch admiral captured the entire Spanish Treasure Fleet. When he brought the vast riches back to Amsterdam, the wealth paid for the entire Dutch Army, then in full-fledged battle, for almost a year. The Dutch seized Spanish and Portuguese possessions around the globe, in the Indian Ocean, in the Caribbean, and in Africa. They even occupied Brazil and tried to attack the Philippines. The Spanish kept pouring money into mercenary armies. But they could never quite subdue that redoubtable little province. It gave them endless headache.

The Dutch were traders. They built Amsterdam into the commercial capital of the world after the Spanish foolishly exiled the Protestants of Brussels. They had no natural resources. They did work, shipping goods, breaking down trade barriers, helping to rectify the massive trade imbalances that existed. They invented new financial instruments like the Stock Exchange. All of this was tangible and highly innovative. And while Spain went into decline, the Netherlands prospered, punching far above its weight internationally for the next two centuries.

What is the lesson from this real-life parable? The Spanish, in acquiring so much precious gold and silver, were briefly enriched but ultimately doomed. Money is not an export. Money does a job in facilitating exchange. But beyond that it has no value; it is a symbol. Goods and services have value. Spain came to rely on exporting the symbol of value rather than value itself. This created perverse incentives, discouraging traditional industries, empowering those in control of the (governmentally centralized) shipment of bullion, and aggravating social stratification. The contrast with the Netherlands, a country with no resources, only daring and entrepreneurialism, could not be clearer. The Spanish reliance on gold and silver, on money, instead of goods and services, sowed the seeds of its decline.

The Features of Currency

As we consider the merits of Bitcoin, we would be well served to distance ourselves from contemporary assumptions about what currency is. The historical examples of wampum and gold should, at the very least, highlight the tumultuous nature of currency over long timescales.

Currency stands in lieu of real value. It is a way of reducing a wildly diverse world, full of so many different goods and assets, into a single metric. If you consider this feat objectively it seems implausible. How can Irish potatoes, Miami beach-front property, and African tailoring all be convertible into a single entity? How does it make sense to convert one into another when they are so different?

In fact, it doesn't make sense. Potatoes cannot be transformed into Ferraris. But the demand for potatoes can be counterbalanced by that for Ferraris. In this way, when I speak of value, what I really mean is the psychology of value. Currency represents the psychological sum of people's desire embedded, however ephemerally, in a certain object or service. Because value is purely psychological, not scientific or mathematically foreordained, its fluctuations are endless and paradoxical. Enter the countless traders who mediate this non-equilibrium process.

While many things have value, few may serve as an effective currency. There must be special properties to currency beyond value. Let us start with a form of money that is plainly wrong and ask why. We may consider a system of money based on Ferrari sports cars. Could we use Ferraris as currency? I could buy a sandwich with 0.2 mFerrari (milliFerrari)! What would be wrong with such a system? While it may seem ludicrous, let us examine exactly why it is ludicrous in order to elucidate the ideal properties of currency beyond mere utilitarian value. In what ways do Ferraris fail as currency?

Standardization

Currency must be standardized. This is absolutely essential. If we used Ferrari as currency, how would one value red Ferrari versus black Ferrari? How would 2003 Ferraris compare with 1995 Ferrari coupes? Little variations between models, colors, etc., would add uncertainty and risk to their exchange. Buying my sandwich for 0.2 mFerrari, the deli-owner might insist on payment in black Ferrari units. If I only had red, we would have to look up the current rate of exchange between black and red. In effect, we would have a separate currency for each little variation in Ferrari.

Historically, heterogeneity in physical money was a constant headache. There were innumerable little currencies exchanged (with Spanish silver, as we have seen, predominating). There were German Thalers, French Louis d'or, English pounds, and many more. Not only were there many national currencies, but the metal content in each coin could vary from year to year, or even coin to coin! There was a great deal of uncertainty involved with accepting money of any kind because of the wide variations between coins. Whole industries sprang up specializing in the trading of different currencies. With such a complex, arcane, and non-standardized system of currency, taking on any currency was itself a risky proposition. These transactional costs doubtless stifled exchange and economic opportunities.

We may draw several lessons. Uncertainty is anathema to exchange. It introduces friction to a process that should be seamless. Currency's job is specifically to mitigate exchange uncertainty. In doing so, an effective currency removes a main barrier to trade.

Standardization is crucial because, when I possess currency, I want to know exactly what I have. If my German 1492 Thalers didn't quite have the silver content of the 1513 variety, this is a complication and a headache that only makes me want to quit business entirely. Similarly, if my Ferrari currency represents the 1992 model, slightly different from the 2007 model represented by someone else's money, I don't know exactly what my money means anymore. Standardization means I know what I'm getting. This is a crucial aspect of effective currency.

Ease of Movement

An effective currency needs to be easy to move. Since we must often perform exchange with distant parties, the speed and security of long distance transmission are essential. If I bought flowers from a florist and promised him 0.1 milliFerrari three years from now, he would be understandably disappointed. He cannot be expected to wait and to endure all the risk in the meantime with no appreciation. Time itself is a key source of uncertainty; a Ferrari now is worth more than one later. Who knows what will happen to the Ferrari market in the future? Since currency's job is to mitigate exchange risk, it must get to its recipient quickly. While currency is in transit, the recipient has no options, and cannot respond to new threats or opportunities. Currency must be quick.

Currency must also be light. In our globalized world, trade flows move massive amounts of money at very high speeds across international borders. For currency to be effective, the burden of physical transport should be minimal.

Before the advent of paper money, the shipment of precious metals was a major problem. Silver and gold are heavy; the roads were poor and dangerous. There were considerable risks involved with moving money even short distances. Gradually an ad hoc system of paper money arose in which bills of exchange represented objects at a particular place. Instead of repeatedly shuffling physical assets back and forth, objects could be **abstracted** away as paper and exchanged more easily. Gold in England could be represented by a certificate in Italy; the real value of that certificate varying with the difficulty of drawing upon it. Generally bills of exchange declined in value the farther they were from their source, when nations were at war, or facing any other uncertainty. Bills of exchange were the historical forerunners of modern paper money, checks, and other financial instruments. They went a long way towards making currency faster and lighter. But as can be imagined, bills of exchange did not fully solve the problem. Long term currency flows could not be represented as paper indefinitely. Sooner or later, actual gold had to be shipped to represent movements of money. To this day, gold held in reserve is occasionally moved between bank vaults, with considerable difficulty.

Longevity

Currency is a vehicle for exchange. But it is also a medium for storing value over time. Someone who holds currency should not be forced to exchange it immediately for a real good. He should have the right to hold it for some time, to save, to wait and see. Indeed, if currency cannot be held for any length of time, why would anyone accept it? It would become a liability. Currency must last.

Historically coins suffered throughout the course of their individual lifetimes. Modern coins are merely representative. But previously coins held value in their constituent precious metals. Renaissance fraudsters used to clip the edges off of large numbers of coins before recirculating them. This way they could accumulate a sizeable amount of gold or silver as profit. In doing so, they progressively degraded the quality of the remaining currency. Some coins were in such bad shape as to be unusable; the currency itself had a half-life. Mints introduced the ridged edges found on modern coins to combat this practice. The ridges would be marred by any clipping, making it hard for the malefactor to pass the diminished coin on unnoticed.

In modern times, physical currency still has a half-life; bills fall apart and coins are worn away. But since they are purely representative, they may be reissued at trivial cost. We generally don't notice the physical degradation of our money anymore.

Ferrari-money would not work well because Ferraris don't last forever. Sadly, they rust and they fall apart. In fact, Ferraris decline precipitously in value. Money backed by something in a constant state of decay would be disastrous. Everyone would try to foist that money on the next person to rid themselves of exposure. This ephemerality would itself become a liability: precisely the sort of exchange risk that currency is supposed to avoid.

Stability

Stability is a paramount prerequisite of money. The risks of holding currency over time should be minimized as much as possible. When the risks of holding currency are low, people will be more willing to receive it and devise a way to spend it later. If the risks are high, there is an impetus to spend immediately on what may not be an opportune investment. Or if the risks are extreme enough, there may be a disinclination to accept currency at all. These are barriers to exchange which needlessly disqualify otherwise worthy trades. When the vagaries of money interfere with economic behavior, then currency itself has failed.

Divisibility

Currency ought to be divisible to small enough units to accommodate the smallest conceivable transactions. Transacting money should be a seamless process; problems of granularity, in which currency cannot be easily subdivided, should be avoided at all costs. If the minimum currency denomination is too large, certain goods and services cannot be easily transacted. Rounding errors, inevitable in any currency regime, become more significant for large minimum units of account. These are headaches that currency ought to avoid. The ideal currency is fine-grained; it is highly divisible.

Ferrari Money would not be easily divisible. While paper representations of Ferraris could be subdivided (but then, to what extent?), the underlying asset cannot be subdivided. Half a Ferrari is worth nothing. Anything less than a full Ferrari is worth nothing. As a result, if we used paper money representing Ferraris, we would constantly be plagued by small leftover amounts. If I bought a milk shake for 0.0001 Ferraris, unless the other party can assemble 1 full Ferrari, their money cannot be redeemed. Complicated mechanisms could probably get around this, but it's not a problem we want to have.

We have seen that a currency based on Ferraris would be disastrous. They would be incredibly difficult to shuttle around the world. They would be extremely coarse-grained, with large, annoying, leftover sums everywhere. Ferrari-Money would be extremely heterogeneous, causing us to constantly wonder whether it is redeemable for the black 1995 model or the defective red 2003. The Ferraris themselves would decay in real value over time. Worst of all, a single party would control the entire world monetary supply. It would be devilishly tempting for them to simply create more. Anyone accepting this monstrous currency would be subjecting himself to a huge amount of risk and inconvenience.

You may not be surprised that Ferraris don't fare well. Fair enough: maybe it was obvious. But at least now we know what we're looking for. But how does a modern currency compare when judged by these criteria?

The US Dollar

Standardization

Today the dollar is highly standardized. There is no question of different variants of dollars. Whether you have a single dollar bill, or a dollar coin, or even a silver dollar from the 1800's, everyone is in agreement that it is a legitimate dollar and completely fungible. This is greatly facilitated by the fact that the value of dollars is purely symbolic. With no silver or gold content, we need not quibble over the precise fraction of metals composing our coin. By virtue of the government's will, a dollar is a dollar is a dollar.

This was not always so. During the Civil War the US issued paper money called Greenbacks representing gold. However they would not be redeemable for gold until some later point in time. This paradox was inspired by the government's simple inability to fund its activities by conventional methods. Although the government claimed these dollars would, in the future, be redeemable for gold at the normal ratio, uncertainty in the government's ability to fulfill its promises led to speculation. Whereas the government pretended a Greenback was worth $1 in gold coin, the real price (i.e. the price free parties chose to accept) was governed by the perceived probability of a Union victory. With victory Greenbacks drew closer to a 1:1 ratio with gold; with defeat they plummeted in value.

The government was paying soldiers, businesses, and people supporting the war effort, in invented money that no one really accepted on the government's terms. An old fashioned gold dollar could in practice always buy more than a Greenback. Crucially, the US government explicitly disallowed the payment of government interest in Greenbacks. They would be paid in gold. Anything less may have set a scare among foreign holders of American debt; they could not be fobbed off with invented money. US citizens with no recourse were less lucky. Interestingly, the South also printed paper money which also suffered from extensive uncertainty. In fact, Confederate money, backed by even less gold and less chance of victory, went through extreme fluctuations in value before finally settling at zero with final defeat.

The presence of Greenbacks coexisting with gold money in circulation created, in effect, two currencies in one country. With the real price always in a state of flux, it must have been a major headache having to calculate the value of Greenbacks at any particular moment before engaging in a transaction. From New York merchants down to lowly frontier shopkeepers, anyone doing business needed to stay current on the exchange rate between gold and greenbacks. Someone buying supplies in gold and selling them for Greenbacks needed to be aware of events on the front-lines. Did the Union score a victory yesterday? How will that affect gold prices? Was there a diplomatic crisis with Britain? How will that affect gold prices? It is not reasonable for regular people to have to worry about currency fluctuations within their own country. The added uncertainty of the fate of Greenbacks added exchange risk: precisely what currency is supposed to mitigate.

Longevity

Physical dollars are manufactured to very high standards. Defective money is practically unheard of. Even as the currency suffers wear and tear, old bills and coins are fully replaceable by the US treasury. This eases any anxiety for users that their physical money, if in a dilapidated state, will lose value.

If the question of physical longevity seems irrelevant, consider certain countries in the Third World. In Guinea-Conakry and Cameroon, for instance, (where the author served as a Peace Corps Volunteer) the physical currency is in very poor condition. Many bills are simply falling apart. Most are made to very low production standards. As a result, people prefer certain kinds of bills over others, introducing obstacles to transactions and risks for holders of the currency. Since the smaller denominations are always falling apart, getting precise change to settle transactions is often a major challenge. That we in America are blithely unaware of these difficulties speaks to the physical quality of the dollar.

Money as Data

A common thread throughout all representations of currency is that it is a *data layer*. Every representation we have seen served a primary purpose as an *informational unit*. Getting hung up on the physical qualities of the medium is a mistake. Even primitive economies need to keep track of value. As Elon Musk put it, "Money is just a number in a database." When gold, paper bills, or Wampum beads are exchanged, what really occurs is an *informational change of state*. Databases are being edited.

The earlier incarnations of money accomplished the same informational purpose as modern money in electronic databases. But without a consensus mechanism, even a centralized one, our predecessors had to resort to the physical scarcity of certain materials to establish incontrovertible consensus. In an uncertain world, gold in hand was the highest form of certainty.

Tally sticks exemplified the need for informational consensus, even in medieval times. Invented thousands of years ago, a stick or bone would have a debt written on each end. It would then be snapped in two. The unique nature of each fracture meant that only the correct ends, coming from the same stick, would ever match. It was the ancient equivalent of a cryptographic signature. The shorter end would be held by the debtor, the longer end by the creditor. If either party tampered with the recorded debts on their half, it would become apparent by inspecting the other piece. Debts could be recorded, in a surprisingly secure way. It was actually quite brilliant and remained in use even into the 1800's. English banks were once stuffed full of tally stick fragments to record debts. They could themselves be traded below par based on the creditworthiness of the debtor, like modern bonds. Although each stick itself was physically worthless, the debt it represented, *as a secure informational unit*, had real value.

Modern money, which is predominantly electronic, further exemplifies the data-based nature of currency. When the Federal Reserve is said to 'print money', the bulk of the invented money is merely credited electronically. Just as one does not worry about the type of computer running a bank's database, or the particular kind of wood composing an ancient tally stick, the physical implementation of money matters far less than its nature as information.

It is in this sense that tinkering with money-as-information is particularly pernicious. The government is a user with admin-level access to the monetary database. That's all it is. Normal transactions, the kind you and I engage in, are edits to a vast database on which we have limited rights. We are peer users with guest privileges. Monetary policy and taxation are sweeping database overhauls by users with root access. When one thinks about money and monetary policy along these lines, not as a physical object but as root level interference in an informational system, government's privileged access seems all the more disturbing. We shall discuss this in greater detail later on.

Money as data is the common thread linking all forms of currency throughout history. Paper and electronic money are transparently informational. But even utilitarian goods, when used as currency, tend to act as symbolic representations of value, above and beyond their original practical purpose. Salt, cows, and cigarettes have all served as currency. As money, the practical component is dispensable, while the informational one is not. Electronic money is just a purer version of the informational role played by utilitarian, commodity-based money. Money can be useful, edible, or shiny, but it doesn't have to be. But it must reliably carry information.

Bitcoin is Born

What is Bitcoin

At the highest level, Bitcoin is programmable money. It is the first truly scarce digital asset. It is both purely informational and tightly conserved. Bitcoin exists on software run by thousands of peers on a decentralized network. It is a system emphasizing governance by reliable protocol rules, and not men. These rules are transparent and symmetrical between all participants. As a system with no center, no one is in charge. It is the first, most successful decentralized entity. It is a network, a dynamic swarm composed of millions of people whose expression is utterly unhindered.

Bitcoins exist, and are agreed to exist, and yet they are utterly ethereal. They are pure information existing within rigidly defined mathematical rules. Bitcoins are abstractions and *only* abstractions. This is not weakness but strength; it strikes to the very heart of what currency ought to be.

Bitcoin is an open source project. Anyone may contribute and nothing about it is secret. All of the code is visible. And yet the system remains intensely secure from outside attack. To achieve this, Bitcoin employs the latest cryptographic techniques.

Finally, Bitcoin is programmatic, digital money befitting the Internet age. It is safer money because it cannot be inflated or confiscated. It is easier to send, transact, and verify than traditional money. It is a well-tuned machine running with incredible efficacy. It is money for savers, for the underbanked, and for machines themselves.

Bitcoin is an experiment: the first foray towards a momentous new paradigm. It poses the question, 'can a decentralized system thrive on its own?' In the earliest days the expectations were suitably low. But the rapid growth of Bitcoin suggested that perhaps something important had been found, and that the answer to the experiment's question would be a resounding 'Yes'. So while Bitcoin is money, and it is a peer-to-peer network, it is a flag-bearer for a new structure of human institutions, a new leitmotif for our times: a decentralized era.

Lingua Bitcoinica

The headlines portray Bitcoin as just another form of money. But this is seeing only a small part of the picture. Bitcoin is a way of achieving universal agreement on information held in common. It is a network of peers following clear rules to achieve consensus. Many clients, run from anywhere by anyone, establish mathematically sound agreement, even in the presence of liars and cheaters. It just so happens that for Bitcoin, this power of consensus is used to represent money.

First and foremost, Bitcoin is a protocol: a set of rules for how to read and write so as to be recognized as legitimate by others. The rules are written in such a way that cheaters, liars, and malevolent spirits cannot pass false information. If they attempt it, honest peers, following straightforward mechanical rules, can always identify illegitimate acts.

Where is Bitcoin? It is nowhere. The same question might be asked for SMTP, the email protocol, or the English language itself. Who controls the English language? Where does it dwell? No one, nowhere, of course. It exists only in our minds. Bitcoin is like a language, except that all the speakers are strict grammar Nazis. It's as if you attended a Grammarians' Convention and, speaking in slang and dropping your R's, everyone ignored you completely. You could always leave, of course, and be understood elsewhere. But to be understood by Grammarians you would have to speak precisely within the constraints set by them.

Because of its unique brilliance, Bitcoin is internally consistent and mathematically sound such that every player is satisfied with its perfect rectitude. Unlike the English Language, in which it is possible to speak untruths, in the Bitcoin Language falsehoods are grammatically forbidden. It is as if you attended the Grammarians' Convention and found that, by some strange laws of the universe, you could not be heard telling a lie. Only truthful statements could be heard by your peers. Falsehoods, no matter how clever, could be conceived in your mind, but not spoken among those present. You might as well be speaking in the slang Grammarians also refuse to hear.

What then is spoken in the language of Bitcoin? The Bitcoin protocol details the movements of bitcoins, the currency, between their owners. Because of the strong consistency and cryptographic security of Bitcoin, it is only possible to speak transactions that are properly owned by the speaker. I may tell you about the time Peter sent Jacob 2 bitcoins (henceforth abbreviated as BTC). I may repeat the words Peter spoke when he sent his bitcoins. But I may not conceive of Peter's words on my own. I can only write transactions that are mine to write. I can only spend bitcoins that are mine to spend. It is trivial for me to hear Peter's transaction and to see that it is legitimate. Each Bitcoin node is a stand-alone Grammar Nazi. Each peer is very good at recognizing whether what the others have spoken is legitimate. But while verifying legitimacy is easy, conceiving fraudulent transactions is impossible. The only grammatically valid transactions that can be written are those one is entitled to make.

If Bitcoin's transactions are its spoken language, the Blockchain is its written history. The Blockchain is the core innovation in Bitcoin. It is the magic nugget in the center. The Blockchain is the record of every Bitcoin transaction ever to have taken place. It enumerates every single instance in which bitcoins have moved from A to B. It takes transactions, written in the correct grammar of Bitcoin, and inscribed them in a long history. By reading the

Blockchain, you can always know the state of the Bitcoin network. You can determine which address possesses how much bitcoin. You can always know when and how much bitcoin was moved in a given transaction. Indeed this is required to gain a picture of the network.

The Blockchain's purpose is to enumerate all Bitcoin transactions, so that any peer can know who owns what where, because he has reconstructed the state of the entire network from foolproof data. Do I own what I think I own? Does this guy sending me money actually possess the money he claims to possess? Did Alice pay Bob? These are the questions that the Blockchain answers. But it is special, because the data has been arranged in such a way that, by looking at it, the client program *knows it is legitimate without asking any higher authority*. Crucially, all records exist in airtight isolation and *had to be the way they are*. In this way, independently verifiable consensus is established. We will unwind this mystery in a later section.

Bitcoin has garnered so much attention because it is both a language and a conserved system. Like the spoken word, it is ungovernable, uncoerced, and robust. It is not administered by anyone, and yet it works. But like the machinations of an internal database, it maintains internally consistent records, even as it is reverberates among countless actors. The absolutism of knowledge in cryptography has been married to language itself. This is a portentous new mode of speaking in which many important matters will be settled.

Bitcoin Addresses

Bitcoins are held by public addresses. A Bitcoin address is a string, appearing as random, illegible characters (known as ciphertext) and obeying certain formatting rules, that 'holds' bitcoins. *18wk94mvPaSDAk7NHgECYRjyf-ExvJCK8YD* is an example of a public address. At any time one can always ask, "How much Bitcoin does a given address have?" For example, as of this writing this address *1EpqtDEYwDMxsNDKQbBjRr7uCUsF2U1T4N* has *exactly* 198.45619757 BTC. I don't know who controls this address. I certainly don't control it. You probably don't either. But whoever does can spend these ~198 BTC at any time. It is publicly recognizable that they are his to spend. Every single Bitcoin address can be inspected in this way at any time and over its entire history. Looking at this particular address, I can see that it has been involved with many transactions, including every date, amount, addresses, and every other detail.

In a sense, Bitcoin addresses are like clear, transparent mailboxes, except there are trillions upon trillions of them. One can peer into any mailbox at any time and confirm its contents. But only the owner has the key to access any particular box. All an owner can do is order bitcoins to be moved from his box to another box. He can never take bitcoins out of the system, only send them to other boxes. Since anyone can inspect any box, everyone agrees on the state of Bitcoin.

If I can see inside the address *1EpqtDEYwDMxs-NDKQbBjRr7uCUsF2U1T4N,* why then can I not take its 198 BTC? This is a large amount of money. Why can't I claim to control this address? After all, all the protocol rules are public knowledge. It's all just data, not fortified bank vaults. Can't I reverse engineer a way to pretend to be the owner? If we are only dealing with information and freely available, open source code, what does the legitimate owner of this address have that I don't?

The answer is one of the unsung miracles of our times: asymmetric cryptography. The owner of *1EpqtDEYwDMxsNDKQbBjRr7uCUsF2U1T4N* has a private key controlling that address. A private key is another long, seemingly random string of ciphertext. For example, *5JX-6aNHDXgt32dV85hNnZRqRfUfCtvdZcmQJy1AwSNKVG8nroyy* is a private key. Each private key in Bitcoin corresponds deterministically to a public address. For instance, private key: *5JX6aNHDXgt32dV85hNnZRqRfUfCtvdZcmQJy1AwSNKVG8nroyy* always maps to public address: *1DBjSwnsy5PFPDVuZU2E2cTexYJFSR8x6H*. There is no randomness; it works every time.

Private keys play a large role in cryptography predating Bitcoin. But as they pertain to Bitcoin, it suffices to know that a private key is sensitive data that *controls* a public address (and any bitcoins it contains). For instance, the address *1i7cZdoE9NcHSdAL5eGjmTJbBVqeQDwgw* is known to possess greater than $47,000,000 dollars' worth of Bitcoin as of this writing. That's public knowledge. But the private key I would need to unlock its 144,000 BTC is unknown. I simply don't know what it is. I also don't know how to go backwards from the publicly visible address. Even though I can always go from private key to public address, no one knows how to start with a public address and go backwards to the private key. Nobody has ever figured it out, *even though every step of the forward operation is deterministic, non-random, and explicitly known.* If I did have the private key, I could take the whole fortune right now. It would be so easy. But I can't.

As an example, what is the private key for *1C3fr43X8u7J5sA2ZkJUpw8VqpuywbdPNv*? No one on Earth can tell you; even the US government cannot know. No one can go backwards. Happily, this is just an example, so I can show that: *5J4MHeG4GKRfHjeNFoK7XcJuY-xMihFzxXEXEABtBVfjDAEejsqh* is the private key which always leads to *1C3fr43X8u7J5sA2ZkJUpw8VqpuywbdPNv*. I only know this because I started with the private key, then computed the public address. I chose the former randomly. But you could prove that they are linked at any time. Notice that the private key, *5J4MHeG4GKRfHjeNFoK7XcJu-YxMihFzxXEXEABtBVfjDAEejsqh*, is such a long string of gibberish that you could never, ever have simply guessed it. A single permutation from the current value would lead to a totally different outcome. But now that I have shown you the private key you control that address, as do I and many others. Since you control the mathematically corresponding key, you can move bitcoins out of this address at any time.

In practice, this particular address is not safe; it is completely compromised because its private key has been exposed. I could send money to the public address. Without a doubt, within seconds, someone would remove that money, since what should have been a *private* key was exposed to everyone. Your actual wallet address will have its private key closely guarded.

When I first learned about one-way functions in math, it bothered me very deeply. How could all the steps be known, be trivial, and yet be irreversible? It still bothers me! It seems dreadfully wrong that simple, nonrandom mathematical steps could be irreversible. And yet they are. Consider

$$X{\char`\^}Y \ mod \ N = A$$

where X,Y,N, and A are all integers.

If given the value of all the variables except for X, how would you ever discover X? If I told you X^32 mod 57 = 42, how would you solve for X (The answer is 3)? You would have to solve it the dumbest possible way, by trying every possible answer, because no one has found a more clever solution. But if I gave you big enough numbers, I could make it so you could never possibly try every possible answer, even in the lifetime of the universe! This is a subject for much more knowledgeable people than me. Suffice it to say, there are bizarre, yet powerful forces at work in math that make astonishing things possible.

Since a private key is all that is needed to unlock one's bitcoins, it must be kept safe at all costs. The asymmetry between the fact that you have access to the key, and that no one else does, is what keeps your money secure. There are no bank vaults, men with guns, or governmental stamp-punching bureaucrats between you and your money. There is no oversight. You are your own bank. That means there's a lot you don't need to worry about from broader, systemic failures in the financial world. But one thing you absolutely do need to worry about is securing your private key.

Managing private keys safely is still quite difficult. It is extremely challenging to secure even a single computer to a sufficient level of security. But there are best standards practices now being offered by Bitcoin companies that greatly decrease the risks of storing bitcoins. These include two factor authentication, multisignature approaches, and others. The ease of use for such services is likely to improve in the coming years. Just as regular people have no idea how their computer works, or why their commercial airliners doesn't crash, and innumerable other underappreciated technological wonders, the sophistication of Bitcoin will eventually be hidden from users, even as they leverage its benefits.

It is trivial to produce additional Bitcoin private-key/public address pairs. You can do it all day long for free. It is just math. It's like asking your computer for 3+2. There are many tools for generating these addresses. You may find this strangely easy. Could a key pair generator chance upon an existing address? Could it randomly find the key to *1i7cZdoE9NcHSd-AL5eGjmTJbBVqeQDwgw*, unlocking its 144,000 bitcoins [at the time of writing]? Yes it absolutely could. But you must grasp again the power of exponents. Given the space of possible private keys for a string such as *5JQc3s4ZhyuWefHEKtshYWzEVANA3TqqCzcWki2Cp VydgYpL8JX*, there are something like 10^{77} different possible key combinations. The key to a multimillion dollar fortune is one of these and can be found randomly. But the chances of doing so are so remote as to be completely irrelevant. This may seem unconvincing. But consider what 10^{77} possibilities means. That means there are about as many atoms in the visible universe as possible private keys. If every person on Earth spent the rest of their lives trying to discover a used key, for about the age of the universe, it is still unlikely a an overlap would ever be found. That's staggering. And stupefyingly, we could make it 58 times harder than that, already unfathomable level of difficulty merely by *adding another digit to the private key string*. It is as easy as that. The take away lesson, which computer scientists are well aware of, is that purely blind brute force methods cannot defeat truly hard problems. Without some clever optimization or analytical solution, but using the dumbest methods, the space of possible answers grows exponentially and always, always overtakes natural constraints.

Thus when manipulating bitcoins across addresses, you employ certain profound mathematical truths without even realizing it. The private key that you control is your sole leverage over your funds. But it is a control that is insurmountable to outsiders, for whom no physical force could ever explore the 10^{77} combinations of private keys that exist. It's like a cliff wall with no toeholds whatsoever; you stand at the top purely in having created a random address from an existing private key. You enjoy that security without having had to do any work. Attackers, by contrast, must either reverse the irreversible, or explore a combinatorial space so vast it defies the laws of physics. They stand at the bottom of a cliff with absolutely no way to climb up. Thus Bitcoin addresses are trivial to create, unassailable from the outside, and essentially limitless in number.

Bitcoin Transactions

A Bitcoin transaction moves bitcoins from one address to another. These are the verbs in the Bitcoin language. They are the actions that define the unfolding history of the Bitcoin network. If Bitcoin is about moving money around quickly and easily, transactions are the vehicles. The ease of writing transactions is one of the prime factors in the currency value of Bitcoin itself.

Each transaction is a message. It says, in effect, that "these previous bitcoins, which everyone acknowledges as mine, will now be moved over here". This message must always be internally consistent according to a particular syntax. It must obey grammatical rules specific to Bitcoin. But it must also be coherent vis-a-vis what others recognize as the legitimate state of the Bitcoin network. In other words, each peer must agree that the transaction message does not contradict what it already knows.

When writing a transaction from a given public address, a node implicitly looks at previous transactions that were sent to that address. Let's say Bob sent me 3 BTC. If I have not yet spent those 3 bitcoins, they are called 'unspent outputs'. Everyone can see my public address and know which unspent outputs it has. Everyone sees the 3 BTC Bob sent me, and even though they don't know me or Bob, they know I haven't spent them yet. I may then use these 3 bitcoins, which were the outputs of a previous transaction, as the inputs for a new transaction.

Every transaction has inputs and outputs. Inputs are the source of bitcoins to be transmitted. Bob sent me 3 BTC, and I haven't spent them yet, so I am free to use them as inputs for a subsequent transaction. Inputs can only ever be unspent outputs of a previous transaction or coins newly created from mining. This means that for each transaction, the source of the bitcoins used is always clear. It is always known that the bitcoins I claim to use do, in fact, come from somewhere legitimate. Going back to the transparent mailbox analogy, an empty 'mailbox' cannot send bitcoins. Implicit to the legitimacy of transaction inputs is a check as to whether the sender's address had the coins it claims to have.

A transaction's outputs send bitcoins to other addresses. Outputs can be sent to any public address. They can also be rendered spendable under more complex criteria[1]. The number of outputs does not need to equal the number of inputs. For example, if Bob sent me 3 bitcoins, I could send 10 people 0.3 BTC each, or 2 people 1 and 2 BTC respectively, or simply 1 person 3BTC. I can arrange it however I want with few constraints. What matters is that the total quantity of bitcoin used, the total in versus the total out, is conserved.

Transactions' inputs come from one of two places. They either originate in the creation of new coins via the Bitcoin mining process (something we shall discuss later) or they are the unused outputs of a previous transaction. If an output from an earlier transaction has not been spent, it is called an 'unspent output' and is then eligible to be used as an input in a later transaction, provided that the correct owner

---

[1] *Transaction Scripts: See a technical resource for more detail information.*

signs off on it. The availability of unspent outputs is always publicly visible (indeed provable).

So what is to stop me from taking someone else's unspent output and using it for myself? I can, after all, witness others' transactions; indeed I *must* to remain aware of the network. So if outputs are never hidden, why then can I not spend someone else's output? Why can't I steal your bitcoins if I witnessed the event in which you received them?

Each transaction's output has a special field called the Script field. This field contains code, which says, 'under what criteria may I be spent'. A Bitcoin transaction sent to my public address has outputs scripts which say, 'only a signature coming from this address can spend me'. Fulfilling this criteria mathematically requires possession of the private key corresponding to the recipient address. It is another bit of cryptographic magic. The criteria for spending bitcoins can be laid out publicly without revealing how to fulfill them. Then these conditions may be met, with a cryptographic signature, in such a way that the sensitive private key is not revealed. Thus I may spend my bitcoins in a way that proves I control the correct private key, while also not disclosing the key itself. Everyone is satisfied in the correctness, but malefactors will have gleaned no additional knowledge.

Each transaction is internally consistent. If your inputs sum to 3 BTC, but your outputs sum to 4 BTC, every peer will identify your transaction as invalid, because you cannot invent 1 BTC out of thin air. If your inputs are not correctly signed, your transaction is invalid; you might not be the real owner. Every transaction must follow a set of strict syntactic rules to even be considered by the network.

Once written, a Bitcoin transaction is broadcast to the network. This means the raw message, a long hex-encoded string, is sent to peers: other people running Bitcoin nodes. They validate the transaction and, if successful, pass it on to their neighbors. In this way, a broadcast transaction is shared from peer to peer, until it resounds throughout the entire network within seconds. False or incorrect transactions are stopped cold at the first peer, who will refuse to propagate them. If a transaction spends bitcoins, but the peer has already detected another transaction spending those very same bitcoins, it will refuse to propagate the transaction. This means that the client has detected an attempt to spend the same money twice, which is forbidden. If multiple conflicting transactions have been broadcasted, only one set of internally consistent transactions will be recorded permanently in the Blockchain. Of all the plausible ways to spend money, only one consistent history can ever become codified as real.

Every ten minutes or so, extant, valid transactions are incorporated in a *block* as part of the *Blockchain*. We will cover this in more detail below. But for now, let it suffice to say that transactions are etched into a permanent record approximately every ten minutes. In the time before a transaction joins the Blockchain, it has been broadcast, and within seconds, has circulated among all the nodes of the network. There are some very specific, technical edge cases for how this works, and attacks that may be done during this time span. But with very few exceptions, once a legitimate transaction has been broadcast, it is destined to be inscribed forever in the Blockchain.

Transactions should include a small *transaction fee*. This goes to the Bitcoin miners who process the transaction and put it in the Blockchain. The fee is automatically the difference between the sum of the inputs and the sum of the outputs. Thus if I write a transaction with 5.0001 BTC of inputs and 5 BTC of outputs, the transaction fee would be 0.0001 BTC. We will discuss the important of transaction fees and mining in a later section.

Every transaction is publicly visible in the Blockchain. I can go back at any time to inspect the full history of transactions. No detail is left out; as we shall see, every proof I need to reconstruct the history, trustlessly, is available. Once inscribed, a transaction cannot be erased. This is another source of great strength. Once funds are received, there is no risk of chargebacks, second-thoughts, or outside intervention. Transactions are permanent.

They are also provable in the record. Identified by a *unique transaction hash*, transactions remain as indelible records in the Blockchain. This is a quick and effective way to reference historical financial events to everyone's satisfaction. There is never any doubt as to whether Joe paid Jill 2 bitcoins last Sunday. The proof is freely available. And no intermediary agency is necessary in providing that proof. It is already mathematically apparent.

A large part of why Bitcoin is useful stems from the nature of its transactions. Whereas most systems *record* a payment in one step and *actualize* it in another, Bitcoin transactions are both. *The record of payment is the payment.* Because transactions exist within a permanent cryptographic record known as the Bitcoin Blockchain, they can be reliably referenced at any time. As we shall discuss further along, they are very fast, they are very cheap, and they are intensely secure.

You can watch Bitcoin transactions as they are broadcast in real-time on a number of websites. Watching nodes from around the world pulsate with data, reverberating with news of transactions, is a staggering thing. Seeing such a map, one truly appreciates that Bitcoin has no center. Transactions are pure data, and yet they manage to function as effectively as a shipment of physical gold: more effectively in fact. Watching bitcoins stream in real-time across the world, ceaselessly and without anyone's permission, one cannot help but be amazed. Money has become a data packet.

The Blockchain

The Blockchain is the core innovation in Bitcoin. It is the special magic part that makes decentralized consensus possible. What is written in it is self-evidently true by virtue of the Bitcoin mining process. The Blockchain has been labored on for years, with astronomical figures of computation done, to hone an immutable, unforgeable history. This history records human acts. The Blockchain was built, designed, and maintained by people. But by design, it has taken on a life of its own. Set off with its own rules, humans may act within its strictures, but never break them. The system as a whole has taken its own course and may not be unilaterally undone, not even by its creator.

The Blockchain describes the entire economic history of Bitcoin. It contains the full details of every transaction ever performed. By reconstituting the history of transactions, it is possible to arrive at the balance of every address. Thus by observing the Blockchain alone, in isolation, one need not consult others to ascertain the state of the network. The Blockchain contains past and present.

The Blockchain is composed of pieces, called blocks which are linked to each other in a chain, hence the Blockchain. Each block is a statement detailing the transactions that have occurred since the block before it. So, for instance, block #100,000 described transactions occurring between 2010-12-29 11:55:31 and 2010-12-29 11:57:43. The block after that, #100,001, described transactions occurring 2010-12-29 11:57:43 and 2010-12-29 12:06:44. The time intervals fluctuate randomly, but they center around 10 minutes on average.

Each block says several things. It describes all the transactions that occurred within its time interval. Nothing is left open-ended. Each block includes everything needed to prove its authenticity, and the authenticity of its substituent parts. Each transaction is fully detailed, with every signed cryptographic proof legible, showing that address A authorized sending bitcoins to Address B.

Just as the constituent transactions are internally consistent, the block itself is consistent within the context of the Blockchain branch it claims to be a part of. Each block has a string, called a hash, which is like its name. For example, the hash of block #100,001 is *0000000000008-0b66c911bd5ba14a74260057311eaeb1982802f7010f1a9f090*. Th at's its unique identifier. Each block also states who its predecessor block is. So block #100,001 says that its predecessor block is *000000000003ba27aa200b1cecaad478d2b00432346c3f1f3986da1afd33e506*. This just so happens to be block #100,000. Every block can be linked back to its predecessor block, all the way to the first block, called the Genesis Block.

Blocks form branches as they refer to their predecessors. There may be many different blocks, telling many different stories of events within Bitcoin. Each branch is its own consistent story. And any contributor may contribute blocks, or refashion his own branch. But of all the extant branches of blocks, it is a protocol rule that the longest branch should be the valid one. Because of the difficulty of creating blocks, which we discuss below, the longest branch reflects the consensus choice of Bitcoin miners. Through their choices on which branches to work on, network participants implicitly vote on which transactional history they endorse.

The Blockchain

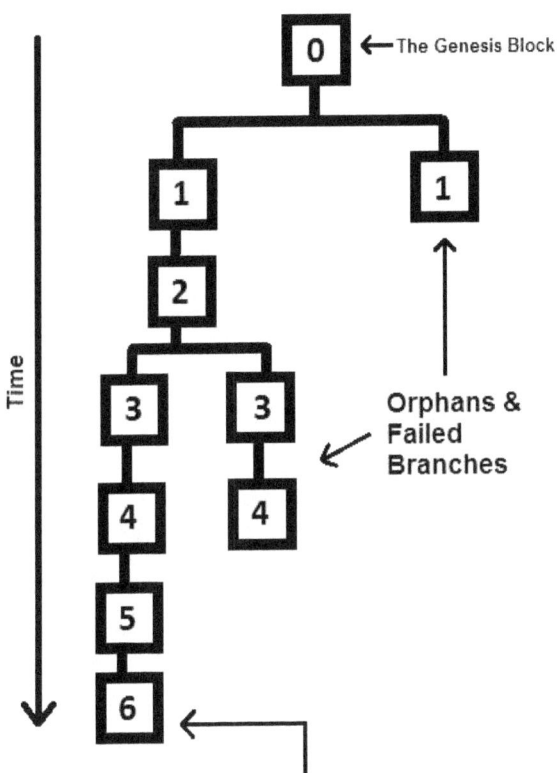

The Longest Branch is the Main Branch

Consensus

The Blockchain is self-evident. It needs to be. The whole point of Bitcoin is that each peer client, you and me running Bitcoin on our laptops, should be able to verify the legitimacy of balances and transactions without recourse to trusting any external source. This is a stupefyingly audacious design requirement. Your Bitcoin client is like a man stuck in a cabin in the woods who, one day, receives in the mail a big stack of books. The books describe every transaction ever performed. As he peruses the stacks, other deliveries arrive containing parallel stacks of books. Thousands of sets arrive. Each stack describes a separate history of transactions. They do not agree. Each set of books is radically at odds with the other. However each set is internally consistent. But the many sets cannot coexist. Only one can be legitimate. Which one is it?

How would you ever solve this problem? This is another version of what is called the Byzantine Generals' Problem. How do distant generals exchanging messages achieve consensus (on when to attack) when some fraction of them are traitors? If there is no trusted authority, and many peers just pass messages to one another, how could you ever come to an agreement? You don't know the total number of generals, or whom to trust. You receive messages from honest and traitorous generals alike. But what if a few generals issued thousands of forged notes, pretending to be a majority? If there is no one to trust, how does one differentiate valid notes from invalid ones? How does a peer-to-peer network with no trusted actors defend itself against cheaters and liars? For years this question stumped the world.

Bitcoin answered the Byzantine Generals Problem with the Blockchain. For the man stuck in the cabin in the woods, each set of books claims to be the real Blockchain. But clearly all but one must be false. Most of them, in fact, are spam sent by a malicious actor. While in the real world it may be difficult to spam tomes and volumes, digitally it is simple. A malefactor could distribute internally consistent, but alternate histories of the Blockchain in such a way as to appear equally valid from the legitimate copy. So how can one separate the junk from the legitimate Blockchain, when all of the junk is syntactically correct? As with the Byzantine Generals, *anyone* could be a traitor; no trusted arbiter can be relied upon to give a stamp of authenticity.

The first part of the answer is that, in an indirect way, peers vote on which Blockchain history to accept. The transactional history with a simple majority of votes may be deemed legitimate; all others are illegitimate. However even something as simple as voting, when migrated to a decentralized, trustless model, becomes quite challenging. As we saw with the malicious Byzantine Generals, if there is no master list somewhere of authorized voters, how does one differentiate between real voters and digitally faked ones?

Imagine if voting in US presidential elections were purely digital via email. What would happen? Surely spammers would decide the election. Without a central repository linking each authorized name, John Smith, to an authorized email address, spammers could bombard the election results with trillions of fake emails. This is called a Sybil Attack. It is easy to fake voters without some form of authorization. For this reason, every voting system before Bitcoin had a central trusted party. When I go to the election booth, there is a list somewhere with my name on it. Whoever controls that list controls the election process. It is centralized and trusting.

Bitcoin is different because it intentionally eschews the centralized model. Recording transactions on a centralized database would have been far easier from the outset. But when such systems break, they break catastrophically. They are prone to systemic risk in a way that decentralized, peer-to-peer networks are not. So how then, does Bitcoin protect itself from Sybil attacks, where all previous voting schemes have adopted the lazy solution of centralized trust?

In Bitcoin, voting on the legitimacy of the Blockchain comes with a cost. The price is computational work. To vote, you must do math. A lot of it. Your influence within the blockchain-democracy scales with the amount of computational work that you do. The people who do this computational work are called Bitcoin miners and the work is known as Bitcoin mining. We shall see that Bitcoin mining, and achieving consensus on the Blockchain, are two sides to the same coin.

By imposing a cost on voting, Bitcoin makes Sybil attacks impossible. It is not possible to spam trillions of votes, because the computational work involved would be astronomical. It is as if, to vote in the US Presidential Election, you had to solve a quick crossword puzzle first, but you never had to show ID. You could vote many times if you wanted to by solving multiple (different) crossword puzzles. But soon you would tire of the puzzles. You certainly could not spam the election with millions of votes. Perhaps an assiduous puzzler would manage ten votes, whereas lazy voters would perform zero or one. But votes could never be mass-manufactured the way spam email can be.

Thus the individuals who devote the most resources to performing computational work get the most say in selecting alternative versions of the Blockchain. Because it is purely mathematical, this work can be done anywhere by anyone. People, as a joke, have even performed these computations by hand. But in practice, computers perform these operations billions of times per second. It's just math, over and over again. Because absolutely anyone can join in on this process, the barrier to entry is basically zero. This means that a lot of people, and a lot of computational power, are currently involved in voting on alternative blockchains.

The more computational power involved with Bitcoin mining, the more secure the network becomes. If I can perform 1 million operations per second, and the entire network only performs 10 million operations per second, then I would command 10% of the voting power alone. But in fact, the network is currently performing approximately 300,000,000,000,000,000 operations per second (that's 17 zeros). That's millions of computations per person on Earth per second. It's such a stupendous amount that any one individual has very little influence.

There's another special bit of magic underlying Bitcoin mining as well. It's the work itself. The work cost of voting comes in the form of a special mathematical function. In cryptocurrencies, this is called its *mining algorithm*. In the case of Bitcoin, the algorithm is called SHA256. You don't need to know how this works exactly. But you should know that it is one of the special one-way mathematical functions that we saw earlier. Remember that your private key leads deterministically to a public address and that this is an easy, straightforward process. However, it is practically impossible to go backwards from the public address back to the corresponding private key. It can't be done without trying every possibility, which is infeasible with so many possibilities. The Bitcoin mining algorithm, SHA256, has similar one-way properties. I can take any piece of text and convert it into a SHA256 *hash*. For instance, the string "Bitcoin" hashes to *b4056df6691f8dc72e56302ddad345d65f-ead3ead9299609a826e2344eb63aa4*. But you could never take that long, intimidating ciphertext and go backwards to "Bitcoin".

Since it is impossible to go backwards from a hash, I could specify criteria for 'solving' a hashing problem with any degree of difficulty I want. For example, I could ask for some input, X, which, when hashed, becomes any string beginning with three "0"'s, such as *00019d6689c085ae-1651831e934ff763ae46a2a6c72b3f1b60a8ce26fe6a2f1*, or others. The *specificity* of the criteria is equivalent to the *difficulty* of finding a solution. Since you cannot predict analytically what the outcome of a hash will be, and you cannot reverse-engineer the outcome you want, you will have to try random possibilities until you chance upon a valid answer. When you try random possibilities blindly, looking for solutions, this is called brute force.

Brute force is the dumbest way to find solutions to problems. But the Bitcoin mining algorithm was intentionally chosen so that it would *have* to be brute forced. If the contest is for pure computational power, the problem should not have easy analytical answers. It should, at its very core, be a problem that *is not* efficiently solvable. This makes it a test of computational power alone. The lack of an analytical solution to the mining algorithm, or indeed, even a minor optimization to finding a solution, makes the problem symmetrical to all participants. This makes it still harder to execute a Sybil attack. The converse, an algorithm with the potential for analytical improvements, would be far more dangerous; some miners could get a massive advantage over others.

Crossword-puzzles would be terrible proof of work algorithms because it would be possible to intelligently optimize the process of finding a solution. Miners with the cleverest algorithms would win, as opposed to those with the most computational power. This negates the point of distributed voting.

The difficulty of finding solutions can be tuned arbitrarily. Let us walk through a simple example. Let's say that the solution I'm looking for starts with three "0"'s. You can't take a valid string like *000aaaaaaaaaaaaaaaaa-aaaaaaaaaaaaaaaaaaaaaaaaaaaaaaaaaaaaaaaaaaaa* and work backwards to the solution. Remember, no one knows how to do that. Instead, you have to try random inputs until you get a winner. If you tried "1" you would get *6b86b273ff34fce19d6b804eff5a3f5747ada4eaa22f1d49c0 1e52ddb7875b4b*: not a solution. If you tried "2" you would get *d4735e3a265e16eee03f59718b9b5d03019c07d8b6c51f90 da3a666eec13ab35*: also not a solution. You would continue on, blindly looking for solutions, until you tried "886" which hashes to *000f21ac06aceb9cdd057-5e82d0d85fc39bed0a7a1d-71970ba1641666a44f530*. This is a solution because it begins with three zeros. At any time, I could make the problem harder by making the solution criteria more stringent. I could demand 4 zeros, or 5, or more, making the solution exponentially harder to find. Since there is no analytical way to devise an answer, you would have to mindlessly hash, again and again, until you found a winner.

The Bitcoin mining algorithm may seem esoteric, but it is a convenient proof of computational work, because finding solutions is extremely difficult, but verifying existing solutions is extremely fast. My computer can hash '886' almost instantly. It doesn't matter how hard the initial criteria was, whether I demanded three zeros, five, or ten. They can all be verified instantly, no matter how difficult they are to find.

Bitcoin uses SHA256 as a way to prove that an individual has done computational work. On the assumption that no one can analytically solve these hashes, i.e., that everyone must resort to dumb brute force methods, a solution to a hash is proof that one has hashed a certain amount, on average. I could only have ever found the "886" solution to the three-zero hash if I had tried several thousand hashes. If I had only tried ten hashes, it's almost impossible that I could have found a solution. Similarly, when a Bitcoin miner solves a hash of extraordinary difficulty, he has proven that he has done a huge amount of computational work. I don't need to mirror that work to verify the correctness of the solution. I only need to take his solution and hash it once, to see that it is correct.

As another example, let's take another hash, from a modern block. The hash for block #300176 was *00000000000000000bd4caae8855a7db92e0e6fa690da4 a05c4f9052e6a6de8b*. That's 17 zeros! The odds of randomly chancing upon a solution with 17 zeros are incredibly low. My computer could never do it. And yet the solution is in the Blockchain now, published for all to see and verify. I could never have found it. But now that it's out there, I see that it is correct. And I know that whoever solved it must have vast computing resources available. It's concise proof they've done work.

Transactions cannot be altered without breaking the solution to a given block. Thus a miner's solution includes his 'vote' on which Bitcoin transactions occurred in which order. Also included in each 'solution' is a reference to the hash of the previous block. Thus a miner, by publishing a valid solution to the mining algorithm, has *implicitly* expressed several opinions: which transactions occurred, and which previous block to append this new block to.

Since each block references a previous block, they are stringed together to form the Blockchain. If disagreements arise between miners, such as on alternate versions of events, or alternate valid solutions to blocks, the Blockchain may branch into separate paths. Many mathematically and syntactically valid solutions exist for any given block. Occasionally miners chance upon mutually contradictory, but valid, blocks within seconds of one another. In this case, one will generally be accepted by the community, and the other will be discarded.

One beautiful feature of this system is that any change whatsoever in an old block will disturb the solution in all of the downstream blocks. For example, changing any detail of a transaction will alter its identifying transaction hash, which in turn upsets the solution for the block it lives in. The old block solution, which had produced a valid hash (think of the requisite number of zeros), will now become invalid. All descendant blocks also become invalid because *their* solutions were premised on a now-invalid block. Since it was incredibly difficult to find a block solution in the first place, finding a new solution under the changed conditions is incredibly difficult. Only someone with massive mining power could accomplish it. This is why the Blockchain is said to be immutable; any change requires recomputing all subsequent block solutions, a computationally infeasible task.

Simultaneously, even if you can recalculate or recreate old blocks under changed terms, the rest of the mining community will have left you in the dust. While you were finding solutions to blocks that already exist, an almost insuperable task, the rest of the mining community was solving the *next* few blocks. If they have more hashing power than you, which they almost certainly will, you have no chance of catching up. The other miners will hopelessly outpace you in the generation of new blocks. Because peers only accept the Blockchain branch that is longest, your version, mined solely by you, will never catch up. And because each block is dependent on the last, you cannot recreate an old block and try to sneak it into the main Blockchain branch. The solutions will not match and it will be rejected.

These forces incentivize miners to collaborate on achieving consensus around the main chain branch of the

Blockchain. No one wants to find a solution while referencing the wrong previous block. Since no one party can outpace the others, every miner works on the newest blocks on the main chain, i.e., the longest branch. Shorter, divergent branches are immediately abandoned; any payouts earned mining on a divergent branch are meaningless. If it's not on the main chain, it's not authentic Bitcoin.

The incentive structure around Bitcoin mining was very cleverly conceived. Even malicious actors are incentivized to mine cooperatively. Without majority hashing power, which we will discuss later in detail, a hostile miner can do little besides mine normally. It doesn't matter what the miners' motivations are; so long as they mine, they increase the security of the system as a whole, *even if they privately would rather attack it*. Because they are not able to attack in isolation, their rational choice makes the system stronger against *still other* potential attackers. It is a positive feedback loop for greater security.

Solving blocks is the only mechanism for bitcoins to be created and for the monetary supply to be increased. Whoever broadcasts a valid solution to a block is recognized to have earned the 'automatic block reward'. This used to award 50 BTC per block, approximately every 10 minutes, but now awards 25 BTC. Next year in 2016, it will drop again to 12.5 BTC per block. In this way the total supply of bitcoins asymptotically approaches a limit of 21 million total coins.

An astute reader might notice that, as hashing power increases, the likelihood of brute forcing a valid solution to a block will increase. For this reason, the block difficulty, the degree of stringency for block solutions, changes approximately every two weeks. Remember the 3 zero's requirement for our hash solution? The strictness of this requirement is a tuneable parameter. Part of the protocol states that, if over a two week period, blocks are discovered faster than once every 10 minutes on average, then the difficulty must increase. This would have the effect of making it harder to find valid block solutions, hence they would be found less often. Similarly, if the average time between block solutions is greater than 10 minutes over the 2 week interval, the difficulty will decrease. This is an automatic process.

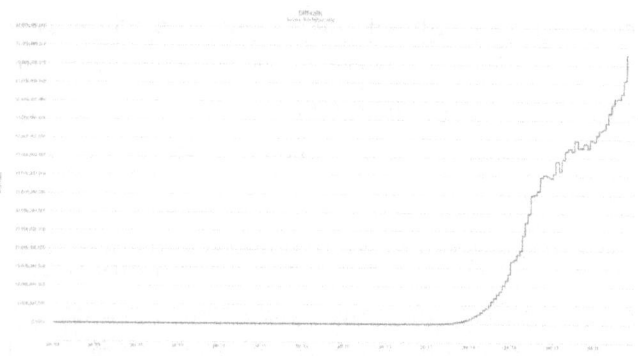

Difficulty vs. Time

Source: Blockchain.info

The effect of this fluctuating mining difficulty is that as more miners enter the system the properties of the system do not change. Blocks are not discovered faster over the long term, even as more miners participate. The difficulty merely goes up; blocks become harder to solve. In the process, the security of the system improves. Due to these forces, the network difficulty is currently 46 billion compared to a starting value of 1.0. This astronomical growth was likely unanticipated by Bitcoin's creator, but it seems not to have mattered. The corrective difficulty mechanism he established has proven resilient despite unpredictably rapid mining growth. The network works the same way as before, but its security has grown by light-years. Because all that are ever found are mathematical solutions whose difficulty is trivially tunable, this approach to security seems highly scalable.

At any one time, mining power corresponds directly to a revenue stream of bitcoins. The amount of money earned depends on the block difficulty, the reward size, and one's own hashing power. Since difficulty is correlated to the total hashing power across the network, and the reward size only changes once every four years, the principal factor governing payouts is one's own mining power vis-a-vis the sum of all Bitcoin miners. If I had 1% of the total mining power, I would, on average, earn 1% of all automatic rewards. If everyone else upgraded their hashing speed by a factor of 2, and if my hashing remained the same, I would then only constitute 0.5% of the network. And I would then only receive 0.5% of payouts. I am thus again incentivized to increase my share of total mining power. In doing so, I increase the total computational power of the network. Thus as one pursues the profit motive the network becomes more secure as an ancillary effect.

The fact that the economics of mining hinge on the relative power of other miners means that Bitcoin mining is the ultimate competitive arms race. Miners are in a constant state of one-upping each other. It is a never-ending slog to outcompete other miners in hardware, speed, efficiency, and cost. And because the barrier to entry is virtually nil, Bitcoin mining has become perhaps the most competitive industry in existence. Profit margins are being relentlessly driven to zero. While this makes mining a difficult profession, it delivers astonishingly good value for money to everyone else. As consumers of the security miners provide, Bitcoin users get an extraordinary degree of protection for relatively little cost.

The success of the Blockchain as a consensus mechanism stems from its clever alignment of incentives for the miners who secure it. Malice in mining is futile, while cooperation is profitable. And that same cooperation renders the malice of others still more futile. Bitcoin miners, in all their diversity of motives, are corralled by their own self-interest into securing the network ever further.

The proof-of-work scheme, whose maintenance is the central devotion of the mining community, has unique properties which make it an excellent verification tool. Solutions cannot be counterfeited; they must be painstakingly brute-forced. Even as they are difficult to find, they are trivial to confirm. Any miner seeking to attack the network, in defiance of his own economic self-interest, faces the monumental weight of the rest of the mining community. So long as mining power remains unconcentrated, as we shall discuss in another chapter, an attack is wholly infeasible.

Most important of all, the Blockchain is unbiased and has no gatekeepers. There are no special privileges or trusted nodes. Anyone may participate. Indeed, the more participants, the more secure and valuable the network becomes. The proof-of-work scheme which underlies the consensus mechanism is completely neutral to all parties. As long as your computer can do math, you can participate. This symmetry between participants makes the system truly decentralized.

We saw the example of the hypothetical man in the woods, alone in his cabin, who wants to ascertain truth. In the era before Bitcoin, to know which ledgers were legitimate, and which were not, would require the seal of approval of a trusted arbiter. But with Bitcoin, to achieve consensus without a trusted center, and still to be 'alone in the woods', is a spectacular technical accomplishment. Bitcoin uses this tool to establish consensus on the order of occurrence of transactions. This alone is the issue which must be agreed upon by all participants. It is a weighted voting scheme, a democracy of computational power, in which votes are self-evidently valid because they solve self-evidently hard mathematical problems.

The Blockchain's success portends big changes in many spheres. It is not just in the matter of money in which consensus should be reached. The man alone in the woods is our computer. It is alone a wild-digital world, under a barrage of malicious misinformation. Establishing the veracity of records in such a dynamic, hostile environment as the Internet is an incredibly important capability. The Blockchain greatly expands the scope of what is possible for a computer to know with confidence. It is programmatic trust. It is the first entity made by people but no longer completely controlled by them. It is the magic ticking heart of Bitcoin.

In Crypto We Trust

Modern Cryptography began only recently, in 1977, with the invention of RSA public/private signing[vi]. This discovery was so powerful because, for the first time, it allowed for strong asymmetric cryptography. This means, for example, that I can verify that you wrote a particular message, but that while I can verify it, I could never forge it. It's like your handwriting. I know that it's yours. But I'll never be able to imitate it myself. Except while handwritten signatures can be faked, with RSA it became computationally infeasible to forge messages. And we have seen already that 'computationally infeasible' is really just a Computer Science euphemism for 'in practice, impossible'.

Asymmetric encryption entails quite a lot and I am certainly no cryptography expert. But I can summarize some of the amazing capabilities it introduces. We will see how these capabilities are leveraged by Bitcoin and its imitators.

With RSA, I can generate public and private key pairs in a manner similar to Bitcoin key pairs (although Bitcoin pairs use a different algorithm, the general idea is the same). I may expose my public key to the world. Then when I write a message encrypted with my private key, anyone can decrypt the ciphertext message back into intelligible plaintext with the use of my public key (which is openly available). But the key bonus here is that, in decrypting unintelligible ciphertext with my public key, you have also proved that only the person controlling the corresponding private key could have written this message. It's a message anyone can read, but only the private key-holder could write.

It's like seeing a painting and saying 'only Picasso could have painted this'. Except instead of relying on a hunch, with asymmetric cryptography there is mathematical certainty. Whoever controls the private key for a given public key can continue to write and encrypt new messages. Each encrypted message will be a different, unintelligible string of gibberish. But when decrypted, they prove that they were all written by someone controlling the same private key. Just like the one-way nature of Bitcoin addresses, exposing a public key in no way compromises the corresponding private key, even though they are deterministically linked. This irreversibility means it is impossible to forge my messages. With private/public key pairs, what you expose publicly is an ironclad shield. What you protect carefully, the soft underbelly, is the vulnerable private key: the part that actually has power.

You can do a lot more with asymmetric encryption too. For example, if I know your public key, because you've posted it publicly, I can write you a message and encrypt it *with your public key*. This seems odd at first. I don't control your public key. I can't read anything encrypted by it. But that's the point. A message encrypted with your public key is readable only by you. This means that I can post the encrypted ciphertext publicly, anywhere, for all to see. But to everyone else it will be indecipherable. Only you will be able to decipher it. I don't even need to know who you are. I just need your public key. That you are the only one reading the message is a mathematical certainty.

Cryptography is the first word in Bitcoin. The concepts inherent to strong cryptography are predecessors to those of Bitcoin. When you encrypt a message with modern methods, so long as you keep your private key safe, you have *absolute* confidence that it cannot be read. It's not confidence in a person or in an institution. It's confidence underpinned by math. This is a very new concept. People still haven't woken up to it.

How Our Nature Obscures Modern Perception

Trusting math goes against the grain of our natural instincts. Evolution has shaped us to greatly value personal interactions over highly formalized, abstract constructs. It is still true today; the vast majority of our interactions revolve around social dynamics of one kind or another. Humans are incredibly fine-tuned to recognize emotions in others. Our historic evolutionary fitness hinged quite a lot on being able to read other people. So it is no wonder that our mindset is, and has always been, about measuring trust in people and the organizations they build.

Humans are, in fact, social geniuses. We're masters at the tasks that mattered over evolutionary time: language, reading other people, etc. It's just natural to us. Just ask someone who works in speech recognition or AI how difficult it is to reverse engineer what we do effortlessly. Stupid people solve problems intuitively that the smartest people in the world cannot solve explicitly.

But while humans are socially brilliant, we're terrible at alien abstractions like math. We weren't meant to do it. There was never an evolutionary need for it. We only accomplish math, and many similarly abstruse pursuits, because we've cobbled together parts of the brain built for other purposes and jury-rigged them for another. I can only speculate, but it is likely that we use a vastly convoluted set of neural pathways, meant for entirely different things, to 'emulate' formalisms like math. It's like running a Playstation on a desktop computer with an emulator. The desktop is much more powerful than the original Playstation. But because the Playstation was built for a different architecture, it wasn't meant to be run on a desktop. The desktop can only emulate the Playstation by mimicking what the Playstation *would do*. But this process, a computer simulating the actions of another computer abstractly, is incredibly inefficient. It's like if I wanted to add 2+3, but to do so I had to translate the words into Chinese, add them in Chinese, and then translate 5 back into English. I suspect that, those areas that we all struggle with, the notoriously hard subjects like physics, math, computer science, etc., are those systems for which we have no instinctive go-to pathway. So we muddle through with makeshift, Rube-Goldberg-like neural architectures.

If evolution has ill-prepared us for many of the most valuable skillsets today, it has also provided a weak intuition for parsing the consequences of new technology. Our instincts, though hallowed over time, don't necessarily coincide with external reality, particularly as technology takes us further from what is evolutionarily familiar. We see this conflict in many fields in which gut feelings are deeply at odds with what is known, technically and scientifically, to be true. Fact and primordial hunch are often deeply unreconciled.

Our evolutionary starting point is an arbitrary bias for what we ought to value. While we are comfortable, through long experience and natural preference, to being impressed by the trustworthiness of people and institutions built by people, trusting math feels alien. Our evolutionary biases do not intelligently inform us when confronting categorically novel concepts. These biases suffer from a 50,000 year lag; the modern era moves far too fast for us to count too much on our intuitions. What feels right in our gut just might not be pertinent in an age of mathematical certainty.

Our gut is wrong about many things. Our gut tells us that relativity and quantum mechanics are ludicrous. Every intuition we possess screams against modern theories: molecular thermodynamics, the scale of the universe, the uncertainty principle, non-Euclidean spacetime, they all instinctively feel implausible. Absolutely no one sane professes to believe these things instinctively in their bones. And yet we have proven scientifically that they are quite real. Our feeble minds were built for a very limited set of circumstances, in which knowing the true nature of things was not necessary. It's like HAL-9000 knowing nothing about circuits. He is composed of them, they make up reality, but conceivably he was not built to grasp that. We humans are the same. And even while scientific evidence exists in huge amounts, most people live with an aversion to the implications of these non-intuitive theories. We walk around pretending that relativity, and quantum mechanics, and mind-bogglingly complex biochemistry are not occurring every millisecond. Such thoughts are too much for us. We have an innate bias against concepts that do not resonate with common experience and our evolutionary past. This leads us to be chronically misinformed about the nature of reality.

As Richard Feynman put it, "The 'paradox' is only a conflict between reality and your feeling of what reality 'ought to be'".

The same basic human failing carries over to math, cryptography, and computers. We should force ourselves to overcome our natural aversion to math, to think around our own inadequacies, to fully comprehend the consequences of technologies that have already arrived. In this book I argue that, with modern cryptography and later with Bitcoin we have entered a new paradigm in which the old assumptions no longer hold. Our instincts may not be right. They were shaped in Africa more than 50,000 years ago; we are hardly equipped to parse the quantitative, abstract world of technology in which we now live.

This tendency manifests itself greatly in the public's perception of Bitcoin. There is a widespread distrust of Bitcoin, surpassing that of other, equally new technologies. It is Bitcoin's greatest strength, its decentralized nature, which also inspires the greatest public worry. Our bias towards trusting people and institutions severely handicaps our appreciation of decentralized trust. Trust based on mathematics, with no central authority, is totally at odds with our experience. Our natural inclination is to ask 'Who?' when we should be asking 'How?' Those who, have asked 'How?' with Bitcoin have discovered a treasure trove of innovation and raw cryptographic power. The majority, who persist in wanting to know who is in charge, have found no one.

'How?' is the question Bitcoin is best equipped to answer. Everything is open-source and publicly available at no cost. At any time you may inspect how Bitcoin works in every detail. The only limit is your own technical ability. Many of the smartest people in the world have delved into these details. Bitcoin has been stress tested by clever hackers many times; none have succeeded in breaking it. Bitcoin excels technically. But it requires a lot of skill and perseverance to recognize this.

Bitcoin is the first institution ever built with no human masters. No person is at the helm. There is no individual with the power to change the network. Only the community as a whole, acting in consensus, has the power to change anything. The lack of central human authority is disconcerting to our sensibilities. We want someone to look to. We want a face to associate with the idea. But Bitcoin refuses us this. Bitcoin exists outside of us.

Bitcoin, having no human master, is intensely alien. It is human instinct to become suspicious at such a foreign concept. This is almost universally the common first reaction. I felt it when I first learned of Bitcoin. It felt wrong. It seemed at first as if such a thing could not possible be real. Only by painstakingly learning about the sophistication under the hood were my doubts quelled.

The inhumanity of the Blockchain suggests that it can have no legitimacy. Why should we relegate arbitration to an algorithmic judge, and not a human heart? Facts with no fact checkers, authority without authorities, the Blockchain is a dizzying departure from normalcy. It feels wrong to set a system off on its own course with no human administration, like a sailing ship with no crew. There is no precedent for this: a thing made by people, but no longer controlled by them.

But our feelings are misplaced. A system governed by open rules will work better than one in which humans' slippery fingers control the levers. It is a very hard step to acknowledge one's own inadequacies, let alone one's species'. But our history proves that humans cannot abide too long by their promises. The temptation to cheat, to bend, to obfuscate, is too strong over long time periods. Humans are too fickle to be trusted. We're too shaped by our recent evolutionary past to have pure intentions. The old metrics, of trusting men with long beards, and institutions with marble facades, and the reverence of certificates, and the pronouncements of experts, are simply too weak. All the dressing up of respectability cannot cover the ultimate blemish, namely, that humans are not to be trusted.

So we've made do, up to now, with elaborate systems of credentials, titles, and ways of assigning authority. Within the space of a few years, they may work alright. And for lack of a better alternative, we've even started to believe in that facade of trust. Institutions impress us. Experts overawe us. We pretend that institutions' promises will endure, or that today's expert consensus won't be ridiculed by tomorrow's changing fashions. But yesterday's heresy is today's orthodoxy. We would be foolish to think that the status quo must remain, or that any human guarantee could be immune from such upheavals. No human institution is truly constant.

But now there exists a competing paradigm. While most facts must still be perceived through the flawed human lens, others may be registered directly. Cryptography is the finest example of a truth untouched by human hands. A cryptographic signature means so much more than any man's word. An encrypted text will withstand any siege. Mathematics is foolproof in a way human promises can never be.

Let us embrace that. Let us change the definition of trust and respectability, from an individual's eminence to a key's complexity, or a protocol's security. Make what must be human decentralized, bound by a common, trustless protocol, so that as many human hands must touch the levers as possible. A new way of achieving consensus has arisen. It leans on mathematics, crowds, and openness. It has no face. We should not let that frighten us. We should stifle the part of us that wants to be reassured by venerable old men. That's the old way talking. Instead let's dig deeper, into truths that, perhaps we have not evolved for, but can nevertheless grasp.

Bitcoin Excels as Currency

If the pursuit of currency had always really been about maintaining a reliable store of data, that purpose has been distilled into its purest form in Bitcoin. As a currency tool, Bitcoin excels in all the ways that matter. It surpasses previous incarnations of money in efficacy and security. Making money merely a matter of well-executed computer code, Bitcoin opens up new payment possibilities that predecessors simply aren't capable of. To try to retrofit legacy systems with the capabilities of Bitcoin would instantly reveal their inherent inadequacies. Because Bitcoin is just code, it is faster, more secure, and more reliable than any human-driven system. If you accept the premise that money is really just information, then it should come as no surprise that its highest form would come from an open-source, crypto project.

And if currency is about trust, then Bitcoin is far more deserving than its traditional predecessors. The old institutional guarantees, for which we have been paying a large de facto premium, have little value in the face of the Blockchain and modern cryptography. The fiat trust we have been buying cannot compete with mathematically perfect and free digital trust. The deadened hand of fiat guarantees has blinded us to what currency ought to be: a creature of the internet, a protocol, open-source, nation-agnostic, incredibly secure, and wicked fast.

Bitcoin is Fast

Bitcoin is insanely fast. Once you have written a transaction and broadcasted it to the network, it takes only seconds before it has reverberated throughout all the peer nodes. This is limited only by latency on the Internet, i.e. loosely correlated to the speed of light. It's blindingly fast. Once a transaction has been broadcast and heard by all nodes, within several seconds, it is only a matter of time before it is included in a block. Within minutes, a transaction will have been *permanently* etched into the public record: actualized and irreversibly complete with no sense of distance traveled.

Bitcoin's speed is one of its major advantages as a currency tool over legacy money. It is simply convenient, extraordinarily so, to be able to send money so rapidly over such large distances. It has the speedy finality of handing someone cash, but extended across everyone on the Internet. In a race between someone fumbling through his wallet for bills, and a transaction being broadcast between Bitcoin nodes, the transaction would win, even as it circles the Earth. Meanwhile the cash you hand a merchant does not enter his bank account for several days. And then its journey has only just begun. Once in a bank account, the delays stretch on for eons by Bitcoin's reckoning.

It is only too disheartening to contrast the speed of Bitcoin payments with that of fiat money. In the US it is particularly bad. It often takes 3-4 business days to transfer money between domestic banks. It's a ludicrously slow process. Email has existed for twenty years, and yet it still takes days to move money within the same country.

Consider the massive amount of waste that results from the delays in moving money. At any given time, how much money is stuck in-transit? It is probably many billions of dollars. This money could otherwise be directed towards productive enterprises. It represents capital that is held in stasis for no good reason other than transactional friction.

The slowness of fiat money transfers likely retards many downstream economic processes. More money must be held in reserve at any given time to act as a buffer. By contrast, in physical manufacturing, the 'lean manufacturing' model (pioneered by the Japanese in the 1990's) minimizes inventory, waste, and lead time. It emphasizes nimbleness in effecting greater efficiency. The world of finance has no parallel. When money moves slowly more of it must be held in reserve in multitudinous bank accounts big and small. I personally keep a sizeable amount of cash in my checking account, equivalent to several months' rent, where it sits idle. I keep it because transferring between accounts, even my own accounts, is too slow to risk failing to pay a bill. This money is accruing no interest and accomplishing nothing. How many other individuals and businesses follow similar practices? The net waste must be massive.

Readers will point out that one must wait until a Bitcoin transaction has been included in a block before it is truly real. In fact, among many Bitcoin businesses, the standard is to wait for several blocks after a transaction is included, up to six. This is to protect against a double-spend attack, or in other words, to protect against the possibility that what they are observing is an illegitimate, orphaned branch of the Blockchain. By the time you get to several blocks, all of which recognize the transaction in question, one can be fairly certain that they are not witnessing an aberrant branch of the Blockchain. If you require multiple confirmations, it can take up to an hour or more to be fully satisfied that a transaction is fully incorporated in the Blockchain.

In the great majority of cases, worrying about Bitcoin block confirmations is unnecessary. If a transaction is syntactically legitimate and agrees with the current history of the Blockchain, it is quite safe. The only case in which requiring multiple confirmations would be necessary is to protect against malicious attacks by the miners themselves. A miner would have to control a sizeable portion of the hashing power to execute this sort of attack. To my knowledge, this has never happened in the history of Bitcoin. Requiring multiple confirmations is protection against an extreme fringe case. It is the equivalent of walking into a bank with a loaded gun as self-defense in case the bank teller wants to rob you.

Simply broadcasting a transaction and waiting a few seconds for it to ripple throughout the network is enough in 99.99% of all cases. If you're handling millions of dollars in Bitcoin, wait 10 minutes, or an hour, for the transaction to be confirmed. In either case, the time scales are incredibly fast. If you bought a coffee at Starbucks, your transaction is essentially completed in seconds. If you are wiring $1 million dollars to Bangladesh, your transaction is fully secured, to the highest possible standard, in about an hour. That's fast.

It is important to distinguish between wiring money via a financial intermediary, like PayPal, and sending money with Bitcoin. When you send money with PayPal, an internal ledger somewhere in their cavernous database changes two decimal values: one to mark a debit and the other credit. While this internal change of state may be nearly instantaneous within PayPal, it will not have been realized in truth in the real world. If PayPal changes your internal balance instantly, it still takes days to actually cement your ownership of that money. It is not really your money yet. It is PayPal's internal representation of what you own. This is not a trivial distinction. Internally, I'm sure PayPal could be made to be as fast as Bitcoin, if not faster. But it cannot be *actualized* in the real world with equivalent speed because PayPal's internal database does not have real-world legitimacy. They must convert to actual dollars for their internal representation to become real.

You see this phenomenon with intra versus interbank transfers. Within banks, money can be transferred very quickly. Between banks, especially for US customers, transfers take days and require tedious up-front verification steps. Internal representations of money within each bank do not translate instantaneously to real money as recognized by the outside world. The actualization step, where database figments become real, is still limited by constraints in the old money system.

With Bitcoin, however, when a transaction enters the Blockchain, the money is cemented as yours immediately. The realization of your ownership is synonymous with the change of state of the ledger. Receiving bitcoins, your possession is enforced immediately, not deferred until later. Unlike PayPal or equivalents, in Bitcoin there is no difference between a change of the database and enforcement of possession. They are one and the same.

Because ownership of bitcoins is self-evident, Bitcoin transactions will always be faster than human-trusted systems. There is no elaborate ceremony of authorization, as there is with current fiat methods, to condone a transaction. Bitcoin transactions are legitimate because they are mathematically consistent with the unforgeable Blockchain ledger. There is never a person approving transactions besides the sender. Since the entire downstream process is mechanical and algorithmic, it is very fast and reliable.

As an illustrative example, consider in the future a highly efficient fiat-based money processor who handles dollars. The company uses the latest high-speed technology to execute transactions as quickly as possible. Somehow, miraculously, the banks have caught on, shaped up their act, and are willing to accept transactions electronically and rapidly. What would happen? Indeed, high speed stock traders already utilize the most advanced technology available to accomplish trades within milliseconds. So they demonstrate that very rapid trading is technically possible.

But it is not the communications technology of Bitcoin that necessarily makes it faster than any trusted, human-based systems. An even faster fiat payment processor could be built. It is Bitcoin's trustlessness that allows transactions to be fully self-actualizing immediately. By contrast, any human system, no matter how rapid the back-end, cannot legitimize money transfers as quickly. For human laws to take hold, transactions must not be self-enforcing.

Slowness would have to be introduced artificially. From the government's perspective, the design requirements of money necessitate that transactions be slowed and that money should never be truly owned independently. A confirmation window would likely be added in which to detect fraudulent or even illegal money transfers. Transactions would not be irreversible. Indeed, as with current money processors, the urge to 'undo' suspicious transactions would be stupendous. Thus at what point would a transaction be truly settled? Whose say-so would be required to actually control one's money? If it can be undone, or reviewed, or appealed, when can it be said to have truly landed in the bank? How long would I have to wait to clear a government-approval window? Or alternatively, would the ownership of money require the cryptographic equivalent of a government stamp? How many requests for permission would be necessary to perform a financial transaction before one knows that it is 'legitimate'? Under a scheme in which transactions may be censored or even revoked, to what extent do I really own anything?

Any human-trusted system carries heavy costs in time and money. Whoever is trusted, under any scheme, can extract extraordinary value from that position. The premiums that must be paid, as well as the regulatory charges which invariably percolate to us all, would likely amount to a significant sum, even in the most ideally efficient human-based system.

By their nature, human-trusted approaches cannot rival Bitcoin in speed. We humans operate on lazy timescales governed by chemical reactions and thermodynamics, whereas Bitcoin lives at the speed of light. And whereas the math involved with confirming the legitimacy of Bitcoin transactions occurs incredibly quickly, any human process to legitimize money must be drastically slower. Those seeking a middle ground, in which the human element in arbitration is lessened, merely describe a system more resembling Bitcoin.

On a final note, experiencing the speed of Bitcoin transactions leaves a lasting qualitative impression. I recall sending a friend of mine some bitcoin to play with. He sat in an adjacent room. I clicked send, and before I could reach the door, he had seen the transaction (albeit unconfirmed). That was it. He was shocked. It was undeniably his now, with the click of a button. There was no waiting. It was simple, irrevocable, and powerful. Just like email. You have to experience it yourself to see how easy it is.

Bitcoin is Cheap

Bitcoin is much cheaper than legacy financial systems. It is cheap both to send money and to secure the network. In Bitcoin, these are two sides to the same coin.

Currently Bitcoin transactions cost about 0.00005 BTC each. This is not a fixed amount, just a suggested one. At current prices, this is equivalent to less than 2 cents per transaction. For 2 cents, you can send anyone, anywhere, any amount of money instantly and securely. You could send $1 million dollars to Timbuktu, or $0.15 to yourself, and the fees would be the same. Bitcoin does not care what the distances or the sums are. Everyone gets charged the same, rock bottom price.

Huge amounts of money may be moved with the same facility as tiny transactions. See this transaction as an example *5d6787b87be7cd240dc4de5e7e5fc048670618bec31022a5b*

8c04bcc45f9952c; $50 million was moved in an instant, just like sending an email. It could have been anywhere in the world. The sender paid $0.06 in fees: actually more than what was necessary. Such sums cannot be moved across borders, instantly, securely, and so cheaply, with anything in the fiat world. The money wasn't just queued to arrive after a few business days. It became final almost immediately. As the transaction reverberated throughout the Bitcoin network, the money became under the new owner's control in a matter of seconds.

Transaction fees go to the miners. The Blockchain, as a purely decentralized entity, must be maintained at some real-world price. The arms-race between miners must be incentivized by real rewards. This is a cost inherent to a purely trustless system. Any more trusted model may omit mining and thereby incur far fewer costs. But the entire aim of Bitcoin is to avoid trust while maintaining veracity. Peers must be purely symmetrical and the consensus mechanism should be open. Anything less and decentralization will have been lost.

The price paid for securing the Bitcoin network is very well spent. The total amount of hashing power among miners is an astronomical figure. Because it is so staggeringly powerful, no single entity can successfully attack the network. Small altcoins with weak mining, by contrast, are highly vulnerable. Indeed, they are often attacked because of their lack of mining power. By contrast, Bitcoin's hash rate is so vast that even major governments would struggle to assemble the resources to attack it.

Bitcoin's fees are spent in the most efficient market on Earth. Because mining is an open system, there are no barriers to entry. Anyone can participate; it's just math. Getting paid is as simple as broadcasting a few kilobytes of data. In fact, the market for hashing power is probably the freest in the entire world. There is zero regulation. There is zero interference. At the lowest level, it's as simple as running electronics from anywhere. As a result, mining has migrated, from individuals' desktops, to highly specialized mining factories sourced near cheap electricity. I will further discuss the nuances of mining and transaction fees later in the book.

You can choose to pay any amount in transaction fees. Higher amounts will guarantee that your transaction is included in a block sooner. A transaction with no fee at all may occasionally enter a block out of the charity of a miner, or it will eventually expire after broadcast. There is a floating market for space in Bitcoin blocks. Transaction fees are prices in the supply and demand balance between transactions and space in the Blockchain.

The Inflationary Cost
While transaction fees are the marginal cost of including content in the Blockchain, the automatic block reward currently constitutes the overwhelming majority of compensation for miners. This amounts to 25 BTC per block. It is a form of temporary inflation that will tail off over time as Bitcoin approaches its maximum of 21 million coins. At least today, the vast majority of the resources for the maintenance of miners come from this inflationary cost and not transaction fees.

We will investigate the long term fate of transaction fees vs. the automatic block reward in a later section. But it should be noted that transaction fees are expected to *increase* as the automatic block reward *decreases*. As fees bear the greater brunt of the cost of supporting the network, the market dynamics for pricing transactions will play out in greater detail.

There are reasons to be optimistic, however, that transactions will remain affordable. If the total transaction volume is large, very low fees can be sufficient to protect the network from outside attack. Because mining equipment is priced in dollars, everything depends on the USD flow rate of Bitcoin transactions.

Today the network costs $1 million to run per day. Greater than 99% of that comes from the invented 25 BTC per block. As that figure declines exponentially in the coming years, the overall cost to run the network may decrease. That is highly debatable. At current levels of approximately $60 million transacted per day, transaction fees amount to less than 2% if you include the inflationary component.

This 2% fraction may still seem too high to satisfactorily compete with legacy systems. Of course the comparison is flawed because we don't count US dollar inflation in our estimation of transactional costs in legacy payment systems. If we did this, taking the average yearly velocity of a dollar (1.5 for M2) and comparing with inflation (charitably 3% according to government figures), we would find that dollars themselves also have an equivalent 'inflationary cost' of 2% per transaction. Normal economists neglect this so perhaps we may also give Bitcoin the benefit of the doubt.

But the situation could dramatically improve. By 2020 the automatic block reward will be 6.25 bitcoins per block. If the network were to grow to $200 million dollars transacted per day and $1000 per coin, then inflationary costs would then be ~0.4%. These are not unreasonable numbers.

The story is actually better than it appears because more transactional activity occurs on the Blockchain than is immediately obvious. Off-chain and payment channel services occur without adding to the visible transaction volume, even as they leverage the Blockchain. So the effective cost per transaction could be significantly less. Moreover, many of the costs of securing the network can be perceived as 'fixed'. Additional transactional volume imposes little extra burden; the marginal cost of additional transactions is near zero. Thus transactional costs may remain very low in practice, and the total volume may grow to take advantage of the already present pool of miners securing the network.

The Costs of Legacy Systems
Whereas with Bitcoin, upkeep of the network is charged explicitly as transaction fees and automatic block rewards, legacy financial systems charge much larger amounts opaquely to the consumer. It may appear inconvenient to have to include any transaction fee at all, but with conventional money tools, such as credit cards, consumers are implicitly playing much more sizeable fees that they cannot see. In fact, these amount to approximately 2-3% for credit card users. These are explicit fees, not the inflationary

cost mentioned above (so add another 2% if you believe the government statistics. Add more if you don't). Needless to say, for large economies such as in the US, these fees sum to a huge amount. In fact, the cumulative fees of credit card processors such as VISA amount to at least an order of magnitude more, yearly, than Bitcoin's entire market capitalization.

International and wire transfers are even more grossly inefficient. Their cost is a shameful statement on our supposed modernity. For the mere service of managing a trusted ledger, companies such as Western Union extract exorbitant uncompetitive fees. Fees can range from 2-20% of transmitted funds. This is stupendous value extraction. The more underdeveloped the country, the higher the fees typically are. It can cost 8% of the total to transfer money between Singapore and Pakistan: two important economies, to say nothing of many small African countries.

The global remittances industry is massive with over $500 billion transferred each year. Most of the money flows from developed to under-developed countries. As such, most of the transfers must flow past the most egregiously inefficient gatekeepers. Consider the sums at stake; if $400 billion dollars flows yearly to undeveloped countries, and fees are on the order of 3% (very conservative) are charged, that makes for $12 billion in fees each year. This sum is 3 times the market capitalization of all of Bitcoin in yearly revenue.

Within the US, Bitcoin is cheaper than the 2-3% fees charged by credit cards, largely as a result of chargebacks and fraud. While the difference within the US may be slight, internationally it is dramatically cheaper. It permits small amounts to be sent anywhere instantly. It costs me $12 to send $100 to Cameroon right now through Western Union. From Cameroon, it costs dramatically more still to send money to another African country. Bitcoin short-circuits all of these inefficiencies. The dilapidated state of financial institutions in Third World countries, particularly in Africa, invites massive off-the-shelf efficiency gains from Bitcoin.

Whereas financial infrastructure must be laboriously built from scratch in many poor countries, Bitcoin, as computer code, is infinitely extensible. So although conventional payment processors do extract too much value for what they provide, their costs of doing business are also higher. Extending Western Union to Senegal requires all sorts of costly investments. Their closed, proprietary systems are costlier to operate, maintain, and to extend. Bitcoin is cheaper in every regard. There is no intermediary capturing profits. But there is also a single network which costs nothing to expand to additional countries.

It is a common trend in developing nations to skip over redundant technologies still found in more developed nations. In Africa, landline phones are extraordinarily rare; but everyone has a cell phone. You will never find a laser disc player in any developing country. For countries that are already severely behind developed nations, it makes perfect sense to adopt the latest and eschew the obsolete. We may see this trend at work in finance as well. Bitcoin is ready-built. For countries with obsolescent banking sectors, Bitcoin represents a massive step up with comparatively little investment required. Many of the hard questions have already been solved by the best and brightest. In many countries, adopting Bitcoin is a question of setting up exchanges and clarifying the legal environment. Virtually all the heavy-lifting has been done; the infrastructure already exists.

Thus while Bitcoin already offers superior transactional utility in the developed world, it offers monumental efficiency improvements for developing nations without commensurately large investment. As software, Bitcoin requires minimal resources to get up and running. What innovations occur, in places such as Silicon Valley, can be deployed virtually for free across a vast economic spectrum. The cost-reward ratio of using Bitcoin is thus most favorable for poorer countries.

We have seen how bitcoins can be sent cheaply, for the price of 1-2 cents. This price outperforms that of virtually all competitors. Competition is strongest in the most developed, efficient markets, such as the US. But even there, credit card and PayPal fees still amount to 2-3%: an unacceptably high rate for the 21st century. Internationally, the price advantages burgeon as they confront deeply uncompetitive modes of exchange. The high fees of Western Union exemplify this trend. These fees grow for more undeveloped markets, such that sending money between small countries like Guinea and Zambia could cost a mind-bogglingly large fraction of the original sum.

Storage

Bitcoin's low cost does not just pertain to the act of sending money. Storing bitcoins is also exceptionally cheap. Because Bitcoin allows one to be one's own bank, a well-versed user could handle his private key totally independently and thus, for free. One could possess many millions of dollars by merely retaining the associated private key, whether encrypted online, stored on a paper wallet, or some combination thereof. The storage costs then are literally zero.

Even if one does not wish to manipulate one's own private key, there are a myriad of tools online to assist with managing an address. One example, by no means the best, is Blockchain.info, a website that offers a web wallet service. One may control a private key through this service whose encrypted form is stored by the company. But the wallet is only ever decrypted client-side by the owner with his password. Thus Blockchain.info reliably keeps the private key, without ever having the means to decrypt it themselves. There are many other web wallets out there with different approaches to security. Coinbase offers a wallet with a 'vault' function whose value is insured by third party agents, and which uses the safest multisignature techniques. This is another extremely reliable storage option. In essence, there is a wide spectrum of choice available in managing your funds. At the one end, you may manage a raw private key yourself and be your own bank in every regard. At the other end of the spectrum, you can trust Coinbase completely to manage everything for you. Somewhere in the middle lie other services like

Blockchain.info, whom you may trust much less, because they cannot actually access your wallet.

One may choose a point on the spectrum of Bitcoin management best suited to one's preferences. I personally retain most of my Bitcoin as a raw private key which I have encrypted and stored myself very carefully. The majority of users will use a well-known wallet service such as Blockchain.info or Coinbase. It is really a special thing that one is free to choose one's own money storage strategy. At any time, a user can change his mind, moving bitcoins from Coinbase to Blockchain.info, to his own private key, or to another service.

These services are also exceptionally cheap. Blockchain.info and Coinbase allow one to store bitcoins with a very high level of security for free. I cannot even think of a web wallet service that actually charges for storing funds. It is such a competitive space that it is hard to imagine users ever having to pay. Perhaps insured, reputable services, such as Coinbase, could someday extract a fee, the same way elite Swiss banks must be paid to store things in their vaults. But even this is unlikely, as bitcoins are already insured on Coinbase for free. Because it's just software, the marginal cost of storing bitcoins is zero.

Storing one's money for free is no small issue either. There are no monthly fees, as there are with traditional banks, merely for keeping funds on balance. Moreover, normal banks do not actually store depositors' money in full. Under the system of fractional reserve banking, some small percent, typically less than 10%

is actually available at any given time. The rest is employed by banks in loans and even in speculative investments. These activities generate income for the bank. But only a fraction of that income is returned to depositors as interest. In today's low interest rate environment, depositors receive virtually nothing. Sometimes, indeed, they must pay outright for the privilege of loaning their money out. The difference in the income derived from deposits, and that paid out to depositors, constitutes the majority of the bank's revenue. Thus, by exposing your deposited money to banks' investments, you subsidize the cost of storage. In other words, part of paying for storing your money is allowing it to be exposed in credit markets, without receiving the full market price for that exposure. Thus the real cost of storing your money is higher than advertised. A bank without fractional reserves would charge much higher monthly sums for storing money. And yet this is precisely what Bitcoin wallet services accomplish for free.

The Fiat-Bitcoin Interface

It is true that there are some costs associated with Bitcoin. It can still be relatively expensive to buy and sell bitcoins into the local fiat currency. This step lies outside the Bitcoin network; it is at the messy intersection of Blockchain and the real world. In the US, Coinbase charges a flat 1% fee for users to buy and sell bitcoins into Dollars. A roundtrip purchase can thus amount to 2%. This is very high compared to transaction fees within the network.

However there is nothing fundamental to this high 1% fee. In fact, it is a symptom of the dysfunction in conventional banking, with which companies such as

Coinbase must interact. We can see this in action; astonishingly, until recently there was no American Bitcoin Exchange. Numerous American exchanges had been shut down, or bullied, or indirectly sabotaged over the years. Virtually every attempt before the Coinbase Exchange had been stymied by an unholy alliance of regulators and bankers. Because of this hostile legal environment, the conversion between Dollars and bitcoins is uncompetitive in the US. Coinbase can charge high fees of 1% because it has almost alone overcome the regulatory challenges imposed by government. This is not a stable state of affairs. It is probable that the business of converting Dollars and bitcoins will become more competitive over time. There is no intrinsic reason why one company should have the regulators' good will. We have already seen this with new Coinbase competitors such as Circle, who already offer lower fees. As competitive pressure grows it will, in turn, push down the 1% conversion fee that currently reigns.

Interactions between Bitcoin and legacy finance remain messy and inefficient. As the number of Bitcoin companies grows, more serious attention is being paid to connecting new with old in a seamless manner. Contrasting the present 1% fee with the torturous ordeal of buying bitcoins a few years ago illustrates how far Bitcoin has already come in this regard. Even as fiat-to-Bitcoin conversion improves, the significance of Bitcoin-Bitcoin interactions will grow in proportion. Transactions internal to Bitcoin operate at vastly greater efficiency than those at the fiat interface. As the Bitcoin network itself grows, there will be less reason to exit the system back to dollars. The number of Bitcoin-Bitcoin transactions already dwarf fiat-Bitcoin transactions (by a greater than 20:1 ratio) [vii], and this trend will continue dramatically as the number of participants grows. Thus the cost advantages of transacting within the network will dominate over any legacy inefficiencies of translating fiat-to-Bitcoin.

That Bitcoin itself is several orders of magnitude cheaper than legacy institutions should come as no surprise. After all, someone must pay for the armies of paper pushers, ATM's, and brick & mortar stores of conventional banks. Just consider all the well paid employees of large financial institutions and payment processors. They extract value from depositors and transmitters of money, i.e. everyone. Bitcoin companies, by contrast, are much smaller, cheaper, and more modest. No company can extract value from customers using Bitcoin to the same extent as in the legacy financial system. The competition is too fierce. The playing field is too flat. Because Bitcoin is only software, a few programmers can build products that touch millions of people. There is no need for expensive, 20th century solutions, such as ATMs or physical stores with tellers, clerks, and managers. Bitcoin has dramatically fewer moving parts. It has (almost) zero well-heeled, expensive executives. Anyone who attempted to extract value to the same extent as PayPal, or Western Union, or Chase Bank, within Bitcoin, would certainly fail; a hundred web startups would gobble them up. With such low barriers to entry, Bitcoin is doing to financial services what software did to many other legacy industries; drive down their profits by offering more efficient, algorithmic replacements. This gives better value to consumers. And it's terrifying to incumbents.

Expect them to raise regulatory concerns to protect their businesses from competition.

Thus via the transaction mechanism, in which enormous sums may be transmitted for pennies, Bitcoin is dirt cheap. In the maintenance of a vast, cryptographically sound, decentralized network which no single entity could overcome, Bitcoin delivers incredible value. In the realm of banking and other financial services, fees are virtually nil. Only at the interface with fiat does regulation rear its nasty head and hence significant fees arise. But even these costs are lower than those of legacy alternatives. And as Bitcoin matures, there should be no expectation for them to last; the space is simply too competitive. It should thus come as no surprise that Bitcoin is cheaper than fiat alternatives. It is software after all. And as Marc Andreessen once said, software is eating the world.

Bitcoin is Blind to Borders

Bitcoin inhabits neither space nor nations. It has no mailing address. Bitcoin transactions occur as pure information within given logical rules. As such, Bitcoin cannot be constrained the way legacy financial services are. It defies physical bounds.

By contrast, governments are routinely involved in restricting the free flow of fiat money. These interventions have had a significant, deleterious effect on capital distribution. Government-imposed limits on the free movement of money disrupt natural human behavior. They infringe on the will of the free market in a politicized fashion. The hubris of such interventions often inflicts large aggregate losses.

Many nations impose controls on the exchange rate of their currency against foreign currencies. Sometimes they do so by fiat legislation; it becomes illegal to trade currencies apart from the dictated rate. Interventions may also come in the form of open market purchases, interest rate manipulations, or the selling of foreign currency reserves. These techniques vary in the extent and the manner by which they infringe on voluntary markets. They are authoritarian distortions all the same.

I can attest from personal experience how damaging currency controls. When I lived in Guinea-Conakry as a Peace Corps Volunteer we lived under a strictly controlled currency exchange rate. The Guinean Franc, perhaps the most inconsequential, poorly made currency on Earth, was controlled vis-a-vis the Dollar at about 3000 Francs per Dollar. All money coming into the country had legally to be exchanged at this rate. All of our living expenses, in addition to all the expenditures by the US State Department, were converted according to this mandated price. However the black market rate, which reflected the true supply and demand relationship, was at that time about 5000 Francs per Dollar. Even this discrepancy pales in comparison to that in other countries, such as in Argentina, where mandated vs. black market rates differ by larger magnitudes[viii]. In Guinea, the skewed exchange rate negatively influenced a broad swathe of downstream economic behavior. It meant that for every dollar foreigners legally brought into the country, someone in the Guinean government was in effect scalping 40 cents.

The government-imposed rate had no bearing on reality whatsoever. No one on the streets would have accepted such terms in reverse. In other words, it would be impossible to buy a dollar for anywhere near that price. There simply weren't enough dollars around; the country could not attract them. Moreover, by mandating such a disadvantageous exchange rate, the Guinean government ensured that foreigners only ever got 60 cents on the dollar. This further discouraged the migration of foreign currency, since it was, in essence, heavily taxed. Since the only reason to import dollars was to buy Guinean goods, the effect was for local exports to be massively penalized by their own government. If they had allowed their currency to float freely a much healthier import/export environment would have arisen.

What Guinea, a desperately poor country even by African standards, needed above all was to acquire hard foreign currency. This was handicapped by exchange rate policies which, on their surface, would appear to bring in more foreign money. By imposing an exchange rate so far from market realities, a de facto confiscatory regime was established. This made it even harder to attract foreign capital: the ostensible object of such policies. It is but one example of many of unforeseen repercussions in enacting policy. Whereas first-order effects may superficially seem to promote a certain outcome, secondary and tertiary consequences may upset one's aims entirely.

The currency in Guinea was atrocious. The largest denomination at that time was a 10,000 Franc bill. This meant that the biggest bill available was worth $2. It was always necessary to carry massive wads of cash everywhere to do anything. No sane person saved Guinean Francs or entered into long-term financial contracts denominated in them. The banking system was so critically broken, on so many levels, that it was almost a barter economy.

In fact I broke the currency exchange law (which theoretically carried a death sentence) on the day we were all evacuated from Guinea. People were only too happy to trade currency at real, market prices. I had to negotiate the exchange rate across a huge range. This reflected the Guinean Franc's illiquidity in a black market. Without transparent, legal markets, black markets become opaque and inefficient. I keenly remember that day; I had a massive pile of $1-2 Guinea Franc bills that I needed to sell. They formed tall stacks, like you see in pictures from Weimar Germany. As I counted the pyramids of money, everyone had to be on the lookout for the Gendarmes (paramilitary police) who would surely have confiscated it if they had seen it. I assumed the death sentence bit would not be taken seriously.

While Guinea may be an extreme case of dysfunction, many more developed countries have capital controls that, because of the greater size of their economies, are even more damaging. China is the most salient example. The Chinese Yuan's exchange rate with the Dollar was forced to fall within a specified range set by fiat. Any other price was illegal. Naturally, the stated rate was not the market one. In fact the Chinese Yuan was seriously undervalued for years. By forcing the Yuan down, the Chinese government in effect delivered value to foreigners and the US in particular, for free. There has been a net displacement of wealth, from Chinese people, to Americans and others, because of their central bank policy. With such a weak Yuan, Chinese exports cannot buy the imports that they ought to be able to buy. The Chinese have been bilked by their own government from the fruits of their own labor. It has been noted by many that the net effect of this distortion, besides a gigantic free lunch for Americans, will be economic turmoil still to come. Cheap Chinese goods and credit continue to wash on America's shores, causing misallocation in the US as well. Any return to equilibrium may itself prove to be a disturbing financial dislocation. In the end, both countries will be worse off.

Indeed, Chinese citizens suffer from a wide array of capital restrictions. For instance, they may not easily take money out of the country. Domestically there are severe restrictions on what they may do with their money. Probably as a result, Chinese savings are largely parked at inefficient, state-run banks, paying low or negative real interest rates. There they finance cronyistic projects in that country's unique brand of state capitalism. China's ghost cities, paid for through loans from hapless depositors with no legal recourse, are unlikely to pay themselves back. Their wealth is essentially held hostage. Under the circumstances, it should come as no surprise that Chinese citizens have exhibited keen interest in Bitcoin.

Other forms of capital controls exist, and they are equally pernicious insofar as they invade the prerogatives of free individuals. In the past, countries have suddenly halted the outflow of currency or gold in an attempt to shore up failing currencies. Others have made even more exorbitant infringements, such as nationalizing industries, taxing savings accounts, and outright confiscation. In fact, many of the most developed nations, with the least need for such depredatory tactics, have been the most egregious perpetrators. Case in point: the United States made it illegal for individuals to own gold, hitherto the world currency, in 1933. Wholesale seizures and prosecutions ensued. The US government promptly devalued the dollar by 40 percent, immediately defrauding savers. If the United States is capable of such outright theft, and indeed, still celebrates it 80 years on, there are almost no limits to the potential confiscatory policies of even the most respected nations.

As ever, Bitcoin stands in stark contrast to fiat money. Bitcoin is blind to borders. No fiat declaration can stop a Bitcoin transaction. The Blockchain is like a parallel dimension in which it is not possible to erect the barriers we suffer here on Earth. It is structurally incapable of discriminating against the nationalities of those involved. Bitcoin's transcendence of borders will doubltess irk the bureaucrats of the world. But such freedom is a much more natural state for money.

Money was once blind to borders. In the pre-1914 era, national currencies were merely surrogates for gold, and in a few cases, silver. Governments could not control capital flows without implicitly defaulting on their obligations. Under a regime tied to precious metals, the proof was in the pudding. Gold either left the country or arrived there. This was a final statement on each nation's trade balance that could not be obfuscated. Exchange rates could not be held at an unsustainable level indefinitely; flows of gold would always bring the monetary supply to equilibrium. Setting one's currency too high would cause gold to flee, effectively bringing deflation and tight credit. Currency set too low would attract gold and loose credit. In either case an equilibrium would eventually be reached by the simple mechanism of profit-seeking gold flows. The profit-motive of arbitrageurs served as a restorative force to monetary imbalances. Long term manipulation of currencies was almost impossible.

The monetary stability of that era was lost and in a century we have not regained it. Money once flowed internationally with great ease. Without fluctuating exchange rates or capital controls, it was possible to invest around the world with much less risk. With all debts ultimately denominated in the one medium which could not be printed by government, gold, currency itself posed less of an obstacle. International investments did not suffer the extraneous risk of fluctuating exchange rates as they do today. One had only to consider the merits of the specific investment at hand. This stands in stark contrast to investing nowadays, in which risk is a complex, multifaceted convolution of factors, only one of which is the base investment itself. Modern investors must worry about the exchange rates, and indeed the inflation rate, of the currency medium through which a deal occurs. Actually that's the ideal case. In practice, investors must also worry about capital controls and central bank interventions. What should be a simple matter of weighing the prospects of a particular investment becomes a bet on a vast constellation of other factors, many of which are intrinsically unknowable. It is not enough merely to assess a prospective foreign business, one must divine the monetary policy of bureaucrats, foreign and domestic.

The principal role of currency is to facilitate trade. The ideal currency should minimize exchange risk. But the current system of floating fiat currencies singularly fails at this, particularly compared to its historical predecessor. Under the current system, nations consistently choose devaluation of their currency over internal deflation. Or in other words, between the twin ailments of deflation and devaluation, the former always proves intolerable, and the latter much more facile in the short term.

During the pre-1914 era, countries just had to make do with expansions or contractions of their monetary supply. Such changes were symptomatic of underlying realities such as trade imbalances or divergent interest rates. But investors knew that gold was gold. Regardless of the nominal form or the nation of origin, it would be the same money as before. By contrast, modern investors have no idea precisely what the meaning is of what they will be paid back in. Or alternatively they must pay a premium for a futures contract to hedge against currency fluctuations. Modern nations have made a conscious choice to tamper with interest rates and their monetary supplies at the cost of volatility risk to international investors. In doing so, they have muted the free expression of the market. And they have done great harm by introducing unneeded risk to cross-border investing. During the pre-1914 era of unfettered financial globalization, European capital built American railroads, Argentinian Farms, and Japanese Steelworks. At that time, almost 50% of all international investments occurred in developing countries[ix]. The modern proportion is dramatically lower; currency exchange risk, among other factors, discourages capital allocation where it belongs most.

As ever, the story of fiat money's failures says much about Bitcoin's promise. What gold once was, Bitcoin can be again in the Internet era. So long as transactions remain within the Bitcoin network, there are no fluctuating exchange rates. The prices I see in Japan, in BTC, are the same units I see in the US. A bitcoin is a bitcoin, regardless of nation-state. Whereas Bitcoin still has tremendous volatility vis-a-vis fiat currencies, and I shall address this in a later section, internally there is no volatility whatsoever. This makes it a superior platform for exchange.

There never was a need for currency fragmentation in the first place. The primary explicit rationale was to empower central banks to plan interest rates. As the Soviet Union centrally planned the number of socks to manufacture each year, modern central banks plan what interest rates should be. A more sinister aim was to endow government with a tool for the surreptitious extraction of wealth. We would have been far better off without such interventions. Bitcoin promises to heal the fracturing of currencies that first occurred in 1914 and reached its ultimate climax in 1971 with the end of Bretton Woods. It is a powerful new tool that eschews the momentary weakness of past leaders; technology may keep us disciplined where nerve fails.

Even now, the advantages of a universal non-national currency are manifest. For example, there are ways to lend out bitcoins around the world. You can lend them to speculators wishing to short the dollar/bitcoin price on

BitfineX, a leading exchange. You can lend bitcoins peer-to-peer via sites such as BTCJam, where prospective creditors and borrowers earn de facto credit ratings. In all these cases, interest rates are fluctuating according to free market dynamics in a manner blind to borders. For instance, on BitfineX (a Bitcoin exchange), the interest rate for bitcoin margin lending typically spikes when there is a heavy bearish sentiment (reflecting the demand to borrow and short bitcoins). At this moment, the annualized interest rate for BTC is 18%. This is an extremely high figure, reflecting the recent downward price movement. But crucially, that interest rate *is the same for all users, regardless of nation*. In other words, it is already happening. Users on BTCJam compete for interest rates regardless of what country they come from.

Loans denominated in bitcoins represent an international consolidation of credit. Interest rates ought to hinge on the prospects of the lender, not the particulars of the country he inhabits. Loans in a currency that is blind to borders, whose monetary policy is already foreordained, can smooth interest rates worldwide. Fiat money, with capital controls and divergent monetary policies between nations, erects additional barriers in the percolation of credit around the world. There is a reason that people in developing countries cannot get credit beyond any analysis of their ability to repay.

Capital flows disproportionately to nations where money is safe, where financial institutions are more secure, and where the risk of capital controls is low. Developed countries such as the US fit this criterion. Despite their heavily-capitalized economies, they continue to attract vast amounts of investment. In Africa, by contrast, not only is the financial infrastructure immature, but currency volatility and regime uncertainty impose additional risks. Thus the parts of the world most in need of capital, where by all rights the returns should be highest, receive less than what they ought to, even in a purely profit-seeking sense. These burdens are not physical; they are needless impositions. Consider the contrast with the 19th century under a gold standard. Under a regime in which money could flow internationally with few barriers, investment in developing countries was proportionately more widespread than it is today. It was safer back then to invest in a remote place; you would be paid back in gold, the same currency as anywhere else. One had only to consider the prospects of the investment at hand.

Bitcoin promises to grease the wheels of international finance in a much safer, healthier way. Because Bitcoin is Bitcoin anywhere, it doesn't matter whether African banks are mature, or whether Indonesia threatens capital controls. A bitcoin on a mobile phone in a village is just as good as anywhere else. There is a perfect symmetry between participants, whether they live in Silicon Valley or Nairobi. It could be a great enfranchising force for those whose economic lives are unfairly sullied by the policies of the nation they happen to inhabit. Bitcoin is a single platform that can be quickly scaled to remote areas without having to build large-scale infrastructure. As an non-national currency, it enables interest rates to harmonize across borders. This could facilitate a more natural diffusion of credit around the world. Instead of clustering where financial institutions make money safe, in a small subset of countries, capital could roam free. The security baked-in to Bitcoin could compensate for local deficiencies in financial infrastructure. The traditional forces dissuading capital from moving where it may earn the highest return, political and currency risk, may be short-circuited by trustless, borderless money.

21ˢᵗ Century Gold

Money with Integrity

Bitcoin today does what gold did for the 19th century. It provides a stable, worldwide currency that is controlled by no government. It is a special resource, a commodity like gold that may not be suddenly printed or created. There are algorithmically predetermined constraints on the supply of Bitcoin which are analogous to the natural limitations in the amount of available gold. Because the supply of gold lay outside the realm of governments, in the 19th century no nation could recklessly print money without the risk of imminent bankruptcy.

The world's monetary supplies were moderated by a self-correcting feedback loop. For each excess or shortage a countervailing force would arise to push things back the other way. As countries ran current account deficits, interest rates would rise of their own accord due to the scarcity of money. Prices would fall with the flight of money. These forces would in turn attract money back. Currencies existed in a natural equilibrium in which trade, fiscal policies, and interest rates obeyed natural laws akin to gravity. Governments had to face the hard reality of trade and fiscal imbalances. Proof of coming failure lay plainly in the flight of gold. The inescapable fact that gold could not be printed, but only slowly mined at great cost, ultimately enforced monetary discipline worldwide.

The Failure of Fiat

Since departing from gold, the world has lost its old discipline. Central bankers have proclaimed an end to the laws of physics. It is as if gravity were suspended by fiat. This is an act of profound hubris. Economic laws did not originate in fiat declarations by men which could later be suspended. Monetary policy has binged carefree, believing hangovers to have been abolished. It is widely believed that we may forever live beyond our means through endless deficits. Nobel-prize winners flatly state that printing money need not lead to inflation, in defiance of basic commonsense. Conventional economics has gone off the deep end; economists today embrace theories that would have shocked their predecessors. As the new orthodoxy is enacted as public policy, the consequences can only be disastrous.

The world needs new monetary discipline. It will get it, one way or another, as inescapable mathematical realities reap the full consequences of our profligacy. Whether through conscientious action now, or disaster tomorrow, monetary equilibrium will be restored. The rock that was thrown will land again. The debts that were raised with such abandon, will take their due, whether in stagnation or inflation, or both.

If fiat currencies reach an inflationary reckoning, as I believe they must, people will seek refuge in stable assets. Gold will surely be one such recourse. But Bitcoin is an even better one. Because it is digital, Bitcoin delivers the supply stability of gold with all the currency advantages the 21st century can offer. As speculators buy and sell gold today as a hedge against the stability of fiat currencies, Bitcoin will occupy a similar niche due to its similar properties.

The day-to-day price of Bitcoin is now only weakly correlated to inflation in fiat money. This speaks to the still speculative and volatile sentiments of cryptocurrency markets. However it is very likely that as speculative fervor subsides Bitcoin's price will start to move inversely with the value of fiat currencies, as the gold price does. In the future large institutional players may trade bitcoins in a manner akin to gold, as an inflation hedge.

It is not impossible for fiat to remain stable under the right leadership. In 1982 Chairman Volcker aggressively raised US interest rates, staunching chronic US inflation, while simultaneously delivering a body blow to the economy. The short term pain was tremendous. The country howled as the economy took a hit. It was deeply unpopular. However Volcker's rate increase was plainly in the best interests of the country over the long run. It stabilized the currency and defeated rampant, destructive inflation. It is now widely seen as a courageous, far-sighted act.

But Volcker was the exception that proved the rule. There is ample evidence, coming from every corner, that the major economies today have no contemporary Volcker at the helm. Nor is there much appetite for the short term pain it would take to stabilize currencies. From Europe, to Japan, to China, and the US, rampant money-printing is the order of the day. There is virtually no chance that monetary discipline will be resurrected under the current generation of leadership.

Persistently low interest rates promote misallocation of capital; they defer the cleansing test of interest payments whose purpose is to signal the economic viability of debt. Simply put, when money is too cheap, bad debts accumulate. And bad debts are what cause financial disasters. In the short term, the sudden realization of the weakness of accumulated debts can cause a panicked run on confidence. This causes a deluge of selling as awareness spreads, almost virally, of the extent of malinvestment. This occurred during the mortgage crisis of 2008. It occurs very suddenly because, as a critical mass of people wake up to the danger, fear spreads with the speed of human panic. It is a sudden dawning awareness that the wealth that was thought to exist *never* existed. Preceding the panic, excessively low interest rates cause capital to be allocated to the wrong places at the expense of the right ones. Because thoughtful investment is what drives productivity growth over the long haul, chronic bad debts lead to lower long-term prosperity. This is what has happened to Japan, where zombie banks were not allowed to die, debts remain massive, and reckoning is constantly forestalled. The consequence has been stagnation lasting generations.

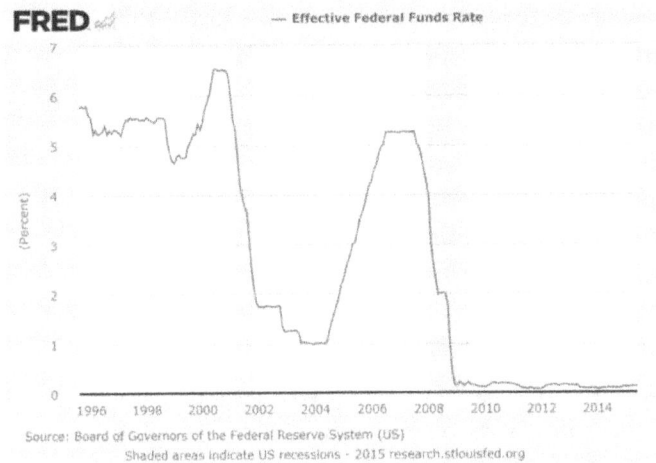

FRED — Effective Federal Funds Rate

Source: Board of Governors of the Federal Reserve System (US)
Shaded areas indicate US recessions · 2015 research.stlouisfed.org

Unnaturally low interest rates sow the seeds of bubbles and concomitant crashes

If private markets stand to lose mightily from increased rates, government debt does as well. The US is constantly accruing new debts through deficits. Most of this debt is being continuously refinanced on a short term basis. If interest rates rise from their current levels near zero to even a modest 4-5%, this will impose a dire new burden on the Federal budget. Consider that this back of the envelope calculation; if US federal debt is approximately 100% the size of GDP, then 4% interest rates impose a fiscal burden of 4% GDP per year. Since the Federal government only takes in about 20% of GDP per year in revenue, interest payments alone would amount to 20% of all federal expenditures! The shortfall could only ever be paid for via still-greater debt, thus propelling a crisis of confidence.

An increase of government expenditures dedicated to servicing interest on the federal debt would only exacerbate persistent federal deficits. Like a bad debtor spiraling out of control, those interest payments would themselves be paid through newly raised debt. This could only ever be paid for through artificially invented money by the Federal Reserve. We have already seen this happen. As newly issued debt is increasingly sustained with printed money, i.e. the debt is *monetized* rather than funded via society's savings, greater burdens are inevitably placed on the Dollar itself. Eventually there comes a breaking point when too much debt is bought through printed money as opposed to savings. While US debts can always be paid nominally, through invented money, the real value of that money would plummet. A panic would ensue, like a run on an insolvent bank, but on a global scale involving trillions of dollars' worth of Treasury bond assets. Just as fear and panic spread virally in 2008, causing a sudden plunge, the same phenomenon could occur with a loss of confidence in the Dollar.

Capturing Value without Consent

Inflation undermines individual liberty as well, in that it provides a mechanism for governments to capture value without having to raise taxes. Because taxation must be debated in legislatures with significant public input, it is an inconvenient way for the government to raise money. What a headache it must be to reach compromises about spending priorities, or to perform careful cost-benefit analyses! Whereas thoughtful weighing of cost versus reward ought to be a primary function of government, all caution may be cast aside when printing money. Inventing money requires no short term losses politically. Inflation steals stealthily, such that the losers don't know it until it is too late. Since nothing nominally has been taken from them, the losers have much less recourse than they do against taxation. Nor is it as obvious an effect. Whereas I may know my tax burden precisely, inflation hits in a nebulous, hard-to-measure way.

If government may raise money without recourse to the inconvenience of taxation, it becomes far less accountable to the citizenry. Ordinarily the government's difficulty in raising money was one of the greatest levers in the hands of common folk. This was best exemplified in the years leading up to the English Civil War, in the 1600's, in which the King attempted to manage the country financially without having to call upon Parliament (who alone could levy taxes). After struggling for years on a shoestring budget, virtually powerless, the government was broke. Ultimately the government's need to raise money required recognition of popular representatives in Parliament. Despite the political animosity, the government simply had no other way to raise enough revenue.

These tensions over money and power, whether in the hands of the King or Parliament, soon erupted into the English Civil War. The king lost and heads rolled. With the Parliamentarians' victory, the democratic stranglehold over the state's revenue was solidified. This throttled the raw executive power of the King; for all his men-at-arms the power of the purse would dominate. The tradition of legislative control over the state's revenue sources was continued in the US, and elsewhere. It has served as a vital bulwark against autocracy. To this day, despite the President's vast powers, he must solicit Congress to raise taxes.

King Charles I would have appreciated Quantitative Easing

Recently the story has changed. Explicit popular consent is no longer necessary to raise money when it can merely be created. Imagine if King Charles I of England could simply have printed money instead of calling upon Parliament. Surely he would have done so. When gold was the world's currency, its scarcity imposed natural limitations on human actions. The corollary to the fact that gold could not be invented was that hard truths had always to be confronted. If there was not enough money for some venture, more had to be raised, whether through debts or through taxation.

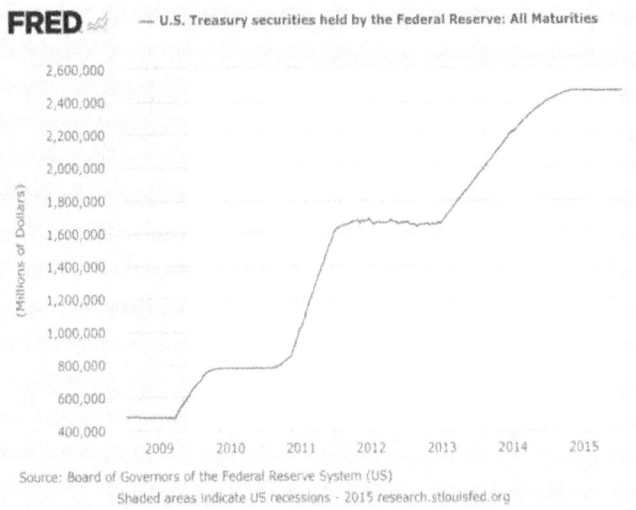

The monetization of US Federal Debt: Government Funding comes increasingly from printed money

King Charles I would surely have resolved his troubles by printing money, had people of that time been willing to accept fiat money. No deal with Parliament would have been necessary. The parallels with today's process for creating money are palpable. We ought to be frightened, not merely on economic grounds, but for our civil liberties when government need not solicit us for its revenue. For there to be a power of the purse outside the representative process is a severe threat to liberty.

Fiat money has wrought much damage over the past century. It has been the ideal medium for the disenfranchisement of savers. It is a way for governments to extract value from their citizens without explicitly taxing them, and hence, without being properly subject to popular consent. Dramatic increases in monetary supplies, no longer bound to physical limits, have promoted malinvestment on a grand scale. When the price of credit hinges mostly on the monetary policy of bureaucrats, rather than the real supply-demand relationship between savers and borrowers, massive economic errors must result. When economic crashes strike, they are only the final realization of the errors that have already been made. The proliferation of bad debts in our era is evidence of the broken credit mechanism as well as a harbinger of further ills yet to come. If money is a measuring stick, then monetary policy is the practice of distorting all measurements.

The lessons of the gold standard ought to remain compelling today. Bitcoin shares the same economic virtues as gold. The same historical arguments in favor of the gold standard should apply to the future adoption of Bitcoin. What currency solidity was lost in the 20th century can be regained, with added advantages, through gold's technological successor.

More Gold than Gold

Most gold traded today is not actually physical but abstract. The vast majority of gold 'holdings' are actually paper claims on others to supply gold. It has been oft speculated that the proliferation of these paper deals has exceeded the base capacity of available gold. In other words, most paper deals could not be honored in physical metal, because in an environment in which paper gold were redeemed en masse, real gold could not be bought in an orderly manner, or indeed, at any price.

Gold is supposed to be sound money: valuable without a counterparty. But paper gold, which is overwhelmingly the vehicle for gold ownership, is by definition just another financial instrument with counterparty risk. Paradoxically, the rationale for owning gold is commonly to escape such exposure. So unless one possesses physical gold at considerable expense and difficulty, paper gold accomplishes very little in insulating oneself from system-wide counterparty risk.

Once again Bitcoin marries the advantages of gold with technology. Bitcoins may be owned on the same principled and self-evident basis as gold. But unlike gold, bitcoins are much easier to own and transact *without* having to resort to the contradictory expedient of paper gold. Thus for those truly interested in owning independent money, Bitcoin accomplishes the same ends much more faithfully.

As a World Reserve Currency?

Bitcoin's unique properties could make it an ideal international reserve asset. As gold, Pound Sterling, and Dollars successively provided internationally recognized stores of value, bitcoins could serve a similar role. The same advantages of Bitcoin in the hands of individual users could equally serve entire nations. The world's choice of a reserve asset is not a fringe or academic question; the currency standard has been overturned several times in the past century. Selecting an efficacious and reliable standard will be a paramount concern. With the state of the US Dollar in flux, the choice of world reserve asset must be reexamined. The amounts at stake are gargantuan, ranging in the trillions of dollars[x].

A reserve asset is a common standard that facilitates world trade. As Chile may sell copper to New Zealanders, neither side of the trade wishes to accumulate the currency of the other. If the fruits of a transaction between disparate parties must be saved, into which currency should it be converted? This is the central question for any prospective reserve asset. What denomination should people around the world save in? When the vast sums commanded by national banks are considered, numbering in the trillions of dollars, these questions take on huge importance.

A reserve asset must, above all, be widely desired. New Zealand and Chile are relatively small countries; to save in each other's currency would be to presuppose that the money will be spent again in that small country. Of all the nations in the world, it is not particularly likely that New Zealand is a pivotal trading partner for any of them. While *some* people are interested in purchasing goods from New Zealand, these are a small minority; for New Zealand Dollars to have any value, these few people must be sought out. It would be a huge headache to amass sizeable amounts of New Zealand Dollars; selling them would be an arduous process of finding buyers. Because New Zealand it itself a small country, with a limited monetary supply, there is only so much demand for the currency. One trillion New Zealand Dollars could not possibly be solid without utterly crashing the value of the currency. In short, there is very little liquidity.

Dollars, on the other hand, enjoy enormous liquidity. There are so many ways to employ dollars. You could sell them in huge amounts without noticeably changing their value. Because the United States is such a large, prosperous country, the number of real investments denominated in dollars is vast; there is a huge market capacity to buy and sell dollars. In this sense, it is safer to hold large amounts of dollars over New Zealand Dollars, because market liquidity makes it safer to execute large transactions.

Dollars are also well-known and thus salable anywhere. Even if New Zealanders and Chileans do not intend to buy American goods, it is trivially easy to find someone who will. It is vastly more probable to find someone who demands Dollars over Chilean Pesos. There may still be some overhead, but if there must be a standard, it might as well be the easiest.

Reserve assets are accumulated and saved around the world in huge quantities. They are the denomination for trading partners of every color. With such large savings, they must generate some yield. There is a limit to money's ability to sit idle; cash is preferably employed in bonds to generate some return. Thus for any reserve asset, in order for it to be attractive to hold, there should be a supply of bonds denominated in it. In other words, while saving gold, or pounds, or dollars, there must be some way to employ them without changing the currency denomination.

The importance of a bond market for any reserve asset cannot be overstated. As with the liquidity of trading currencies, bond markets also have their own measure of liquidity. For example, there are far more bonds denominated in Dollars than in Swiss Francs. Even while the Swiss Franc may be an attractive reserve asset for other reasons, only so many bonds exist denominated in it. If everyone were to rely exclusively on Swiss Francs, the supply of bonds would vanish. Bond prices in Francs would rise as the supply proved inadequate to demand. This has actually happened in practice to an extreme degree. But were Switzerland a larger country with a larger pool of bonds, the attractiveness of holding Swiss Francs would grow commensurately. In fact, it would not be an overstatement to say that the liquidity for bonds in a particular currency and its liquidity on FOREX exchanges are two sides to the same coin.

Throughout the 1800s and leading up to World War One, British Pound Sterling was unquestionably the dominant reserve currency. It was widely used around the world. Foreign nations took on debts in pounds. A huge array of financial instruments was denominated in it. Because it was pegged to gold, nations that would otherwise have merely stored gold, saved Pounds instead. Since they were freely convertible to gold, pounds were functionally equivalent, except that you could also buy bonds with them. Thus you could enjoy the security of gold, while also earning a decent rate of return. This was a very appealing safety. So long as the Bank of England maintained the peg to gold, the pound was a safe and attractive asset.

During the First World War, Britain suspended convertibility of pounds to gold as an exigency of war. In the pursuit of victory over the next four years, Britain and virtually all the main participants printed an excess of paper money in relation to their gold reserves. With a surfeit of paper theoretically tied to gold, the maintenance of the old peg became a pretense.

Britain found itself unable to support the weight of debts incurred during the war. It chose to devalue the currency rather than endure the painful, deflationary era of austerity necessary to repay its debts. This meant breaking the peg to gold. While this proved a temporary relief to Britain, it was essentially a national default. As the issuer of the historically foremost reserve currency, Britain's default had massive international consequences. The many savers who had amassed large quantities of pounds saw their value evaporate overnight. Financial arrangements around the world, carefully calibrated to their particular economic conditions, went haywire. Virtually all the calculations embedded in financial contracts presupposed the stability of the currency they were denominated in. When the world reserve currency failed, the measuring stick for countless transactions failed as well.

The dollar became the de facto world reserve currency in 1944 under the Bretton Woods arrangement. The dollar would be pegged to gold; all other currencies would exist in relation to the dollar. Thus only one gold peg would support all others. Holding dollars became as convenient as holding British pounds had been. Dollars were strictly correlated to the price of gold, meaning they could not be recklessly inflated. But they could also earn a nice return. As the currency of the world's dominant industrial power, enjoying a massive fraction of total global economic output, the dollar had exceptional liquidity. The US was also the world's foremost creditor nation. Gold had flowed to the US for decades as European nations indebted themselves during the World Wars. With such liquidity, size, and the backing of a huge quantity of gold, it was inevitable, at the time, that the Dollar would be the world's reserve asset.

Since 1944 the economic landscape has changed dramatically. The Dollar is no longer tied to gold. As we have seen, that link was severed by Nixon in 1971. Since then, a huge quantity of dollars has been produced, greatly diluting their real value. The US, while still the world's largest economy, does not hold the same, overarching, dominant position it had in the 40's and 50's. The US economy, while still enormous, will never compose the same fraction of world GDP it once did. In the past 15 years the Dollar's role as the world reserve currency has slowly waned. This is an observable fact. The proportion of foreign reserves held as dollars has declined from over 70% in 2000 to about 61% today. What caused this decline and what the future holds are highly contentious.

The Dollar Today

Today the Dollar has problems. There was nothing foreordained stating that the Dollar had to fail. There is no such thing as historical destiny. But the appeal of the dollar on objective grounds has deteriorated since 1944. The relative decline of the US economy is actually probably the least important rationale for dollar weakness; it is still big enough to support a reserve asset. No, the Dollar's problems lie deeper.

There are simply too many dollars. We've printed too many of them. With the break of the peg to gold in 1971, there have been no limits, besides our own sporadic sense of responsibility, not to print money. It has proven all too easy to (literally) paper over our problems with invented cash. This has come in various forms: artificially low interest rates, interest payments held by the Fed and refunded back to the Treasury Department, Quantitative Easing, guaranteed loans, etc. The exact mechanisms differ. But they all share a simple similarity, printed money solves problems. Balancing budgets is no longer necessary.

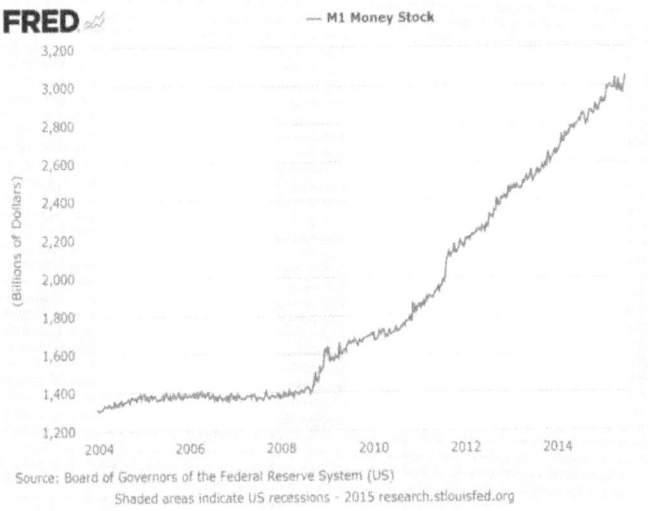

Total US cash: M1 money supply

Simply put, fiscal problems in the US have led us to print too much money. This fundamentally domestic issue has had deep international repercussions. Printed dollars, once spent, cannot be retracted with the same fiat magic with which they were created. They are simply out there. Vast hoards of dollars are held by private and governmental organizations alike. Abroad, foreign governments possess huge reserves of dollars, in such large quantities that they can hardly be sold without breaking the market. Even the US

Treasury bond market, with all its vaunted liquidity compared to that of competitors, could not withstand a sale from the huge dollar holders around the world. China alone has assets worth over a trillion dollars in US dollar denominated instruments. These cannot be safely sold.

Foreign reserves of dollars continue to grow at an astounding rate. The US trade deficit, approximately half a trillion dollars each year, is paid for through the export of dollars. We literally export paper money to pay for real goods. This is not a transient fluctuation but a trend lasting decades. Foreigners accept these payments, year after year, without complaint. Were the dollars spent, they would inexorably find their way back to the US where they would produce inflation. But they are seldom spent. They sit idle abroad.

The willingness of credulous foreigners to buy American Dollars has contributed mightily to the absence of inflation in the US. Persistent trade deficits should be corrected by countervailing changes in the exchange rate. A negative feedback loop should take place, in which foreigners sell dollars more than they buy them. The weakened dollar should encourage exports, as well as offer more attractive bond yields. But for decades the opposite has happened. Trade deficits persist and grow. Debts have exploded without any reckoning. Bond yields are near zero. Why is the corrective mechanism absent?

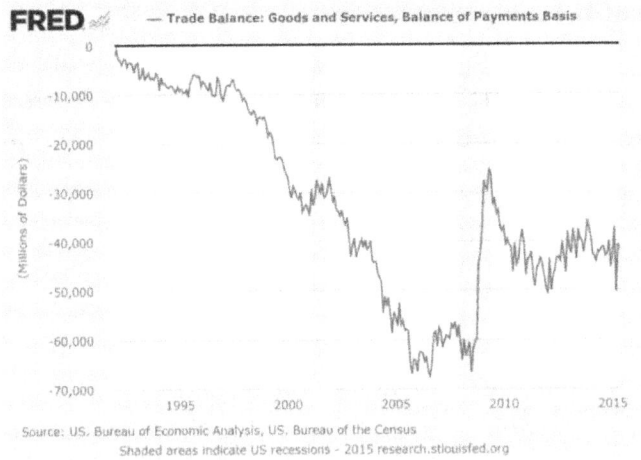

Monthly US trade deficit: Getting billions of dollars of stuff in exchange for paper... over decades

Until recently, the world has practiced exceptional self-delusion with respect to the US dollar. Because it is the world reserve currency, so many assets are already denominated in it. So many national banks have already committed, in a big way, to dollar holdings. There is a sort of inertia of practice by which these old habits cannot be turned. Selling dollar holdings at a loss would expose decades' worth of folly. It is better not to stir trouble. In the meantime, more dollars are printed and the problems are exacerbated.

Disturbances in capital markets worldwide encourage flight to safe assets. The dollar, as the world reserve currency, has historically been the foremost such asset. Thus the dollar has been immensely strengthened by currency troubles in Europe and Japan. Other currencies, such as the Yen or Euro, to say nothing of smaller currencies, do not enjoy the same reserve status as the dollar. They enjoy much less historic confidence around the world. Thus they are much more responsive to shifts in the underlying reality. A small nation, Ecuador for instance, could never run trade deficits year after year, push its interest rate to zero, or aggressively print money without witnessing a massive flight of capital. Its currency would be immediately crushed. That's reality responding to immutable economic forces. But the dollar, in which so many parties have such a vested stake, has proven far less responsive. Inertia in the minds of others makes the dollar respond less well to fundamental economic forces. This is actually a bad thing. It doesn't mean the dollar can defy hard realities, only that it may delay their consequences.

The historic lack of consequences for US monetary decisions has created a pain-free culture, in which the US can print money, and foreigners are expected to accept them. This surely cannot last. Indeed, China, which once followed a policy of accumulating dollars, has reversed course, and has now stalled its dollar holdings. They are rapidly acquiring gold now. Nations that once amassed dollars willingly are now beginning to question their reliability. What can they really buy after such a growth in the monetary supply? Current exchange rates are not the best indicator; there is insufficient liquidity to *safely spend* the vast hoards of dollars that have been amassed abroad.

The US dollar system started to fray even while it remained pegged to gold. In the 60's, before the peg was broken, US deficits drove the flight of gold from the US. Nations such as Germany acquired large portions of the

US gold reserve during these years, in which American paper spending required forfeit of physical gold. Only when this process came to its logical conclusion, years later, when foreigners began to doubt the physical viability of the gold peg, did the gold outflows become a surge. This occurred quite like a bank run except the principal players were central banks and currency traders. Rather than reap the consequences of its profligacy in the 60's and 70's, the US defaulted on its obligations, much as the British did in 1931. This was considered a positive economic step by Keynesians and statists, for it seemed to unshackle government spending from any accountability. The stimulus of default appeared to outweigh the pain of honestly paying one's debts. In the meantime, the currency itself was sacrificed in the name of expediency.

The US dollar is on track to fatally undermining itself. Schemes such as Quantitative Easing have done incalculable damage to its credibility. Foreign and domestic creditors alike cannot be expected to accept real losses on their dollar holdings indefinitely. Money printing in the US is accomplishing what no outside power could possibly do; undermine the dollar's reserve status. This decline has only been masked by the still-greater folly of foreign central bankers.

It is in the context of the failure of the 'old gods' of finance that Bitcoin arrives at a propitious moment in history. Bitcoin could redress many of the historic problems with reserve assets. Bitcoin answers the most pressing problem of dollars, namely, that dollars can be conjured out of thin air. Bitcoins cannot be invented; the supply is ineffaceably limited. Thus the foremost weakness of dollars, that the moral hazard to inflate the supply is too strong to resist over historic time scales, fades away. Bitcoin holders enjoy cryptographic guarantees that no central bank can equal.

As a reserve asset, Bitcoin could offer the best of both worlds. If scalability issues are addressed, as we shall explore in a later chapter, the reserve asset could also be a reserve commodity. Whereas gold was a convenient store of value that was difficult to inflate, it was a difficult medium for credit. It was difficult to have bonds directly denominated in gold. Rather, it was more convenient to peg pounds and dollars to gold, and then earn interest on those currencies. Gold is not easily transmitted. Naked gold is not an optimal currency tool. Money mechanisms, such as gold-pegged Pound Sterling, had to be built around it with the right properties of currency. It was these currency layers over gold that financial instruments were built upon: bonds and profit-generating assets. But with Bitcoin a much more elegant solution has been found. The asset representing value serves also as a currency tool. This was something gold could never quite do. The need for an additional layer, such as gold-pegged dollars, is obviated. Bitcoin is scarcer than gold, because the supply is actually finite. And it is faster and more secure than dollars. It enjoys both sets of properties in a historically unique way.

A world reserve system based on Bitcoin would look a lot like the gold standard of the 1800's, except there would be no substituent national currencies. They would simply become unnecessary. The interest of the consumer in sound money would trump the government's interest in extracting value via money-printing. A normalization in the relationship between consumers and their money would occur, not through the altruism of governments, but by the leveraged endowed by technology. Such a tool has never existed before. Whereas historically one had to own physical gold to exit the system of fiat currencies, now one has only to control a Bitcoin private key. Regular people could never manage physical gold safely or in the requisite quantities. But they may hold Bitcoin as easily as they control an email address or a password. Opting out of inflationary money has never been so easy.

World Money Should not be Nationalistic

Today's world reserve currency, the Dollar, is anything but neutral. It is employed as a policy baton according to America's short-term interests. The same government that wages war controls the blood of world finance. One government exerts immense influence on purportedly international organizations such as the IMF. The SWIFT network, where wire transactions are cleared, is heavily influenced by American policy. So many economic levers are in the hands of one administration; entire nations can be forced out of international trade by the controller of the world's reserve currency. Such a unipolar financial world is historically unprecedented.

A truly neutral economic framework would be far superior to a politicized, national one. A currency that is itself open-source, stateless, anonymous, and cryptographic cannot come under any one national jurisdiction. This is as neutral a concept there ever was. One nation could not censor transactions, as the US does via SWIFT against Iran, with neutral money. One nation could not browbeat its partners into accepting endless trade deficits. Economic power should be economic, not geopolitical. The interests of a nation should not trump economic commonsense as reflected in free market behavior. Endowing one nation, however powerful, with monopolistic powers of money cannot be wise. It is a function merely of the technical inadequacies of the past.

Neutral money will be a huge net boon. As gold was blind to national borders, a reserve currency should always be fundamentally neutral. Technology has made it possible to unify the commodity-like scarcity of gold with the transmissibility of electronic fiat money. Bitcoin is scarcer than gold and faster than paper money.

A neutral world money will make interest rates fairer between nations. The US would not enjoy artificially low interest rates from its reserve status; interest rates would compete more honestly across borders. Pricing capital correctly in the US will bring its own benefits. Capital will flow more equitably worldwide to where the return is best, in a manner reminiscent of the 1800's era of globalization. Prices will be fairer too. Chronic trade deficits will not be possible; local prices will have to adjust instead. This would be a much healthier economic state of affairs, in which prices adjust dynamically to currency inflows and outflows. Rendering money tamper-proof would make it a much cleaner, more honest signaling mechanism.

To be sure, Bitcoin is not yet ready to be a reserve asset. It is still extremely volatile. It enjoys very little liquidity. It is still used by only a relative few. And its scalability issues are not resolved. And yet only the question of scalability should give us pause. Volatility, liquidity, and awareness are very tractable problems for Bitcoin. If scalability can be addressed, Bitcoin will be in a position to possess all the properties of an ideal reserve asset.

Bitcoin is Pseudonymous

Bitcoin is aware of cryptographic signatures rather than people. Human identities are not laid out on the Blockchain. What we see instead are addresses, scripts, hashes, and cryptographic proofs. It is not at all clear how to discern individuals from these records. While the history of your actions is written ineffaceably, it is not explicitly linked to you.

Bitcoin can be best described as pseudonymous. On the one hand, it appears to be anonymous in that addresses, appearing as strings like *1PAdeffiD61ouuVcH1nhwkhBM-aY7zK9fAT*, say nothing overtly about their owner. What can one conclude about a transaction between *1PAdeffiD6-1ouuVcH1nhwkhBMaY7zK9fAT* and *1Ffza91-2ka2Vc9V-Y1JYuEwfMpbVY3yxhN*? How would you ever know that the former belongs to Alice and the latter to Bob? It appears on the surface as intractable and purely anonymous.

We have seen that the entire record of transactions is, and must be, permanently written on the Blockchain. Addresses are pseudonyms for their true owners, not camouflage. Since the tangled historical web endures, it is very likely that identity will slowly be teased out through complex analytical methods. Algorithms may crawl the Blockchain, looking for relationships between addresses. If the owner of a particular address is known, whether through admission on the Internet, the purchase of physical goods, or otherwise, his other addresses may be guessed based on the pattern of transactions. Sets of addresses owned by the same entity, such as a large corporation, may reveal their interlinked relationship through a high rate of reshuffling of bitcoins. It is likely that quite a lot can be inferred from the Blockchain.

What has not been figured out yet, may be figured out tomorrow by someone still more clever. Because the Blockchain cannot be edited, anonymity must stand the test of modern investigators and future ones as well. The smart algorithm that uncovers your spending habits has not yet been conceived. But it need not hurry, because your transactional history is not going anywhere.

The identities behind addresses can already be determined in many cases, at least in theory if not yet in practice. Ownership is revealed in many places heedlessly. Some websites exist specifically to advertise one's name as correlated with a particular address. In fact, the trend towards the representation of identity as a cryptographic entity is already apace. Many users have already left behind the fatal clues that will, or have already, been uncovered by prying eyes.

I can look at my own Bitcoin habits to see that the identity behind my own addresses has already been largely compromised. User profiles that are plainly mine, based on something I've publicly said, link my name to a large array of Bitcoin addresses. In the process of soliciting tips, I unwittingly left behind evidence of my bitcoin addresses. Any tips I received were shuttled into one of my main Bitcoin addresses. These few central addresses have been involved in many transactions with one another, or with third party sites that are themselves highly coupled to my main addresses. With the link between my tipping address and my real name, and the transactions linking the tipping address to my heavily used, central addresses, the identity of nearly all my addresses can be guessed with some level of confidence.

I have compromised my anonymity in many other ways as well. Whenever I bought something with Bitcoin and had it shipped to my location, I was inadvertently advertising my identity. It would be a simple matter for my merchant to sell that data to a 3rd party identity processor who could then figure out the rest. In fact, it is strikingly difficult to spend one's bitcoins without opening oneself up to this sort of search. The act of spending one's bitcoins is admission that they were yours. At that moment, upstream bitcoins become traceable; all correlated transactions acquire a probabilistic taint of identity.

There are ways to make your bitcoins much more anonymous. They can be repeatedly shuffled with others' bitcoins, introducing intrinsic uncertainty into the owner's identity that no algorithm may beat. This is facilitated by

'Bitcoin Mixing' services. These are run by third parties and are not entirely safe; the operator could retain a record of identity. *Trustless* bitcoin mixing, in which bitcoins are shuffled without resorting to a trusted human party, is a new concept that promises to make bitcoins truly anonymous. By mixing bitcoins with peers and trusting no operators, the resulting bitcoins are dispersed into shiny new addresses and cannot be reliably traced. All of the mixers are plausible candidates until, extending backwards in a series of mixing events, an exponentially-growing, vast pool of plausible owners obscures identity completely.

Other approaches exist to hide the ownership of bitcoins addresses, such as circulating coins through a large series of intermediary sites, all of which would have to be compromised to reveal the identity of downstream addresses. Virtually all of these methods, while disassociating any trace of personal identity with Bitcoin addresses, make evident that an attempt at securing anonymity was made. While Bitcoin mixing may be strong, the act of mixing is itself a signal; these bitcoins were washed.

Thus while Bitcoin is natively pseudonymous, it can be made more strongly anonymous with sophisticated new tools such as trustless mixing. This is an ongoing field that has yet to reach a state of maturity. Surely there will be attempts back and forth to defeat and to strengthen anonymity. Perhaps if trustless mixing proves robust, there may be an attempt to discredit bitcoins that can be traced to mixing-transactions. This would create a two-tiered state of Bitcoin, in which some coins are 'clean', whereas others are 'dirty'. The latter would be linked to 'undesirable' activities, such as mixing or crime. It has been theorized that the government may try to taint, or segregate, bitcoins based on their individual histories. This would be akin to declaring some ingots of gold guilty and others innocent. Segregating bitcoins into arbitrary categories would be a massive uphill battle. Legalisms won't be easily imposed over the Bitcoin network.

It is still unclear, however, to what extent individuals will seek out perfect anonymity. And if the technical tools prove sufficiently robust, it is debatable to what lengths governments may go to differentiate bitcoins into licit and illicit.

Even if the majority of users do not seek out strong anonymity tools, their mere existence is a boon. Just as TOR exists, but is not used by most Internet users, its availability presents users with a spectrum of choice. In both finance and in communications, mathematically strong privacy ought to be a prerogative. Even if most users do not use such tools, what matters is that they are available.

Conversely, I could intentionally reveal my identity on the Blockchain at any time with a cryptographic signature. This would be a mathematical proof beyond question. This capability could itself be useful. I could prove, mathematically, that I had paid my taxes in full, or that the amounts I report to the IRS or to investors are the right ones, purely by referencing transactions in the Blockchain. The immutability of the transactional record makes it easy to perform audits or prove that one has paid his taxes.

The desire for financial anonymity is a noble one. As we may enjoy privacy in other parts of our lives, so too should it extend to our financial acts. I cannot exercise true privacy in a world in which my deeds at home, or my words, or even my thoughts, may be private, but in which my economic decisions are not. It should be seen as a disturbing trend that authorities may peer into one's financial history so easily, and thereby discern things that would otherwise require a gross invasion of personal privacy to establish.

Nor is the purported privacy offered by conventional banks truly sacrosanct. As these promises live and die by human trust, and exist within fickle and flawed human laws, they cannot be truly trusted. Your bank may expose your financial history to the government at any time, without even your knowledge. It is all supposed to be for the greater good. Or for our safety. But equally grotesque violations in any other sphere would have us in revolt.

With Bitcoin, the pseudonymity you enjoy out of the box intrinsic to the system, and relies on no human guarantees. The lack of human discretion is a pillar of value. The pseudonymity of native Bitcoin is superior to the privacy endowed by banks. At the very least, others must painstakingly piece together trace data to reconstruct your identity. While in the long term, it is likely that these attempts will reach a high level of efficiency, insofar as the public is concerned, they have not reached an advanced state quite yet. Pseudonymity alone is by no means safe in the long run. But it is already a step above the fickle assurances offered through traditional institutions.

Stronger guarantees of financial anonymity can be attained through new developments in trustless bitcoin mixing. With proper diligence, your bitcoins can be made truly anonymous. It is likely that the technical burden on the user to secure these capabilities will diminish. As with many things Bitcoin, what is now a challenging endeavor for computer nerds will become increasingly accessible to the masses through the efforts of third-party entrepreneurs. The general streamlining of Bitcoin will continue to offer ever-more sophisticated technical tools to novice users. As a playboy dilettante does not know how his Lamborghini works, the grandmothers of the world will need not understand how their anonymity is secured, but merely that it is.

Some will doubtless demonize Bitcoin for the anonymity it offers. What does one have to hide, after all, if one is not a lawbreaker? This is a particularly noxious argument because it presupposes the malleability of civil rights. The desire for privacy should need no explanation. If privacy should be surrendered, it should be a voluntary act. By contrast, the root mechanisms underlying the present financial infrastructure do not intrinsically support privacy. In fact, privacy has been rendered anathema by the government through laws such as KYC (Know Your Customer). A slew of regulations ensure that banking can never be done anonymously. These strike against the very concept of financial privacy. The government has no doubts about the legitimacy of prying into your financial life. The bar for violating your privacy has become inordinately low. The authorities can easily get what they want by leaning on banks, whom they have turned into complicit partners. Because traditional banking is built upon human trust, human threats may move it to do unprincipled things.

Banking nowadays is designed to extract your identity, and those you do business with, to the utmost detail. Anonymous banking has become an oxymoron. This is not in our interest. Excessive financial prying presages other abuses. The power of the purse is all. Surrendering that power to institutions so dominated by government is dangerous. Money percolates into all facets of our society. If there cannot be privacy of money, we will not have it in any sphere.

Critics will argue that nefarious groups, such as terrorists or drug lords, will use financial anonymity for evil. Certainly they will. But while money has been involved in many evil acts, most of us do not call money itself evil. It is a vehicle for the deeds and misdeeds of others. And while anonymous money may make it harder to interdict groups engaged in subterfuge, particularly against governments, who can count the value of privacy to the human dignity of the rest of the population? The civil rights of billions should not be overridden by the actions of so few. This is a grievous net loss on balance. Moreover, while governments may hunt nasty folks such as terrorists, they have also hunted quite admirable people as well, such as dissidents, freedom fighters, intellectuals, whole ethnicities, and many others. The tools the US uses to interdict funds for Al Qaeda could equally well be used by China to clamp down on internal dissent, or by any number of unsavory regimes. The assumption that anonymity is bad because it is not in line with the interests of our government, at this time, is not only generally naive, but it is a distinct undersampling of history, which is replete with counterexamples. One need not look far in history to find gross misuse of government power. Natural checks on that power, in favor of personal liberties and in the form of cryptographic guarantees, will be a massive boon for society.

As I have reiterated in this book, Bitcoin is a system not controlled by people. It is preternaturally resistant to compulsion by government. Its truths are mathematical: its guarantees cryptographic. The anonymity it provides, particularly with new mixing techniques, delivers the privacy so sorely lacking in legacy finance. One has, at the very least, the capability of anonymity, if one chooses to exercise it. Those who would argue against anonymity itself are taking the narrow view, spoon-fed to them by the perpetrators. The loss of civil liberties will always, on balance, be of great harm to society. Whatever noble goals to the contrary will be subsumed, as they always are in the course of history, by the wiles and petty interests of people with authority. As a result, our trust should reside in math, and not in people. And we should opt, to the greatest extent possible, for a system which maximally protects our property and our liberties.

Bitcoin is Safe

From the beginning, Bitcoin was designed with security in mind. Its inherent openness meant that no vulnerability could be hidden from malefactors. No trusted server could be assigned to run vulnerable code. Rather, every component had to be so strong that it could not be broken, even though the code lay wholly available to attackers. In the absence of physical gatekeepers, it had to excel in informational security. This marriage of security with openness is one of Bitcoin's signal accomplishments. In an environment in which a single core flaw would have led to the demise of the entire system, Bitcoin's technical excellence has been extraordinary.

Bitcoin is simply the most secure money ever made. Gold held in subterranean vaults manned by armed guards is less secure than properly implemented, multisignature Bitcoin wallets. Whereas gold and fiat can be seized, no army can crack the elliptic curves upon which

Bitcoin addresses are based. When Bitcoin private keys are correctly managed, stealing bitcoins becomes a problem of mythic proportions: a computational task beyond our civilization. Invading Fort Knox and seizing thousands of tons of gold, by contrast, would be much easier.

The core Bitcoin protocol is exceptionally strong, but at the edges, at the interface where Bitcoin meets other systems, idiosyncratic flaws invariably arise. If private keys are held in a vulnerable state, they may be hacked, as any other server is hacked. Coins entrusted to the untrustworthy may still be stolen. Ponzi schemes, fraud, and outright scams may proliferate. Even merely weak passwords securing private keys may be expose coins to theft. In practice there are many ways in which bitcoins can be compromised. But all such failures have occurred at the periphery, not at the core, and have humans to blame.

There have been many incidents involving the theft of large amounts of Bitcoin. The greatest by far was the now-infamous MT.GOX scandal, in which hundreds of millions of dollars' worth of bitcoins were stolen. So cataclysmic was this event that it seriously tarnished Bitcoin's image among the general public. Many others as well have had their bitcoins stolen or lost due to poor key management practices.

Such instances should give one pause. But importantly, a distinction must be made between Bitcoin the protocol and Bitcoin private keys as handled by any particular operator. Bitcoin the protocol has never failed. Bitcoin at the interface has failed many times.

Securing private keys and following best practices have proven essential skills for Bitcoin users and businesses. Increasingly, security standards have arisen to ensure the safety of private keys. There is no reason why these techniques cannot reach a very high level of efficacy. As time goes on, the trend has been for improvement in the security of Bitcoin wallets; in the earliest days they were generally far more vulnerable than they are today. Users following simple instructions can now make extraordinarily secure wallets, involving 2-factor authentication, complex passwords, and multisignature techniques.

The technical perils of using Bitcoin are in fact a double-edged sword; as bearer items, such as stock certificates or bearer bonds, possession is equivalent to ownership. Bitcoins cannot be recovered if lost. There is no higher authority to solicit to 'undo' a transaction. Just as there is no appeals court for the laws of physics, there is no appeals process for Bitcoin. This stands in stark contrast to virtually all financial instruments which are claims on other parties that can be legally arbitrated. In Bitcoin, the law is not necessary for enforcement; ownership is mathematically self-evident and thus self-enforcing. Thus while possessing bitcoins carries a profound finality, so too do mistakes.

Bitcoin allows you to be your own bank, and that comes with tradeoffs between complexity and independence. The bearer-item quality of ownership makes mistakes costly. On the other hand, the advantages of self-evident ownership, namely obviating the human element of enforcement, are profound. This trade-off is becoming increasingly one-sided as user-facing complexity is eased by new companies looking to simplify Bitcoin. While the technical difficulties of using bitcoins can be addressed through friendlier-tools, the fundamental transformation in ownership is unchanged. The technical risks of using Bitcoin, such as key mismanagement, will feel increasingly irrelevant to normal users, just as the details of IP addresses and SSL certificates are wholly irrelevant to normal Internet users.

While there are ways to make grievous mistakes with Bitcoin security, bitcoins are nevertheless fundamentally much safer than existing money. Because Bitcoin is underpinned by cryptographic proofs, the core essence of the protocol cannot be broken. Only human error at the edges can cause failures. Just as I may forget my wallet at a restaurant and lose all my cash, there is no perfect protection against human failings. However in Bitcoin, such failings can only have a *local* effect.

Bitcoin is much safer than existing solutions because, while individuals may occasionally make catastrophic mistakes, large aggregates of people are not under *systemic risk*. The risks to my bitcoins are self-imposed. They are compartmentalized from the risks incurred by other people who may protect their money less responsibly. If I have taken the correct measures, no one else's decisions will affect the security of my money. My bitcoins are in an invulnerable escape capsule. Even if large institutions make disastrous mistakes, my money is completely safe.

Fiat money is not compartmentalized. As institutions fail, like a large sinking ship, their mass pulls flotsam and bodies down with them into the depths. One bank failure can cause another. Virtually all financial instruments are subject to counterparty risk. Deals with even large institutions can unexpectedly fail if their creditworthiness is in doubt. We saw this in 2008 with AIG and other major banks. Large institutions whose ability to honor agreements had never been in doubt, whose word essentially traded at par, suddenly experienced a sharp and unexpected liquidity crisis. Financial instruments involving these banks as counterparties suddenly turned toxic. This effect permeated to still other banks who may otherwise have been healthy; excessive exposure to a bad counterparty can itself make one a bad counterparty.

In the current climate, in which highly-leveraged banks invest in dubious bonds that yield virtually no interest, counterparty risk should be a serious concern. Universally, the greater the leverage ratio, the greater the risk one incurs. However if basically all financial institutions maintain very small collateral against such high debts, and if they hold assets on each other's books, their fates become exceptionally correlated with one another. If one bank suffers a crisis of confidence insolvency can quickly spread to the other banks. The risk of one becomes the risk of many. By exposing themselves so recklessly to large debt ratios, banks have put themselves in a potentially precarious position. This is the very definition of systemic fragility.

All fiat money is a debt instrument vis-a-vis a counterparty. A bank deposit is not cash; it is the right to demand money from a bank. Even a dollar bill was once the right to redeem gold (In fact, dollars are still considered a 'liability' by the Federal Reserve; this is a historical artifact). Quite a large fraction of the total monetary supply (M2) is subject to non-central bank counterparty risk. Money sitting innocently as a bank deposit may serve as collateral for loans up to even 30 times its magnitude. These loans may in turn serve as collateral for still more loans. This process of rehypothecation in effect expands the monetary supply. However such dollars totter on an unstable pyramid of debts. They are not real, physical dollars, but an extensive chain of IOU's between leveraged, private institutions. The effective supply of credit hinges dramatically on the credit-worthiness of the original, heavily rehypothecated dollar. In such circumstances, counterparty risk should be a paramount concern.

Even if you store your dollars under your mattress, the mistakes of others still affect you. The recklessness of bankers and their ignoble pleas for rescue induced the government to bail out the major banks. Not only were billions spent directly on banks, but trillions more were spent on stimulus and propping up asset values. This money had to be invented out of thin air. These trillions weakened the real value of your dollars no matter how safe they were physically. As money is printed to paper over problems, the real cost is born across all existing holders of dollars.

The interconnectedness of the financial world means that, in practice, the fate of your money is tied to that of others. You are swimming across a river tied to people who can't swim, and still to others would like to swim too fast. Systemic risk comes in many forms. It may come directly through inflation and the weakening of money. It may also come in highly-leveraged, dangerously over-extended banks whose mutual entanglements doom all. The mortgage crisis illustrated this only too plainly. Your humble deposits are collateral for 30:1 leveraged loans somewhere else. You hailed a taxi, but James Bond picked you up and is driving like a madman.

More perverse still, your money is at risk even innocuously. The FDIC depositors' insurance you enjoy imposes yet another moral hazard on money managers. It subsidizes excessive lending risks using Uncle Sam's credit. Since losses are, in practice, freely insured, extreme risk-taking becomes perfectly logical. Once again, endless printed money distorts natural behavior. Even by participating in FDIC insured banks, you are fueling this perversely-incentivized, precarious system. While your dollars may be *nominally* safe under FDIC, the existence of such a guarantee increases the *real* risk to dollars everywhere.

By contrast, owning bitcoins is to be your own bank. If you have secured your bitcoins correctly, you'll never need depositors' insurance. You are insulated from whatever machinations speculators are up to. Because you are your own bank, your money is not acting as collateral for someone else's heavily leveraged debts. You're not a part of that. What they do does not affect you. There is no counterparty.

Security
There have been numerous high-profile data breaches recently in which large amounts of users' sensitive data were

leaked. Credit cards are particularly susceptible to these security lapses. There have been many incidents in which millions of credit card numbers were exposed; it virtually goes without saying that this payment method is insecure. This is reflected quite transparently in the charges imposed on merchants; the 2-3% fees they pay largely pay for covering theft and fraud. This is a stupendous sum of money; credit card fraud is utterly rampant.

It should not come as a surprise that a system with so many diffuse vulnerabilities has led to such spectacular failures. One should not have to trust Home Depot or Target with one's own private information. Payment data ought to be encrypted in such a way that the recipient can redeem money without revealing anything sensitive about the sender. This is precisely what cryptography is capable of providing. Every time I use my credit card, I must completely turn over all the keys to the castle. Any one vulnerability in any of the merchants I frequent can lead to a catastrophic loss. Such a fragile system is begging for abuse.

Admittedly, new fiat payment systems such as Apple Pay do encrypt transaction details such that vendors do not possess all the 'keys to the castle'. Fiat systems could certainly be improved to lessen the exposure of sensitive information to vendors. But Bitcoin already has this baked in. If the contention is that Bitcoin is not secure, and yet it practices data security to a degree envied by fiat operators, there is a clear contradiction. While fiat could be improved to more resemble Bitcoin, many of the old problems remain. Underlying Apple Pay are still the old credit cards. Chargebacks remain an annoyance for merchants and a rationale for lucrative processing fees. And even if Apple Pay is used by an individual for 80% of his transactions, exposure of credit card data in the other 20% of cases is enough to reintroduce the same risk of catastrophic loss.

Fiat clumsily aspires to the informational security already possessed by Bitcoin. In a historical sense, this should come as no surprise. Traditionally money could rely on centralized systems: proprietary databases, official money-printers, and governmentally sanctioned legitimacy. These were enough; the informational threats, such as physical counterfeiting and check fraud, were easily combatted. In such a world, fiat processors could afford to be relatively lazy in data security. Before the era of paper money, one could be even lazier; gold is exceptionally difficult to fake. The rise of electronic fiat money, ranging from credit cards to online bank accounts to wire transfers caught the existing system off-guard. Physical security was not enough. Data had to be secured to a much higher standard.

The centralized models of data management employed by modern banks offer a separate set of pros of cons versus those of Bitcoin. Centralized systems are much easier conceptually to build than decentralized alternatives. They can be faster and cheaper to operate. Trust in a single party obviates the need for proof-of-work mechanisms as employed in the Bitcoin Blockchain. Most of the time, these systems work well.

But the convenience of centralized solutions comes at a steep price. Because so much is dependent on one trusted source, when something does go wrong, it goes cataclysmically wrong. Vulnerabilities in the trusted center affect everyone. Centralized systems are brittle in that they are excessively dependent on the integrity of one or a few nodes. In the long run, this is a weak, less robust model.

Decentralized systems such as Bitcoin are far more resilient. A failure at one node remains isolated at that node. A security lapse in any one place does not have systemic consequences. So long as the governing protocol remains strong, the fate of the many is independent of any one player. This is an incalculable advantage of decentralized systems generally. Their resilience and symmetry between participants justify the costs.

Because Bitcoin is purely digital, the only form of security that pertains to it is informational security. In this, as we have seen, it singularly excels. Indeed, it excels because it must; any less and it would be undone entirely. Fiat, by contrast, has lazily relied on centralized approaches and the enduring aura of governmental sanction. This approach is inadequate for the modern era which is so rife with cyber threats. Moreover, because fiat itself is invariably managed within centralized systems, small flaws in trusted nodes are magnified unto millions of people. The Bitcoin model is far safer in that, if anything does go wrong, the direct impact is confined to that one party.

We can easily observe this in the effects of the collapse of MT.GOX versus those of the 2008 financial crisis. In the case of MT.GOX, the world's biggest Bitcoin institution went bust in epic fashion. Those who held money with MT.GOX lost it. But those outside remained wholly unaffected.

Compare this to the banking crisis in 2008 in which the risk to banks spread like contagion. Failure in the Bitcoin world is remarkably compartmentalized, to the envy of the counterparty-bound fiat system.

As a general trend in the 21st century, the central importance of digital security will become increasingly obvious. The significance of other forms of security will wane commensurately. This is precisely the space in which Bitcoin was designed to excel, and for which fiat systems are largely unprepared.

Bitcoin Cannot be Confiscated

When money cannot be raised, it is taken. Confiscation has been the norm for governments to a much greater extent than most people would like to admit. History is replete with instances of seizure, fraud, and inflation stretching back centuries. Whether by hook or by crook, through outright force or by subtler means, authorities have repeatedly managed to extract value without the consent of citizens.

It is easy to dismiss the threat of governmental confiscation, but it is a much nearer threat than we would like to imagine. Even in very recent years, and with strikingly little cause, it has already occurred. Nor are the lessons we may draw from history isolated from our times. What was unimaginable when it occurred in the 1930's will be unimaginable if it occurs in the 2020's. Our intransigent expectations have no bearing on what may come to pass. In fact there may even be a negative correlation, as our preconceptions of what *must be* render us feeble to new events. It is foolish to rule out what has occurred throughout history because we fail to imagine it now; what is impossible is impossible until suddenly it happens.

Bitcoin is extraordinarily resistant to confiscation. Fiat bank accounts may be simply debited by government *diktat*. Taking dollars is as simple as editing a database. Banks fear the legal authority of the state and must comply. But Bitcoin cannot simply be seized. Only the holder of the right private keys may take funds. Nothing violates this principle. So long as the private keys are secure, no force on Earth can confiscate the underlying funds.

By using multisignature addresses, bitcoins can be further secured by distributing keys among various stakeholders. It can thus be required that multiple parties must be compromised before funds may be released. The exact requirements and allocation of private keys can be designed case by case. In practice this means that properly secured bitcoins may never be seized.

Historically bitcoins have only ever been confiscated by government when they were improperly secured. Ross Ulbricht lost a vast hoard of bitcoins to law enforcement agencies when they seized his computer in a vulnerable, unencrypted state. More careful measures could have prevented this. Otherwise bitcoins may be seized if their owner is under duress. Access to bitcoins may then have been traded for his freedom.

It could be a dark day when an individual is tortured or extorted into releasing his otherwise secure bitcoins. There is reason to fear that the government will resort to these measures as they confront the impregnability of Bitcoin. They will have to find human weaknesses where they fail to find cryptographic ones. Governments and criminals alike, frustrated with their powerlessness against so powerful a system, may apply pressure on people instead. Such is the shining future that may yet await. In the face of sublime sophistication, brute methods, more suited to another age, will come to the fore.

Safety against confiscation should be a vital requirement for money. It is in the people's interests that their property cannot be easily seized. That power has historically not been in the hands of governments. In past times, seizing the gold and property of citizens was a challenging logistical endeavor. But in our current era of fiat electronic money, it has never been so easy to confiscate funds *en masse*. This is a dangerous, historically abnormal power that is begging for abuse. The sanctity of one's property should be a natural check on the intrusive powers of others. Unfortunately, property today is virtually indefensible. In many places, private property rights have been diluted into a pale ritual. The vast reach of governments, in whose eye property solely exists, constantly undermines the premise of personal ownership. Today we own things with the leave of government, according to legal interpretations that could at any time change.

It need not be so. Bitcoin defies the rule. Bitcoin ownership is self-evident and subject to no interpretation. This is what property was meant to be. It is outside of the fickle whims of magistrates. For this reason, government will despise it. But this is how ownership always should have been: self-evident, like a force of nature, true without anyone's permission. Two plus two equals four in every country. Gravity obeys no dictates. Equally certain is that my bitcoin are my own.

Bitcoin Empowers the People

One of the best things about Bitcoin is that no one is in charge. It is totally decentralized. Unlike virtually every other system ever devised, every participant who runs a full node is equal. There are no trusted few. There is no special caste of caretakers who must be trusted to do the right thing. It's pure peer-to-peer. This is Bitcoin's defining feature, even surpassing its role as currency. Its decentralized nature makes it more robust, more egalitarian, and safer than centralized models. If we could reproduce all of Bitcoin's functionality more cheaply on a centralized model, we would be at a steep loss. Decentralization is the very source of Bitcoin's strength.

It is remarkable in the first place that, as a peer-to-peer network, Bitcoin survives at all. How does a complex system survive with no codified leaders? If the Blockchain is set off on its own, how is it not continually foiled by hackers who may game its rules? Those rules are, after all, public knowledge. It should be surprising at first that a relatively inflexible system with no human direction can nevertheless survive human wiles.

The answer lies in the fact that, from the beginning, Bitcoin was designed to operate in a hostile environment. Bitcoin was built on the assumption that some fraction of peers is composed of malicious liars. It was in wrestling with these problems that the Blockchain was born. Only because it was made for the hostile wasteland that is the Internet, in which there would be no trusted landmarks, has Bitcoin survived. Had it been built more naively, perhaps with more optimistic expectations, or with anything but security as its foremost goal, it would have perished long ago. The innumerable hackers who have tried, and failed, to find vulnerabilities in Bitcoin are proof enough.

As a purely decentralized network, Bitcoin enjoys numerous advantages over its predecessors. Because no peer is irreplaceable, things can go hideously wrong with one node without undermining the whole network. Contrast this with the prevailing server-client architecture, where problems with the server spell immediate doom. In decentralized networks, such as Bitcoin and BitTorrent, as one node fails, others pick up the slack. Participants may join and leave transiently without affecting the health of the greater whole. It is like skin cells, in a way, in relation to your whole body. Skin cells replicate and die in massive numbers. No one cell lasts very long. Together they accomplish a purpose. But individually they are all replaceable; otherwise a single defect would bring down the billion-cell-whole.

The Blockchain is indifferent to the fate of individual nodes. It does not even need to exist on Bitcoin nodes; it is a cryptographically linked ledger document that can stand-alone and remain equally valid. As nodes come on and off line, or as their number dwindles, or if the network is populated by malicious, cheating nodes, none of it matters. They cannot touch the Blockchain.

Without a central point of weakness, there is no way for the Bitcoin network to suddenly experience an outage, or an attack from an outside party. Unlike virtually all web services, which inevitably experience technical problems at a requisite server, Bitcoin is never 'down for maintenance'. Even as numerous parties on the Bitcoin network experience their own technical problems, there are always more peers, and so the network never just shuts off.

Similarly, Bitcoin has no central hub that is vulnerable to outside attack. There is no office building the authorities can visit to influence Bitcoin. There is no person that can be arrested who is 'in charge' of the network. One could arrest all the lead Bitcoin developers. But that would be like arresting English Professors in the hopes of outlawing the English language. It's utterly hopeless. Just like English, Bitcoin is a language: an idea that once released cannot be contained.

The fact that there is no central point of weakness makes Bitcoin infinitely safer from the most pernicious form of systemic risk in existence: other people. Governments in particular have very few ways to influence the Bitcoin network. In fact, it's an almost comical coincidence that there has been so little discussion within government circles of 'shutting down Bitcoin'. Certainly the desire is there. One of Bitcoin's less advanced predecessors, E-gold, was not so decentralized; it was shut down in the 1990's by the US government on spurious licensing charges. Certainly the government would claim far greater cause to shut down Bitcoin than it had for E-gold. But Bitcoin has no weak points. It is everywhere and it is nowhere. It is a protocol surrounding a common public ledger that cannot be forged. The government cannot shut it down without a truly massive mobilization of resources.

It continues to surprise me how often it is stated among journalists that Bitcoin 'may be shut down by the government'. Although we rarely hear that mentioned by knowledgeable governmental officials, since they should know better than to suggest something they cannot accomplish, it is a popular refrain among Bitcoin's wider critics. This is emblematic of a failure to grasp the new paradigm Bitcoin represents. Pundits speak as if Bitcoin is something that is subject to the government. It is as ridiculous as the suggestion during the 1990's that cryptography should not be exported. While government erected barriers for a time, the effort to resist the spread of ideas was futile. Criminalizing ideas is folly and cannot succeed. You could no more ban the English Language or mathematics, than you could ban Bitcoin.

Even besides attempts at outright criminalization, Bitcoin's independence from authorities is a great asset because it spares Bitcoin the regulatory and legal baggage that would otherwise be forced upon it. The government's vision of the ideal financial product may not agree with the consumers'. For example, it is likely that the government, if it had a say, would demand less anonymity. Or perhaps they would enforce taxes, paid natively as part of the core software, to government addresses. Surely they would expect the right to undo and censor transactions. It is hard to imagine the cornucopia of requirements that regulators could impose. But surely they would impede the operation of the protocol as desired by users. One has only to look at modern finance, so overburdened by regulations, to see the desired ends of bureaucrats.

The proof of Bitcoin's appeal lies in the open nature of the system. There is a free market of ideas in which cryptocurrencies compete. The government could, at any time, make its own cryptocurrency with whatever regulations it likes. It is obvious that, short of compulsion, such a currency could never compete in the realm of ideas. Being unable to throw their own party, they feel compelled to ruin someone else's.

So because of the countless ways Bitcoin could have been tampered with were it not a decentralized system, the currency gains immeasurably from its intangible, ethereal nature. While Bitcoin's success points out the lie in fiat currencies, envious governments cannot murder the Wunderkind in its cradle. If they could destroy Bitcoin, they absolutely would. Because it does not exist within the realm of human control, at least as we know it, Bitcoin does not suffer the additional burden of constant human intervention.

Rebuttals

Bitcoin is a Ponzi Scheme

When I was first told about Bitcoin by a friend in 2012, my instinctive reaction was to say, "It's a Ponzi Scheme". I said it immediately. It was obvious. How could a purely invented currency ever be valuable? It had no sound basis in anything. It came from nowhere, under no one's authority. It was just make believe, like monopoly money, except worse, because it was pure data. Monopoly money, at least, had to be printed on honest-to-god paper. Bitcoins, as solely 0's and 1's, were pure fiction.

Bitcoin was practically a joke. In those days, it had such a low value and so little public awareness. It was a laughable distraction at the edges of the Internet. Almost no one had heard of it. I saw it as basically the equivalent of video game money. It's as if someone wanted to give you World of Warcraft gold as real-world payment: money with no legitimacy for people with no lives.

Bitcoin reeked of absurdism the way Internet Memes must appear to my grandparents. The pretension from Internet nerds, to have their own fringe currency, appeared like a purists' open-source project run amok. It addressed something so fundamental in such an esoteric way. It was like installing some off-brand Linux distribution, so obscure as to be somehow special. Honest dollars weren't good enough for these people.

The enormity of the task that lay before them, and their apparent hubris in thinking that they could accomplish it, made me assume that Bitcoiners were either stupid or fraudsters. Currency could not be conjured up out of thin air. It required value and authority that no hacker could command. I assumed immediately that, as play money, Bitcoin would be a running joke whose final punch line would be the last people holding them. Surely this was a clever trick by elite hackers to trick gullible people on the Internet. Something entirely born and conceived online could not translate into real world value. It was doomed to fail, I felt. So only then did I backtrack, in my mind, for the reasons why it must.

This was my original impression of Bitcoin and Bitcoiners. I simply didn't take it seriously. I arrived armed to dismantle its rationale from the beginning. I had judged it guilty; it would be merely a formality to gather the necessary evidence. How wrong I was. I could never have imagined how my doubts would transform into interest, which would snowball, and snowball, until I was completely entranced. Nor did I ever imagine that a single idea would lead to such blossoming of thought, around the world, and that I would be enmeshed in it.

Bitcoin is not a Ponzi scheme. A Ponzi scheme is a system in which participants are paid solely out of the entry of new entrants but with the illusion of some legitimate profitability. Only the older cohort can avoid loss. Each new wave of members sees the success of the previous wave, but fails to realize that there is *no external source of value. They* are the profits. In aggregate, there is only a net loss. There is no profit-engine; one man's profits are another man's losses. But this fact is concealed until a critical mass is reached, whereupon the illusion can no longer be maintained. Ponzi schemes blow up spectacularly and enfranchise only a few.

As I began investigating Bitcoin, one of the first things I realized was that the system was symmetrical for all participants. There are no gatekeepers. There are no users with 'special privileges'. As a peer-to-peer system, you are truly a peer under Bitcoin, particularly if you run your own full node. There are no special keys held by the elect few. No one can systematically game you because *everyone* operates under the exact same set of rules. There are no exceptions, no amendments, and no special cases. This should strike you as unusual. It is. Organizations run by people are ridden with little exceptions and special privileges; you would be right to be on the lookout for that in Bitcoin. But worry not. The Bitcoin protocol touches all equally.

False promises about profitability are a hallmark of Ponzi schemes. How else to convince new participants without at least a facade of independent value? If I sold Andrew Shares, with promises of rich profits from Andrew-related activities, I could feasibly sell a Ponzi scheme. The profits would come from buyers of new shares, not the underlying Andrew-related activities, which are worthless. This is how Ponzi schemes work; you never tell the truth about the purported value source, else no one would ever buy.

Bitcoin makes no false promises. Bitcoin fans claim it is really excellent as a currency tool. That's it. And as I describe in this book; Bitcoin *is* excellent at what currencies are supposed to do. You don't need to take my word for it. Use it yourself or look at the source code. Everything is open. There is nothing hidden about the value proposition behind Bitcoin. A Ponzi scheme in which everyone may inspect the books and question the accountants would be doomed to premature failure.

Some Bitcoiners may make hyperbolic claims, such as that 'Bitcoin is going to $10,000 next week'. The fervor with which many Bitcoiners describe Bitcoin suggests that they are trying to sell you something. The Bitcoin community has made countless false predictions in the past. As a heterogeneous mass of people, it is bound to indulge in all sorts of fantasy. However it would be a fatal mistake to conflate the prognostications of Bitcoiners with the underlying content of the Bitcoin protocol itself. Just because a Bitcoin enthusiast proclaimed $10,000 bitcoins for next week, does not mean you need to hold a grudge against Bitcoin itself when the prediction fails.

It is an easy mistake to confuse the folly of individual Bitcoiners with the merits of the underlying protocol. Bitcoin the protocol is computer code. It is pure and deterministic. It is also, still, a work in progress. Anyone may inspect it, run it, edit it, at will. You may understand the technical aspects to the last iota. Those who do so see the power behind the protocol. Bitcoiners themselves, however, are people, and thus prone to many well-known bugs. Know the difference. It is too easy to knock down the straw man, the Bitcoin enthusiast who said something ridiculous, as a way to target the protocol itself, which is infinitely more robust. This is a cheap approach. But, as we have seen, it is in our nature to think more of the human face than mathematical truths. Resist that temptation. If you would like to discuss Bitcoin, you must have a basic handle on the technical aspects. The flaws of Bitcoiners do not extend to the protocol itself, which has endured with exceptional success.

Bitcoin probably felt more like a Ponzi scheme in its earliest days, when bitcoins were almost free, the prices were *wildly* volatile, and there were almost no places to spend them. With so few users and so few ways to use them, bitcoins essentially *were* play-money in the early days. This was reflected in the extremely low price. However it was a play-money with special properties that would allow it to metastasize into a real, useful, spendable currency. But that lay in the future. In the earliest days, 2009-2012, Bitcoin was a hobbyists' venture.

Bitcoin markets were so illiquid that prices would be subject to mind-bending springs, spurts, and undulations. With so few buyers and sellers at any one time, and so little agreement on what a bitcoin's value should be, all sorts of market antics were possible that have since become impractical. A single buyer or seller could overwhelm orders and engage in blatant manipulation in what were, in the early days, immature exchanges in unspendable Internet play-money. While vestiges of these tactics remain today, their magnitude pales in comparison to the primal early days.

One could have observed the erratic market behavior and concluded that Bitcoin was a scam designed to enrich early adopters. In the very first Bitcoin bubble, the price skyrocketed from pennies, to $30 a bitcoin. In proportional terms, this was the greatest Bitcoin bubble ever. It was the first and the greatest. And it popped in a similarly spectacular fashion. The price plummeted to $2 a bitcoin: a 93% loss from the peak. Countless hopeful investors were burned and disenchanted with Bitcoin, even as the price lay in the single digits for over a year.

At the moment of the first bubble, the human reaction at such market devastation would have been that the Ponzi scheme had been exposed. You could have said that the Bitcoin adopters had fooled new entrants into Bitcoin, selling at the outrageous peak of $30, for what were essentially worthless digital tokens. At this time, many people believed just that: that Bitcoin the Ponzi scheme had been finally exposed.

And yet, why did Bitcoin not die that day? In its darkest hour, with its greatest ever proportional loss, with almost no ways to use it, with scarcely any users at all, how did Bitcoin endure? The answer lies in the protocol, which was unmoved. The code was indifferent to the wild gyrations of human thought. Bitcoin still worked. Bitcoin still retained its core value proposition, namely, as a currency tool. What made Bitcoin valuable in the first place had never changed, even as market turbulence had erupted in the world of men. Human thoughts did not matter as much as expected. Opinion could not doom the Blockchain. If it could, it would have killed Bitcoin years ago. In spite of incredible catastrophes striking the Bitcoin community and ecosystem, the protocol and the Blockchain are resilient as ever. Despite so many setbacks, the protocol survived to fight another day, its value undimmed, because it was subject to math alone, and not human whims.

Bitcoin recovered, from $2, to $15, to $266, in the second great bubble. And then it crashed in a paroxysm of market terror. And the Ponzi scheme was unveiled a second time as the price hit a $50 floor. Soon Bitcoin rose again, all the way to $1100. And then it crashed, again. And the Ponzi scheme was exposed for a third time, when the price hit a $200 floor. You see the trend. Speculative bubbles aside, the utility value of Bitcoin the currency has not gone away. In fact, it has grown immensely.

It is a well-known adage among computer people that the number of connections in a network scales by the square of the number of nodes. As the Bitcoin community has grown, the number of ways to use one's bitcoins has grown immensely. Since Bitcoin's core value proposition is as currency, its underlying value strongly scales with the number of users. While Ponzi schemes also make more money the more users they have, so do basically all viral startups. This is not a defining characteristic of Ponzi Schemes as much as it is one of network-based systems, which include countless successful businesses. Facebook's value scales exponentially with the number of users it has. The Internet itself became more useful only as more users went online; there were simply more things to do on it.

As more users are attracted to Bitcoin, the protocol delivers more value by allowing fast, easy, secure transactions with more and more people. Meanwhile new companies are constantly arising offering clever new ways to use Bitcoin, such as tipping on Reddit or paying for streaming video. Such capabilities arise from the core utility offered by Bitcoin. It is doing its job, precisely as advertised: as currency. Critics who identify the similarity between the growth in Ponzi schemes and the Bitcoin user base are making a superficial observation which would be equally inappropriate with any successful startup.

Bitcoin was built to be mathematically, provably fair. It has no gatekeepers. It has survived 3 massive bubbles and crashes, each one accompanied with proclamations of 'The End of Bitcoin'. It's open source. And it's doing its job, as currency, extremely well. Bitcoin is demonstrably not a Ponzi scheme.

Bitcoin is Illicit

Bitcoin has had a reputation as a reserve for criminals and hackers. This belief is widely held. I've met people who were shocked that I owned bitcoins, as if they were an inherently unsavory thing to possess. Even such luminaries as Bill Gates have implied that, while the technology is great, Bitcoin itself is simply too sketchy. Its close association with drug trading, cybercrime, fraud, and other unsavory acts has tarnished Bitcoin irrevocably, so the argument goes.

Police agencies, the FBI, and other governmental bodies have expressed concern at the rise in the use of Bitcoin. Bitcoin alarms them because the old methods for interdicting money do not apply. It is a scary, new world in which they have little expertise. Users are pseudonymous through public addresses. Transactions require approval from no one but the bitcoins' rightful owner. There is no central weak point to control the flow of money. Bitcoin was designed from the start to be above the control of governments. This makes it a natural tool for those who wish to escape them. Evading the reach of the government, they say, is itself inherently nefarious. Conventional money methods are more above-board. The police know how to handle them. Using Bitcoin, by contrast, suggests that you have something to hide.

By using Bitcoin, you are certainly in the company of some sinister figures. There have been many incidents of criminal use of Bitcoin. It has been the central currency for the sale of illegal drugs online. Sites such as Silk Road, their successors, and many others, have sprouted up to cater to the drug trade. They have all used Bitcoin to the chagrin of government. More sinister things such as child pornography and even purportedly assassination hits, have even been traded using Bitcoin.

Within the Bitcoin universe, there has been a rash of instances of fraud, theft, and deception. Millions of dollars have been connived or stolen from hapless bitcoin owners. Bitcoin Savings and Trust was a Ponzi scheme built on top of Bitcoin. It promised 7% weekly returns to investors who, in the end, became hapless victims when millions of dollars' worth of Bitcoin were stolen. Exchanges have been hacked, resulting in losses in the hundreds of millions. Bitcoinica, a sophisticated Bitcoin trading and leverage platform, was hacked, resulting in the loss of millions of dollars' worth of bitcoin. It later collapsed due to insolvency. The list goes on and on.

Most ominous in the history of Bitcoin is a dark chapter called MT.GOX. Its very name hangs like a shadow over the Bitcoin community. It was the first exchange. And for much of Bitcoin's history, it was overwhelmingly the largest one. It had a lucrative business as the ultimate Bitcoin brand. Originally "Magic the Gathering Online Exchange", it embodied Bitcoin's early roots at the fringe of the Internet. As Bitcoin (unexpectedly) grew, MTGOX became a large and prosperous business. But it was hit by multiple troubles. It had millions of dollars confiscated by the US government on dubious grounds. It suffered from attacks by hackers and, more seriously, the technical incompetence of its owners, which in no way matched its dominant place in the market. These failures came to a catastrophic conclusion in early 2014, when MTGOX declared insolvency. This resulted in the loss for depositors of 100,000's of bitcoins.

With the collapse of MT.GOX, a non-trivial percentage of total extant bitcoins that were believed to be owned went dark. They had been stolen by hackers, or possibly, stolen by the administrators of MT.GOX itself. It was a massive shock to Bitcoin. It incited a loss of confidence in the nascent system. Many former enthusiasts left in disgust. The protracted demise of MT.GOX was a bleeding wound that refused to heal. While its market role has been replaced by far superior exchanges, the damage done to confidence remains much less easily restored.

There is no question that many distasteful things have occurred in the Bitcoin universe. Criminals have employed it to great effect. Fraudsters have run scams. Hackers have stolen millions. Thousands more users have suffered sudden losses when their private keys became exposed or lost. The history of Bitcoin is filled with many corpses from many battles. Of that there is no question.

But one should not judge Bitcoin by the bad apples. Just as you cannot judge Dollars by the deeds committed for them, Bitcoin is innocent of the misdeeds perpetrated by people. The correlation between Bitcoin and a malicious minority is a false association. It does not capture the essence of Bitcoin. It is such a limited subset of the uses to which Bitcoin is employed. It is seeking out the bad to spoil the good.

Are diamonds any less lustrous because a few of them are "Blood Diamonds"? Are cars any less useful because they sometimes kill people? Many things can be associated with evil, if you twist your vision to see only the bad and never the good. Those painting Bitcoin with the brush of illegality are showing you a narrow vision of what Bitcoin is.

And if Bitcoin is sometimes used to skirt onerous regulations, capital controls, and other 'legal' mechanisms imposed by governments, then we should see it as a sort of Robin Hood situation, in which we sympathize with the criminals. Just because a law exists does not make it right. Financial privacy ought to be a basic right, as well as immunity from confiscation, no matter what the laws say. Insofar as Bitcoin empowers people to escape immoral laws, we should celebrate it. In the struggle between people and domineering government, many words will be slung, such as 'illicit' and 'criminal' to describe behavior that is perfectly valid. Don't be distracted by *who* is saying what; measure the content of what they say.

Bitcoin is too Volatile

Another common criticism leveled against Bitcoin is that it is too volatile to serve as currency. Its price often undergoes dramatic swings over short time scales. A thousand dollars of bitcoin can be worth seven hundred the next day. Or perhaps fifteen hundred. Even over the course of minutes it can jump up or down by several percentage points. This extreme volatility, the argument goes, makes Bitcoin unsuitable as currency. Anything whose real-price oscillates so violently introduces exchange risk to participants in a transaction. I can't hold bitcoins and be sure about their value the next day, or even the next hour. This uncertainty itself causes waste. It undermines the fabled currency utility of Bitcoin.

It is true that Bitcoin's present volatility weakens its currency utility *at the present*. But this says little besides that the currency is at a nascent stage. This is a short term observation, not an equilibrium outcome.

Let us first look at the present. The price of Bitcoin is extremely volatile. Prices can jump 10 or 20% within an hour, albeit under exceptional trading circumstances. Over the course of a single day purely stochastic surges and crashes are entirely possible. Most days are uneventful. But when turbulence hits Bitcoin markets, it hits hard.

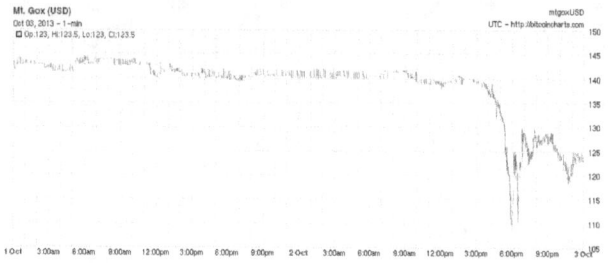

Bitcoin price gyrating 20% within hours after the arrest of Ross Ulbricht

Bitcoin is volatile for several reasons, foremost of which is that it is currently *very small*. The market capitalization of bitcoins actually circulating (as opposed to lost or burned) is only about $3 billion as of this writing. The depth of limit orders on any particular market is thus only ever in the millions of dollars. Thus, with a few million dollars, one could cause a sizeable disturbance to the price of Bitcoin, on the order of a 5-10% spike. That's an enormous price movement. Try moving a publicly traded stock on the New York Stock Exchange. You would need stupendous sums to move the needle for big companies like Intel, Apple, Exxon.

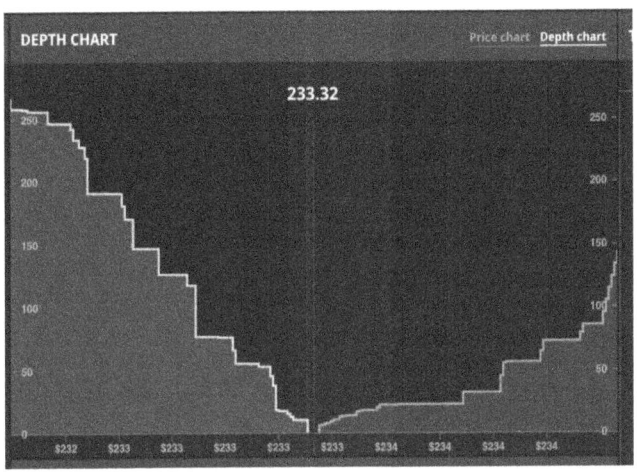

A depth chart on the Coinbase Exchange. Even small amounts of money can move the price substantially.

Source: exchange.coinbase.com

Bitcoin's non-standard financial status means it has much less liquidity than comparable stocks. Fewer traders and big institutions monitor the Bitcoin price. The armies of algorithms and traders on Wall Street hardly interact with Bitcoin. Whereas on the New York Stock Exchange, trillions of dollars provide deep liquidity to equity markets, comparatively little money sits on Bitcoin exchanges. This means that the forces that ordinarily moderate sharp price swings are much weaker in Bitcoin than in conventional markets. Simply put, less cash and fewer eyeballs are monitoring Bitcoin. The oceans of cash that stand ready to correct, and profit from, stock market jumps don't exist in Bitcoin.

There is nothing fundamental about Bitcoin's comparative lack of liquidity. Rather than an intrinsic feature of Bitcoin, it is a function of its immature status as a financial instrument. This can hardly be a surprise; entire markets, exchanges, and complex trading tools have arisen to cater to Bitcoin trading demand. However with such a small community, and relatively little money involved, these tools have only come so far in their 2-3 year lifespans.

In fact, Bitcoin's liquidity has improved by leaps and bounds compared to that of the early days. To gain insight into the primitive trading patterns of early Bitcoin, one need only visit an altcoin exchange. In such underdeveloped markets, bid-ask spreads are enormous. Volume is erratic. Price manipulation is a very real thing. Altcoin exchanges are not happy places. Bitcoin was once like this.

Today, Bitcoin's exchanges are dramatically superior to those of just 1-2 years ago. They continue to improve due to the intense competitive pressure. When Bitcoin may equally be exchanged in China, Slovakia, or anywhere, exchanges must innovate to keep their fickle clientele. They are getting cheaper through reduced fees, now on the order of 0-0.2 %. And indeed, the quality of modern Bitcoin exchanges is greatly improved. Exchanges have even done cryptographically rigorous audits of their Bitcoin holdings. This is an accounting feat that even well-established, international banks cannot equal.

Trading algorithms now ply the Bitcoin exchanges, providing constant market depth. You will hardly ever find Bitcoin's bid-ask spread rise to its previous levels, except perhaps for brief windows during particularly heavy trading. This is a demonstration of the growing sophistication of Bitcoin trading. And it is a symptom of the openness inherent to Bitcoin. This is the result of an open, meritocratic free-for-all of algorithms.

In fact, arbitrageurs are another example of the increasing maturity of Bitcoin markets. They keep the prices across various Bitcoin exchanges in sync with exceptional efficiency. In the old days, Bitcoin exchanges often drifted apart, showing sharply varying prices from one another. Algorithms constantly seek to correct price divergences. The sort of slippage that used to occur is rectified by diligent traders. These inglorious tasks are essential to well-functioning markets. That Bitcoin has attracted traders and arbitrageurs of such sophistication is a sign of financial health, if not of maturity.

Bitcoin trading is not like other markets with set hours and multitudinous rules; it is *de facto* unregulated. In practice if not in law it is a free-for-all. You can dump millions of dollars on a Chinese exchange at 3 AM. No one will stop you. You can design a trading bot that tries to play manipulative games versus other bots. The trading never stops. It goes on 24/7. Historically many of the greatest trading antics occurred late at night when no one was awake to respond. The fact that no regulatory body is capable of interrupting trading, interdicting certain kinds of trades, or even setting defined trading hours, makes Bitcoin trading less predictable than its conventional cousins. It also makes it freer.

This is actually another parallel with gold; as a non-national, neutral asset, it is traded 24/7 like Bitcoin. As opposed to other financial transactions, both gold and Bitcoin do not require a legal framework for the settlement of transactions. Thus they may be traded wherever there are buyers and sellers. That's why you can always get a running price quote on gold, as opposed to stocks, because a market for it is always open.

Besides the technical aspects to trading, Bitcoin is currently so volatile because, ultimately there is little objective agreement as to its true value. It is devilishly hard to value Bitcoin using hard numbers. There is such a broad diversity of thought; widely varying views coexist in the marketplace. Sometimes one extreme view may dominate the market as the other sits out. The optimists carry the market to bubble prices; the pessimists drag it down into despair territory. Since there are so few hard facts that would guide a valuation of Bitcoin, the price is today largely driven by emotional and speculative forces. Over its turbulent history, psychology has had an undeniable role in setting prices.

It is evident that Bitcoin's price at any given moment is a combination of its utilitarian purposes and speculative forces. Whereas the sudden onset of parabolic bubble heights is surely a function of excessive euphoria, the price at the despair-ridden lows reflects Bitcoin's core value proposition. No matter how low the price falls in moments of panic, Bitcoin retains its utility value as a unit of exchange. You can see that, even as the price falls, the dollar-denominated transaction volume typically remains steady.

As Bitcoin attracts more users, the growth of the network further accelerates its utility to future users. As users conduct non-speculative transactions, they indirectly create a hard price floor for Bitcoin. Thus the growth in the scale of the network increases the price contribution stemming from utilitarian purposes as opposed to speculative ones. Conversely, the speculative proportion of the price will diminish in importance. If, when Bitcoin was first released, its value was 0% practical and 100% speculative, the current price may be 50/50. Further growth will drive down the speculative component, and thus also the observed price volatility.

If Bitcoin's practical use acts as a minimum base layer of value, we can easily measure this on the Blockchain. We will observe that, extreme price movements notwithstanding, the network has been growing steadily. The number of users is starkly up, as are the number of transactions per day, and other technical metrics. These trends are not as exciting as the price rockets. But they represent Bitcoin's value proposition in action. We should expect prices to rise with these metrics as volatility diminishes.

Historical Transactions per Day, Averaged per Month. Source: Blockchain.info

The transaction rate is much less volatile than the price

Looking backwards in Bitcoin's history, we see these trends as well. Bitcoin had virtually no use case in the early days, with almost no users. Any value it commanded was purely speculative. As a result, bubbles and crashes were cataclysmic. Measuring these undulations in proportional terms, there is a clear decline in volatility with an increasing market cap.

Bitcoin's volatility says nothing fundamental about its future. It is a by-product of its nascent state as a financial instrument. In the future, if comparable resources are dedicated to trading Bitcoin, as in other currencies, we could see volatility dramatically moderated. When the base use case is widespread and broadly recognized, there will be less room for speculative booms and busts. As the facts of Bitcoin's use trump the opinions of speculators, their influence on prices will wane. Bitcoin need not always be as volatile as it is now.

Life: More Volatile than We're Used to

The mere fact of Bitcoin's dramatic rise triggers the suspicions of many. How can something increase in value by orders of magnitude so quickly? How many stocks increase by 100x multiples within the space of a year? Surely something nefarious is at work. Such growth is unnatural, so they say.

Whereas experienced stock market traders will see the explosive growth of Bitcoin with surprise and dismay, experienced venture capitalists will be unfazed. Comparing the growth of Bitcoin to that of large, publicly traded companies is an inappropriate comparison. As any venture capitalist can tell you, new ideas can experience sudden and exponential growth that would be unfathomable for large, $200 billion dollar companies. Bitcoin's price moves like that of startups.

Individual companies on the stock market can experience substantial volatility. Apple stock since 2002, one of the greatest growth opportunities in recent times, grew by 30X over the course of 10 years. But this rate of growth pales in comparison to that of successful startups in their early growth phase; they can increase in value by 10x-100x in a very short period of time. Across startups, an extreme potential for growth is counterbalanced by an extremely low-chance of success. Most startups fail. But a few become supercharged into fabulously lucrative investments for their original backers.

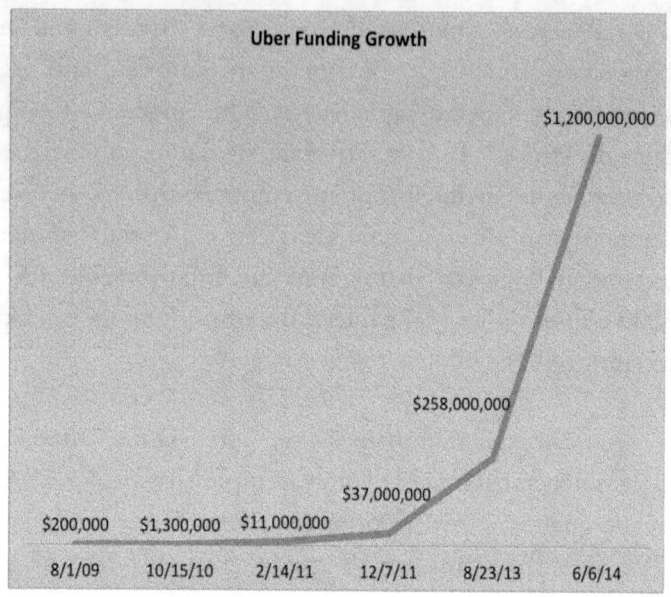

Source: Venturebeat.com

Startups, by definition, are pre-IPO stage companies. They have market capitalizations and equity distributions. But ownership is not actively traded. Hence there is no price discovery. Whereas publicly traded stocks constantly voice the market's opinion of the underlying value of their respective companies, infrequently traded equity, such as that of startups, is highly illiquid. Thus you cannot tell me, from one day to the next, what the current valuation of a small startup is, as you can for a larger, public company. Startup valuations are established only infrequently, typically when new capital enters the business. When equity is exchanged, only then must a valuation be established. For startups, the rarity of these events and the subjectivity of valuing an unproven idea make valuations imprecise best-guesses.

How would one have valued Facebook in 2004 when it was run by a few kids and served only a few thousand college students? Let us imagine that traders could have publicly traded Facebook equity at that time, without, of course, the foreknowledge that Facebook would be hugely successful. If Facebook had somehow been publicly traded when it was run out of a college dorm, what would its price have been? How would that price have undulated over time?

Surely Facebook stock would have suffered intense, fighter-plane G's of volatility. Perhaps Mark Zuckerberg would have gotten sick one weekend. As the only employee, getting sick could have sent the stock tumbling. Perhaps with a total market cap in the thousands, or low millions of dollars, a few traders could have manipulated price movements, causing massive pump-and-dump price upheavals. Surely the stock would have been highly illiquid with a massive bid-ask spread. Who would have bothered providing liquidity? At times the share price would have sky-rocketed, such as when Facebook spread to the first neighboring colleges. At others, it may have plummeted, perhaps when Zuckerberg got in trouble at Harvard. Every little event at Facebook in those early days could have had a proportionally massive effect on the underlying share price.

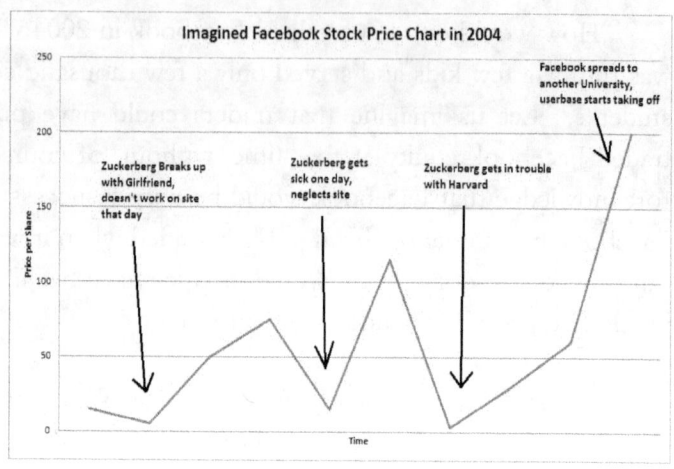

But because Facebook was not a publicly traded company, we never got to see the vast gyrations in its value from minor, early events. Nor did we ever get to see the exponential, 10,000X growth period when Facebook morphed from a college dorm room into a large, significant company. Naturally Facebook had shares with some price, at least from the moment of its first investment round. But we never got to monitor that price, in real time as we can with Bitcoin, through all Facebook's tribulations and successes. It wasn't publicly traded.

If we could have watched Facebook's share price from the earliest days, we could have leveled arguments similar to those used against Bitcoin. The dramatic price rise is unnatural, some might have said; nothing normally grows that fast. It's too volatile, others would say. Nothing should gain and lose value so suddenly over such trivial events. Normal investors are not habituated to the epic fluctuations of startup valuations, because they are illiquid and rarely publicized. People are used to the *comparatively* tame movements on the New York Stock Exchange. This is misleading. Most investors have only been exposed to a subset of business trajectories.

Bitcoin is a startup currency. It's a raw idea that has grown exponentially, the way any good startup should. It's getting traction and it has a devoted user base. But it's still in that frantic, unstable, upward trend that (sometimes) ends in mainstream stability. There is a disconnect between the reality for startups and the more even-keeled experience of most people that leads many to judge Bitcoin by the wrong standard. Bitcoin cannot grow as most things in life do, ploddingly by 5% a year. As a new idea it has something to prove, a chip on its shoulder, that means it should go big or go bust.

In contrast to startups, we've been able to witness Bitcoin's price all along. Bitcoin IPO'd in 2010, when the first exchanges were set up. In addition to IPO'ing early, Bitcoin invented its own set of parallel exchanges which were assumed to work perfectly from the get-go. It's as if Facebook had IPO'd in November 2004 and then went on to found the Boston Stock Exchange. That's asking a lot. And yet the Bitcoin community has done it.

So as we witness Bitcoin's price acrobatics, its mad dives, its exuberant highs, we ought to judge it by the standards of an adolescent startup, not a wizened ExxonMobil.

The mere fact of its volatility says nothing. Many successful companies have trodden that path already; it is a symptom of small stature. And in Bitcoin's case, since its devotees have literally reinvented the requisite financial infrastructure, the nascent state of the trading technology also plays a part in volatility.

While there may be good reasons for Bitcoin's volatility in the here-and-now, nothing about the current state of things is in equilibrium. Bitcoin's central role as a currency tool will not be threatened, in the long run, by the volatility which presently affects it. This volatility is transient and in historic decline. As the Bitcoin network grows in use, the speculative fevers it endures will diminish in significance. As the trading technology continues to improve, illiquidity and exchange failures, such as MT.GOX, will fade. With more financial players in the game, we can expect prices to be better moderated by profit-seeking traders, as they are on the stock market.

All of the factors that contribute to Bitcoin's present price instability are in decline. This leads to a self-reinforcing pattern in which the network becomes more valuable in its core purpose. As volatility declines, Bitcoin becomes more viable as a currency tool. This leads to more use, which in turn further reduces volatility. The amazing thing was that people still found Bitcoin useful during its most extreme price gyrations. With that established any subsequent reductions in volatility drive a positive feedback loop. Just as the utility of the network scales dramatically with the number of participants in turn attracting still more users, volatility, price, and the currency utility exist in a similarly virtuous circle. Improvements beget still more improvements. This is the very definition of viral growth.

No one contests that Bitcoin has been volatile, or that it has suffered numerous bubbles, or that its trading systems were once rudimentary. And there is no doubt either that volatility hinders Bitcoin in its present use as currency, particularly for non-speculative savers. But here I've sought to make the case that, none of these failings are actually intrinsic to Bitcoin. Some degree of uncertainty is inherent to any asset class, even immensely liquid ones such as the dollar. More importantly, any new idea experiences hairpin turns of volatility in its birthing process. Startups are volatile, but this in no way predestines them to always be so. The novelty of the Bitcoin experiment necessitates that price volatility will remain, at least until the underlying questions are finally answered in the mind of the market.

Bitcoin has no Intrinsic Value

There are still a few hard-money advocates left in today's world. They are a sad breed, having been forced to witness the sharp deterioration of the US Dollar since the 1970's, and as follows, nearly every other world currency. Their goals were laudable and their logic sound. But they were fated to be Cassandra: cursed to see the future, but never to be believed. Their lot in life was to constantly be the killjoy at the party, the unwanted naysayer who wishes we'd all be more responsible. For being so completely right in the time since Bretton Woods, real sound money advocates have predictably earned widespread hatred.

Modern proponents of gold take inspiration from the long-lost days of sound money. They tend to approve of Bitcoin's fixed total supply at 21 million bitcoins. Since the monetary supply of Bitcoin is guaranteed by the protocol, not by people, it is a promise that cannot be broken. The management of the monetary supply has been taken out of fickle human hands. Instead it was fixed from the outset in such a way as to disallow tinkering. The supply of gold, by contrast, while stable relative to that of fiat currencies, is imprecise and non-constant. Gold may be mined from the Earth at unexpected rates. Perhaps a massive gold vein will be discovered tomorrow. In the 19th century, the world's gold supply abruptly increased with massive discoveries in the US and South Africa. As much as goldbugs like to think that the supply of gold is immutable, it is in fact dynamic and dependent on geology. This is an inelegant correlation; the fortunes of geologists shouldn't impact the supply of money, especially one that claims to offer superior stability.

Goldbugs and libertarian Bitcoiners have much in common ideologically. However one criticism consistently leveled against Bitcoin by gold enthusiasts is that, while Bitcoin and gold may superficially have similar properties, gold is valuable because it has *intrinsic value*, whereas Bitcoin, as pure data, has none. This argument comes in two forms.

First, gold has been widely recognized as valuable for thousands of years. This long history is so indelible that it gives gold a permanent aura of value. To ask why gold should be objectively valuable is to peer back into the distant past, into the Bronze Age, behind a dark shadow of prehistory best left unquestioned. Gold has always been valuable. There is a worldwide consensus. This is a self-perpetuating truth. It is true because others believe it, and it has always been so.

Gold also has intrinsic value because gold is physically used for productive, non-monetary purposes. Gold is used in electronics, in jewelry, and a range of industrial applications. Gold's unique chemical properties, such as its electrical conductivity and resistance to oxidation, make it genuinely useful. Because of these uses, gold has intrinsic value underlying its role as currency. Even if all assumptions about money broke down in a massive collective amnesia, we would still find ourselves desiring gold for its alternative uses.

Bitcoin, goldbugs say, has no intrinsic value. It has no history. There is no consensus on its worth. And as a non-physical abstraction, Bitcoin is not useful for anything besides as money. You can't make anything out of it. If all our currency assumptions broke down in one instant, or perhaps in an apocalypse, Bitcoin would be valueless.

I will argue that gold is not actually valued for its physical utility to anywhere near the extent that its price would suggest. Some of gold's idiosyncrasies are differentiating factors between Bitcoin and gold rather than fundamental, irreducible qualities of money as some would suggest. They do not strike at the heart of the matter of what money is. They are not why gold is valuable.

Historical longevity is a poor argument for intrinsic worth. It's circular reasoning; something is valuable because it has always been valuable. We should not have to resort to this sort of logic. There should be a more objective rationale than simply 'it's valuable because everyone agrees it is'. This may explain behavior over short-time scales, but certainly not long-term outcomes. We know empirically that currency regimes may change over time, but also that people care about what their peers value. The psychology of value may take hold over short time frames; but it cannot dictate long-term outcomes as if they existed in some sort of perfect equilibrium. In fact, gold deserves better treatment than such circular reasoning because there are more objective reasons for its historic success.

Why was Wampum valuable to the Iroquois? What would modern goldbugs, if transplanted to the 1600's, have said about Wampum? They could have made exactly the same arguments. They could have pointed to its utility value in jewelry and decorations. People did want Wampum for its own sake. They still do; to this day it is actively traded for its artistic value. They could have pointed to its longstanding status as an object of value. For the native people of that time, and even the colonials, Wampum was widely perceived as valuable and as money.

And yet Wampum is no longer very valuable. Its value now corresponds to its physical utility only. Previously, when Wampum served as money, its value derived from its physical utility *and* its utility as a medium of exchange. It accomplished two things. Now, having lost its currency purpose, wampum is much less valuable. What does this mean? It means that serving as money is inherently valuable on its own. Money is a tool, like any other, and that tool has value.

Certainly not everything can serve as currency. Wampum and gold, among other things, fit certain criteria to be useful as media of exchange. Different items have different levels of effectiveness as money. Wampum and cowrie shells weren't great as money because they could be manufactured or shipped from overseas.

Consider the value of the big round stones once used on some Polynesian islands as money. As currency these stones were relatively ineffective money because they were too hard to move. But in their time and place they were considered valuable, far beyond their physical utility value, because as money itself they were useful tools. Thus they commanded value from their informational role as money over any physical, utility function.

Goldbugs have conflated gold's physical utility with its utility as currency and thereby assumed that these two properties must come hand in hand. This is a fallacy. Gold was effective as money because it was scarce and durable. While rare, it was not so rare as to make for an illiquid monetary supply, such as if one used rare earth elements. Gold is also very difficult to fake with cheaper alloys. It was both divisible and highly standardized. There was only ever one form of gold, whatever its origin. It was also very value dense, making it relatively efficient as a means to move wealth (try moving cows or salt of comparable value!). These properties made it effective money, completely independent of its other uses.

If gold were valued solely by its uses in jewelry, electronics, and industry, its market price would be *far* lower than it is today. It would be like any other rare metal. The percentage of its current value derived from its physical uses is a trifling fraction of its present market value. This really shouldn't come as a surprise. Much of the world's gold sits idle in bank vaults. If its value really derived from its physical utility, and not its purpose as currency, that gold would be actively employed elsewhere.

That gold's value derives so heavily from its use as currency illustrates that the currency function is itself valuable. The precipitous fall in the value of wampum, or Polynesian stone money, after they ceased acting as currency also demonstrates this. Is it any surprise then that a return to the gold standard would skyrocket the price of gold (in real terms)? Why then can Bitcoin's value not also derive from its role as money, rather than from shininess, conductivity, weight, saltiness, or any of the other useful properties of previous forms of money?

When proponents of gold argue that Bitcoin cannot serve as currency because it does not have intrinsic value, they are missing the point of why gold is valuable. They are looking for something to differentiate Bitcoin and gold. Seizing upon this difference, its physical utility, they claim that this must be the fount of gold's value. But in fact they have confused two separate attributes of gold. This is a case of correlation, not causation. In the pre-digital era, physical utility often coincided with currency utility. But this was never written in stone, nor essential to the nature of currency. Remember the tally sticks recording medieval debts; the sticks they were written on were worthless versus the informational value of the debts they stored. Money is valuable because it serves an *informational purpose apart from the physical medium it inhabits.*

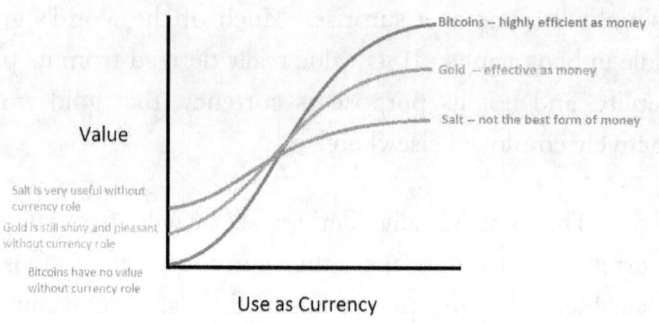

Consider if wampum traders had argued that bead-based money is the only legitimate form of money. Because the currency of the time, wampum, consisted of beads, *beadness* must be an essential aspect of money. Their history *proved* it. It had always been so. Bead-ness is an inescapable part of sound money!

Bitcoin illustrates the difference. Bitcoin has no physical utility. But it is exceedingly excellent as a money tool. It is scarce, durable, secure, instantly transferrable, and as lightweight as data itself. What currency utility gold had, Bitcoin far exceeds. This is the criteria by which it should be judged. Bitcoin handily defeats gold in gold's own true purpose: as effective money.

Goldbugs are the equivalent of Polynesian islanders hoarding big round stones. Yes, they're better than fiat money because the monetary supply is constrained, limiting the moral hazard faced by modern central banks. But nevertheless, gold is the big round stone money of our era. Gold was not meant for the age of the Internet. Its currency utility, which constitutes nearly all its value, has waned dramatically with the advent of sophisticated new technologies. Gold does not compete with Bitcoin as shiny jewelry, just as gold did not compete with wampum as pleasant beads. They compete in the realm of currencies, where exchange efficiency, durability, and monetary stability are the real criteria.

Historical legitimacy is not the deciding factor in settling on the right form of money. No historical precedent is so long-lasting that it can be counted upon to defy a compelling logic or even the normal upheaval of events. This was proven with the departure from the gold standard in the 20th century. The public consensus, while seemingly monolithic at any given time, has proven incredibly malleable over history. Our current regime of fiat money, which is now the largely unquestioned norm, was unthinkable only 50 years ago. I'm sure Iroquois trading wampum were assured by its long history, its veritable status, and its obvious legitimacy. But none of that mattered over longer time scales. We are blinded, by our own nature, to measure things by excessively short time scales, such that things undergoing gradual change appear to be static.

Goldbugs will point to gold's long history as an inviolable source of value, beyond question. In their view, gold is valuable axiomatically. But axiomatic arguments are generally unconvincing. I have pointed to currency utility as a superior, less subjective measure of an object's efficacy as money. I have tried to distill the ultimate essence of what we are trying to accomplish with money, separating apart historical coincidences, such as that gold is shiny, or that wampum makes for lovely beads. These details are idiosyncrasies that do not point to the heart of the matter.

The common theme of what constitutes money is information, scarcity, standardization, and transmissibility. These are not accidents of history, but the core features of a currency tool.

Unlike gold, Bitcoin does not need to resort to the mythic past to justify itself. It has no traditions or vested interests. It stands on the strength of raw ideas alone. Because it excels in the core domains of currency, it wins the meritocratic case over gold. No amount of tradition will protect gold from a currency competitor that is not only more far more scarce, but infinitely superior as a tool for the exchange of value.

Deflationary Currencies are Undesirable

A common argument against Bitcoin is that, as a deflationary currency it removes the powers governments have to intervene in the economy via monetary policy. The capacity of the Fed and other central banks to manipulate the money supply introduces new policy options to alleviate economic pain. Since central banks can intervene countercyclically in a way that private actors cannot, they may moderate booms and busts for the benefit of society. They may boost downturns and restrain excesses. The economy is like an engine that can be run more efficiently with the additional lever of monetary policy. Bitcoin, a currency that intrinsically disallows such interventions, removes these capabilities. The economy would then, the argument goes, veer like a rudderless ship. Why needlessly neuter the golden goose? Why disempower the economy's guardians?

This argument is where the Keynesian rock meets the Bitcoin hammer. It is the crux of the disagreement once the outright fallacies have been swept aside. Orthodox economics states unequivocally that counter-cyclical interventions, both fiscal and monetary, are net positives for society. To accomplish such interventions the money supply must remain malleable in the hands of central bankers. Thus any scheme involving a fixed currency, one whose supply is governed by constraints outside human control, is deeply unpopular among economists.

On this issue, the facts are not in doubt. Bitcoin *does* remove monetary policy as a tool for central bankers. It *is* a deflationary currency. Central bankers *would* be impotent in a Bitcoin-dominated world. The disagreement does not lie in the facts. It lies solely in interpretation of the consequences.

Mainstream economists believe that control over the monetary supply is a useful tool in promoting economic growth. They notice that GDP numbers go up when the monetary supply grows. When times are hard, such as during the Depression, economists similarly noted that the monetary supply had contracted. These observations led them to conclude, in significantly more verbose form, that a decline in the monetary supply *causes* economic pain. Similarly they concluded that, because GDP numbers went up when the monetary supply increased, loose money must be good for the economy. With these conclusions in hand, they had only to rationalize ex-post facto. While I simplify their perspectives here for the sake of brevity, this is a generally accurate depiction.

There is a major logical fallacy in this line of thinking. It is so common as to be a cliché, but it must be named anyway; it is the problem of causation versus correlation. It was over-eager to associate a declining monetary supply as the *root cause* of the hard times of the Depression. Keynesians constantly offer this particular example in defense of their theories about deflation; thus it must be addressed.

Correlation does not imply causation. If deflation is observed in hard economic times, should one then conclude that the former caused the latter? It would be very unscientific to do so without further evidence. Although history does not afford us double-blind experiments, or answers to counterfactual questions, theories must at least be stress-tested for rigor. The most elementary way to test a social theory, for which hard data may be difficult to acquire, is to attempt to falsify it with counterexamples from the historical record. Any theory that is unfalsifiable, or has not been subject to attempts at falsification, cannot be considered rigorous.

Deflation has been observed in many times and places, in good times and in bad. Throughout the 19th century, prices generally trended downwards. It was veritably a deflationary century. And yet economic growth was tremendous. How this can be reconciled with modern theories of deflation? In fact, throughout American economic history, many deflationary events occurred without coinciding with an economic downturn. A Federal Reserve study wrote, "Our main finding is that the only episode in which we find evidence of a link between deflation and depression is the Great Depression (1929—34). We find virtually no evidence of such a link in any other period. [xi]

Keynesian economists have conflated separate phenomena in their conclusions on deflation. Downturns naturally cause a decrease in prices; all else being equal, this is the inevitable conclusion to a sudden decrease in demand. But downturns may equally be inflationary, as we saw in the 1970's in the US. Could one then not say that inflation causes downturns as well?

Deflation is merely a decrease in prices; it is a function of numerous factors, not all of which may be related to an economic downturn. Increased supply can decrease prices just as much as decreased demand. Should an increase in supply, perhaps through productivity gains or through new trading partners, be considered equivalent to a decrease in demand? Is new technology that reduces prices really ever a bad thing? Surely these cannot be lumped together, even as their effect on prices may be identical. Similarly, a decrease in the monetary supply vis-a-vis real goods may produce the same deflationary effect. While we may be predisposed to like productivity gains, why should we then be biased against decreases in the monetary supply, when the observable effect on prices is identical?

The velocity of money may also decline which, with all else being equal, leads to deflation. There might be good reasons for this, such as paying off old debts or saving for future investments. Should the rule be that money must always fly fast and never slow? Is that really tenable? Keynesians would suggest that money should fly on a pinwheel faster and faster. It should be spent immediately;

saving is not legitimate. Because it reduces spending, it is bad for the economic numbers. Hence saving is bad for the economy. This is a classic case of optimizing what you measure, not what really counts. Of course saving can be good for the economy, particularly in unfettered capital markets. And yet you will often hear economists complaining about too much deleveraging and not enough spending, *as if Americans weren't already the most profligate consumers on Earth.* If anything, we are desperately in need of more saving. To the Keynesians intent on improving the short term numbers, this is anathema.

Regarding deflation, the conceptual difficulty arises from the fact that, when one discusses virtually any economic metric, it is a convolution of numerous other metrics. Everything sits on shifting sands. There is no solid rock upon which measurements may be made unadjusted. Everything must be adjusted. Everything is a product of multiple variables. Deflation is a product of the monetary supply, the supply of real goods, and the velocity of money. To conclude that "deflation causes X" is to miss the wide space of varying circumstances in which deflation may occur. It is to subsample this space for the example that carries the most emotional resonance and that may most easily be recollected: the Great Depression.

It is not at all clear that the historical record suggests that deflation causes economic pain. It seems much more likely that the causal relationship is reversed. Because economic downturns surely decrease the velocity of money, it requires no leap of the imagination to see how deflation could result. The opposite view, that deflation inspired economic failures first, requires fairly tortuous logic and vastly more improbably assertions.

Keynesian economists have attempted to explain why deflation is such a negative force. As money itself gains in real value over time it becomes rational to hold money instead of spending it on real goods. As time goes on the money will buy more, so it is always logical to delay spending. As a result, spending declines, leading to further price decreases. Prices accelerate downward in a self-reinforcing cycle referred to as a 'deflationary death spiral'. According to this logic, the desire to hoard money becomes self-perpetuating until virtually all demand has frozen. This theory is constantly trumpeted by Keynesian economists as the reason why deflation *must* be avoided *at all costs.*

But the deflationary death spiral theory suffers from major flaws. First of all, it has never happened. Despite many historical instances in which deflation coincided with economic malaise, there is no clear example in which deflation became a self-reinforcing phenomenon able to choke off demand. Secondly, everyday experience disproves the fundamental assertion: that a regime of declining prices will *lead to* a sharp reduction in demand. It is too easy to falsify this assertion; many goods experience constantly declining prices. Computers are always declining in price. So are cars. Next year's version will always be better bang for buck than today's. Sometimes this effect is particularly extreme, such as with electronics. But people buy them nevertheless. Why is this so?

Economists may be right in theory, that declining prices can logically induce people to hoard money. But this may only occur in a situation of *extreme* deflation which has never been witnessed in modern times. Whatever the rational impulse on spending from inflationary or deflationary forces, that impulse exists *in equilibrium* with ordinary human demands. In maximizing my own personal utility, gratification itself has a clear time value. I will not be dissuaded from owning a computer for years because I know that they will be cheaper. People are very good at balancing their own wants within time scales that make sense to them. Were food experiencing sharp deflation, people would still buy food, because their need for food is inelastic compared to rational optimizations of wealth. Whereas food may be a particularly sticky requirement, demand for all types of goods will have some measure of responsiveness to long term price movements. It is within this context that people will adjust their consumption relative to deflation expectations. What is the time differential for gratification now versus later? What is the spread between the time cost of happiness and deflation rates? In observing consumers' behavior, it seems highly unlikely that deflation rates within our experience can appreciably impact demand. There are simply too many counterexamples of people buying goods that they could have bought tomorrow for much less. In fact, the "Gratification Curve", like the yield curve, may be immensely steep in practice. Our cultural inability to delay gratification suggests that only the most extreme deflation could impact our spending habits.

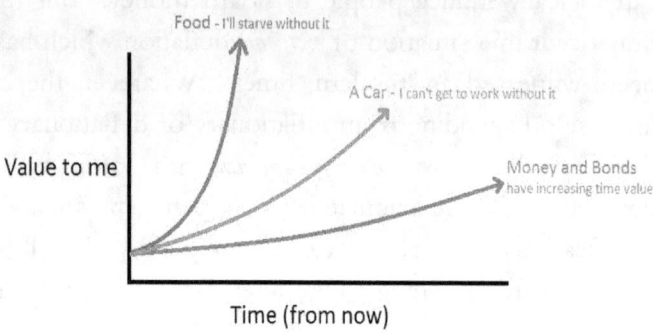

The Gratification Curve

Food - I'll starve without it

A Car - I can't get to work without it

Value to me

Money and Bonds
have increasing time value

Time (from now)

The Government-Knows-Best Theory

Keynesians will rationalize fiscal and monetary interventions on the grounds that the government knows best when to stimulate a downturn and blunt a euphoric high. By intervening countercyclically, the government can rein in the intrinsic excesses of the market. Because it is generally acknowledged that economic highs and lows are undesirable, the government performs a useful public service in moderating erratic market oscillations. For government to have the right tools to intervene, they must have control over the monetary supply. Fiscal interventions are paid from deficits. Deficits are paid from government bonds. And government bonds are bought with printed money by central banks, at least in the current era. Under a more stable currency regime, such as gold or Bitcoin, governments cannot print money to buy their own bonds. This makes it more difficult for them to finance the very same deficits that must stimulate the economy. Hence the government must not be prevented from increasing the monetary supply, because what it buys with printed money is absolutely essential.

This line of reasoning is dangerous for two important reasons. First, it makes expansion of the monetary supply a vehicle for raising money for the government. In printing money, governments indirectly tax savers. This is a non-legislative way of raising money. The people need not consent through their elected representatives as they must with taxes; it simply happens via the expansion of the monetary supply. And it disincentivizes savings by targeting them for de facto confiscation. This is to penalize virtuous behavior. Governments should raise money more transparently via taxes that are honestly debated. By printing money to extract value, government has a powerful revenue collecting mechanism that it *does not acknowledge*. Monetizing government debt is *not considered* an official revenue stream, *even though it is in practice*. The government is living a lie about where it gets its (real) money.

Consider, as a thought experiment, an explicit tax on savers. This has been done to a minor degree in Europe. The outcry would be enormous. Seeing one's balance decline in *nominal* terms would spark mass outrage. Experiencing a decline in *real but not nominal* terms is much less perceptible, even as it accomplishes the same thing. If the government's actions are valid, let the tax on savers be explicit.

Second, the premise that governments can intervene countercyclically is deeply flawed. Why should governmental officials be any more qualified to judge the economy than private actors? If anything, they are far less able to do so. Unlike in private markets, within government there is much less of a feedback loop from results, i.e., rewarding success and punishing failure. Traders must constantly reevaluate themselves based on undeniable profits and loss. Politicians and bureaucrats may remain much more insulated; their decisions affect someone else's money after all.

History is replete with examples of governmental misallocation of resources. This has often occurred on an epic scale that no private, financially constrained private organization could match. The Federal loan programs, for instance, are particularly rotten. A full exploration is beyond the scope of this book. But generally speaking, federal interventions to pick winners or make strategic investments are often economically unviable. While its intentions may be benevolent, without financial constraints government cannot be counted to make wise investments. Without the discipline imposed by the need to worry about financial sustainability, or the need to satisfy shareholders, and no hiring/firing process linked to the economic viability of one's decisions, how can we expect any outcome but failure? It's not like the bureaucrats who administer such programs are another species. They are people just the same. But their incentives are different. The reward feedback loop they experience is different. Thus a bureaucrat may push policies or economic ventures that make no sense, because he is paid to do so. And if humans do anything well, it is to respond to incentives, no matter how insane the outcome.

Government shouldn't respond countercyclically because there is no way for them to have superior information over market participants. One has only to read *The Big Short* by Michael Lewis to see the mass delusion within financial and official circles alike before the 2008 crisis. Why does government mandate the use of the ratings agencies, who contributed so much to the mortgage crisis, if government officials have superior knowledge about the economy? Why didn't officials make bearish bets, and make a veritable killing, if they knew better? Why doesn't government just buy the low's and sell the high's, as any market player should, if it knows better? The answer is that government is no more equipped than anyone else to do so. To grant them the right to invent money as a tax on savers, in order to speculate in a game they have little hope of winning, is recklessly irresponsible.

The Multiplier Theory

Keynesians also propound the multiplier effect theory, which states that a single dollar spent by government, at the right time and place, has a stimulating effect on the economy worth some higher multiple of that dollar. In other words, a dollar spent by government can generate 2, or even 3 dollars' worth of economic activity. Because government spends money on long-term investments or during downturns, it can get extra bang for its buck. And if it's true that government spending has a multiplicative effect on the wider economy, the government can make its expenditure back in future taxation. Thus it is reasonable to go into debt to spend that dollar, because it will be earned back through taxes on the increased economic activity it created.

The multiplier effect is essentially another version of the government-knows-better-theory. If it were true that government spending delivered better returns than capital allocation in private markets, we ought to disband capitalism entirely and run the country like the Soviet Union. It can't be both ways. Investors are constantly trying to create new forms of useful economic activity for which there is no better evidence than profits. There is no reason why government would show superior foresight than private players.

Indeed, the multiplier effect was used to rationalize the TARP bailouts in 2009, in which the government wrote a massive check to stimulate the economy. It is a rationale for government spending virtually without limits. While this does constitute demand, which can indeed "create jobs" and "stimulate the economy", such spending might not necessarily be *efficacious*. Insulated from real costs, we could equally well pay people to dig holes and refill them; *mere activity does not imply the creation of value.*

It seems likely that the TARP and other bailouts generated pennies on the dollar in terms of economic activity. But unlike a private enterprise, the government pretends it cannot be held to account. The dollar is spent, generates pennies worth of real value, and is eventually defaulted upon. The government cannot bear the real cost of that dollar, and must thus print it instead of earning it. Meanwhile politicians claim victory over the few pennies worth of real stimulus that the dollar generated, even as it is misspent on economically unviable projects. The real burden of such waste is imposed diffusely on society through the debasing of the currency.

So yes, Bitcoin and gold-backed money disarm the government's ability to intervene in the economy. This is not a bug but a feature. The government is in no position to act *wisely* in the economy. It is a lumbering behemoth with immense power and little brains. Disempowering central banks from determining interest rates will restore capitalism to capital markets. This can only be accomplished with money independent of governments.

Governments will still be able to raise debts under a Bitcoin standard, as they were in the 19th century under gold. There is nothing intrinsically wrong with that. But they will have to pay fair, market-based interest rates to do so. Debtors and creditors alike will have to grapple with difficult questions of *actual* credit worthiness instead of resorting to the god-like power of inventing money. We have avoided the difficult matter of price discovery in credit markets since at least 2008, if not earlier. In papering over our insolvencies, we have only rendered them more potent in the long run.

A stable currency, beyond the reach of bureaucrats, will impose honesty on capital markets. It will be a sobering up of epic proportions. It will be a painful withdrawal, an excruciating coming to terms with the errors of the past. The old debts must be faced with a combination of deleveraging, defaults, and stoicism. There will be temper tantrums and paroxysms of economic pain. But it's the only (sane) way. In the face of such disarray, only a mathematically solid currency, with guarantees that are cryptographic, can impose the necessary discipline. Anything less than a cryptographic standard will not be strong enough.

Cryptocurrencies are not Scarce

Bitcoin is limited to 21 million coins. Bitcoins may be scarce. But cryptocurrencies are practically free. I can trade bitcoins for litecoins for dogecoins for primecoins, and a thousand other coins you've never heard of. They all use some variation Bitcoin's core innovation, namely, the Blockchain. But they're all separate. And while each coin is parallel and non-intersecting with every other, internally each coin is also scarce.

I can make 'AndrewCoins' right now. It's so easy. All I have to do is fork the Bitcoin source code and start making changes. Anything that speaks the Bitcoin language, but disagrees with the history, is by definition incompatible. Since it is merely computer code, it is trivial to copy Bitcoin as a separate 'AndrewCoin' currency. AndrewCoins may have the same properties as bitcoins, but no one on the Bitcoin network acknowledges anything reported by AndrewCoin. AndrewCoin transactions aren't legitimate Bitcoin transactions, even if the protocol is identical, because they exist on a divergent, parallel-universe transactional history.

But if cryptocurrencies are completely free to make, why should I value Bitcoin at all? While internally bitcoins are limited, the premise of a digital currency is utterly open. Since there are no gatekeepers, there can be as many coins as there are foolhardy individuals. What then distinguishes Bitcoin from all the rest? How can something be valuable when it can be trivially copied at any time? Why should I value Bitcoin when just another cryptocurrency can come along at no cost?

It is true; cryptocurrencies are not scarce. There are countless unheard-of coins. There is no monopoly on cryptocurrencies generally. The underlying technology can be infinitely duplicated. However, because none of these alternate coins (altcoins) touch Bitcoin, their prevalence does not affect the scarcity of bitcoins themselves. Each altcoin has some separate blockchain that, superficial similarities notwithstanding, says nothing about the Bitcoin Blockchain.

Some might worry that the ease of creating alternate digital currencies makes them all worthless. But in a world in which digital currencies are so easy to make they are meaningless, *what becomes meaningful is scarcity within an accepted standard.* It does not objectively matter what that standard is. Instead of Bitcoin, it could have been Litecoin. Or perhaps Dogecoin. Who knows? But once a standard is chosen, powerful network effects come into play incentivizing use of the winner.

To claim that cryptocurrencies are not scarce and that therefore bitcoins are not valuable is equivalent to saying that paper is not scarce and that dollars are not valuable. Dollars and monopoly money have paper in common. Things that superficially resemble dollars are not scarce. But dollars themselves are (sort of) scarce. It is not right to confuse the medium (paper) with the object (dollars versus monopoly money). It is thus not valid to conflate Bitcoin with cryptocurrencies generally. The proliferation of monopoly money in no way diminishes the value of dollars. Similarly the plethora of altcoins do not diminish Bitcoin.

Indeed, the ease with which one can fork cryptocurrencies starkly illustrates the need for a common standard. Following our analogy further, the excess of monopoly money only makes dollars that much more recognizable. One can even express this mathematically. Exercising the by-now-well-worn adage that networks scale in connections by the square of the number of connected nodes, numerous small networks are worth less than the sum of their parts. One big network with a million nodes is worth far more than a thousand networks with a thousand nodes each. This simple principle drives self-interested actors to the same platform.

As can often be said of Bitcoin, it's like language. You are free to speak any language you want. You could speak German, and be understood by perhaps 100 million people. Or you could speak Romansch, a language spoken only in a single valley in Switzerland, and be understood by about 100,000 people. You could even just speak gibberish, your own language, and be understood by just you! Or you could speak English and be understood by perhaps 1 billion people worldwide. Speaking English is much more than 10,000 times more valuable than speaking Romansch. And it is much more than ten times as useful as speaking German. In theory we could wander off and choose to speak obscure little dialects, or our own personal brands of gibberish. But the network effect of wanting to be understood drives us to choose mainstream languages. Whereas the network effects between languages come into play only slowly over the course of generations, competitive forces act very quickly between software protocols; a single software standard can establish total dominance in a short space of time.

Network effects are so significant that they may even trump underlying technical quality. Bitcoin, as the first cryptocurrency, may have constituted the greatest innovative leap of them all. But on a technical level, it is certainly not the best finished product. How could it be? Whereas Bitcoin has had to cater to the conservative interests of thousands of stakeholders, altcoins of every different stripe have flourished. The diversity and experimentation in the altcoin world is breathtaking. On a pound-for-pound basis, discounting miners and network effects, it is almost certain that one of the recent altcoin incarnations is technically superior. Perhaps its mining algorithm is more ASIC resistant. Perhaps its block-time, or incentivize structure, is more cleverly thought out. We need not quibble over the details because they don't matter. Bitcoin wins anyway. Cryptocurrencies are competing on a vastly unfair playing ground. The established network, Bitcoin, has every advantage. There is virtually no incentive to leave that network.

Comparing the technical schemas of altcoins is like comparing Esperanto to English. Esperanto's grammar may be more logical, and thus, in a perfect world, it would supplant English. If history always trended towards optimal outcomes, we could count on a 'stable equilibrium' in which Esperanto would surpass English. But human behavior does not trend towards equilibrium; it is extraordinarily path dependent.

Some might argue an opposite point, that the network effect of Bitcoin is so overbearing that innovation is stifled. Some have expressed concern that the centralizing influence of a single standard may snuff out new ideas. There are those who have sought to swim against the tide of unity under Bitcoin. Projects such as Ethereum promise advanced new features, albeit on a separate blockchain. While the technology is compelling, they face a steep uphill battle. They will likely not succeed in replicating the community and infrastructure of Bitcoin. One could just as soon found a copycat Facebook 2.0 and defeat the original. The whole cryptocurrency community needs to unite behind a common standard to advance the technology in mainstream use. Constantly diverging in little separate branches, albeit technically meritorious ones, is a counterproductive distraction. By straying from the network effects of Bitcoin, altcoiners are fighting on the wrong side of history.

Critics will argue that Bitcoin is Napster, or MySpace, waiting to be defeated by the next Facebook. This is a classic analogy. The classic response is that, rather than MySpace, Bitcoin is SMTP, or HTTP. In other words, Bitcoin is not a company that may rise and fall, it is a protocol, a language, that endures, even as technically superior approaches arise. Protocols can quickly establish dominance because the network effects of 'speaking the right language' totally trump minor variations in efficacy between competitors. What everyone else is doing, so too must you do.

Others complain that Bitcoin's features are limited, and that altcoins are necessary for unlocking additional functionality. There is some truth to this; there are certain things Bitcoin cannot do, or cannot do efficiently. Most attempts to introduce new features to Bitcoin have involved creating altcoins abstracted on top of the Bitcoin Blockchain or on blockchains entirely separate from Bitcoin. But regardless of which blockchain they inhabit, these parallel systems involve separate units of account.

In my view, having to translate between floating assets to unlock functionality is too onerous. A floating exchange rate between different feature-sets is a major impediment to their use. Using an altcoin specifically for escrow, only to convert back to bitcoins, is a tedious process. It also contributes to exchange risk. Altcoin-based functionality also leverages none of the network effects of Bitcoin.

In the struggle between embracing a common standard and encompassing the broadest possible feature set, there is a potential answer. It's called sidechains. Sidechains are parallel blockchains, with their own sets of rules, just like altcoins. However the currency units in sidechains are two-way pegged to Bitcoin. I won't go into the full technical details here. But it has been shown that one may get the best of both worlds: diverse functionality and a link to Bitcoin. Currency on sidechains, since it is cryptographically pegged to Bitcoin (and not by human guarantee), is essentially a surrogate for bitcoins, but with added features. Sidechains allow for greater technical experimentation while also piggybacking on the network effects of Bitcoin. Holders of bitcoins lose nothing by the introduction of sidechains. In fact, they gain, because the option to move into sidechains, and back out again, means your bitcoins have more potential features available to them. These features include things currently missing from Bitcoin such as escrow, asset issuance, betting, contracts, and much more.

Imagine if Bitcoin were gold, altcoins would be all the other metals: silver, copper, iron, etc. While they may be interesting on their own merits, none of the others will reach critical mass to replace gold as currency. But let's say, while you want gold most of the time, occasionally you want copper for its chemical properties. You could sell your gold for copper on an open market. The price of copper in gold would fluctuate constantly. If, after playing with your copper, you wanted to return to gold, the price may have moved. Thus, if your goal is to settle all values into gold, holding copper inherently gives unwanted exchange risk. This is the situation currently with Bitcoin vis-a-vis other altcoins. Similarly, copper may be mined at a much faster proportional rate than gold, meaning you lose value by merely holding copper due to inflation. The same goes with

Bitcoin versus other altcoins, which sometimes come with steep inflation rates.

However, taking the analogy further, what if you could magically transmute gold into copper, and back again, at a fixed and predictable ratio? It could be 1:10, or 1:100, or even 1:1, it doesn't matter. If gold could be transformed to copper and back again with complete safety, there would be no risk to holding copper. You could freely morph from one metal to the next, taking advantage of the properties of all, while still knowing that you may always return to a given amount of gold. Thus you would gain access to the properties of all, while experiencing no exchange risk.

This two-way conversion is precisely what sidechains accomplish. Allowing bitcoin holders to convert to sidechains, and back again, at fixed rates, sidechains become much more attractive than altcoins. They open up to Bitcoiners the possibility of accessing interesting new features, while retaining their investment in bitcoins.

The pegging mechanism, moreover, is not administered by people. It is cryptographic, meaning that all the moving parts are trustless and provable. While this has posed an extremely difficult theoretical problem, great Bitcoin minds have demonstrated that a two-way peg is possible and feasible.

This is not to say that sidechains do not have their own risks. They do. And in fact, the technology is still conceptual and unproven. But it seems plausible that this technology may bear fruit in the coming years. The consequences for all cryptocurrencies would be profound.

Even without sidechains, altcoins will still lose to Bitcoin because of the overwhelming strength of network effects. Any technical innovations altcoins may have will probably be swept under the tide of rising Bitcoin adoption. But with sidechains, that pace may be vastly accelerated. Innovations among altcoins may be assimilated into sidechains which benefit from the growth of Bitcoin. Rather than existing as orthogonal, parallel universes to Bitcoin, sidechains will be parallel universes, with cool new laws of physics in each, but connected via reliable doors back to Bitcoin. Instead of competing as separate entities, the world of cryptocurrencies may be tethered under Bitcoin. Whereas currently the creative energies poured into disparate blockchains diffuse the momentum of cryptocurrency adoption generally, an ecosystem of pegged sidechains will promote itself far more coherently. The success of each sidechain would make the others more valuable. By contrast, the practical incentive of using an altcoin will approach zero.

For those primarily concerned with the financial implications of Bitcoin, the proliferation of altcoins poses no risk whatsoever. The ubiquity of meaningless altcoins only accentuates the value of the common standard: Bitcoin. If there were, somehow, only 3 or 4 cryptocurrencies, then they would truly compete, as gold and silver competed historically as money (even then gold won out decisively due to network effects). But if there are a thousand altcoins, they become meaningless. It's like that Stalin quote, "A single death is a tragedy, a million deaths is a statistic." Well, a million altcoins are a statistic.

Network effects don't just exist in people's minds, they exist as very real physical investments as well. As the infrastructure around Bitcoin continues to grow, the extent of investments in Bitcoin grows much faster than comparable investments in competing altcoins. Far more capital, both human and otherwise, has been poured into Bitcoin than into its competitors. One only has to look at the total market capitalizations, or the average daily transaction volumes, to illustrate the dominance of Bitcoin. It exceeds its nearest competitor in total valuation by a factor of 20^{xii}. Barring an unforeseen technical catastrophe, this is a head start that cannot be overcome.

Interest in altcoins will never hit zero; in absolute terms it will likely increase. Altcoins will continue to represent a healthy, unfettered form of experimentation. But relative to Bitcoin, competing altcoins are likely to diminish. If cryptocurrencies hit mainstream and become actively traded, through a myriad of complex financial instruments by traders on Wall Street, it will be Bitcoin that is traded, not Litecoin (the leading altcoin). Regular folks aren't going to want to learn about Bitcoin versus Litecoin. Software developers aren't going to want to develop another parallel set of architecture to handle Dogecoin in addition to Bitcoin. Remittances won't be worth sending in Litecoin, which is far more volatile (owing to its smaller size and immaturity), when Bitcoin offers all the same advantages, but with a more mature trading and technical community. Where cryptocurrencies really shine, as a money tool with exchange utility, there will hardly ever be a reason to opt for a less mature competitor over Bitcoin.

Perhaps some technical innovation will overturn Bitcoin. Maybe something brilliant will be conjured that is so compelling, we decide we cannot live without it. Via sidechains, we will be able to incorporate new features into the Bitcoin ecosystem without breaking Bitcoin. Like the Borg from Star Trek, resistance is futile. Innovations will be assimilated and make the whole only stronger.

The ease of creating another altcoin is just too easy. The community has already, even at this early hour, become jaded against the advent of yet-another-altcoin. What matters in the end is extracting the maximum currency utility out of cryptocurrencies. It appears clear that a single common standard is the best such path. And due to its overwhelming lead, that standard can be none other than Bitcoin. From a financial perspective the manufacture of endless altcoins only reinforces the importance of a single standard that rises above the fray. It is the scarcity of bitcoins that counts.

Bitcoin and the Blockchain are Separable

It is a common refrain that, while Bitcoin the currency is doomed, the underlying Blockchain technology will have as yet undiscovered value. Even the most vociferous skeptics would admit that blockchain technology is novel and potentially useful in some future incarnation. But in attempting to remake currency technologists have overreached. The argument basically states that Bitcoin is an aberrant, first iteration of something which may in the end be useful in some other form. It is a foreshadowing of some later purpose, one that uses the admittedly novel aspects of the Blockchain. What that form may be is left unsaid, but it is certainly not as a separate currency. In short, the idea of a blockchain is valuable, but bitcoins themselves are not.

There is a sense that the Blockchain heralds new opportunities. This is a significant admission. Blockchain-technology may be intriguing, say the critics, and yet the foremost exemplar, Bitcoin's Blockchain, is not valuable. Blockchains are important, and yet the crucial, conserved quantity across them, bitcoins, have no value. This does not make sense.

If a blockchain is valuable, the fuel that makes it run will be valuable. When that fuel is a scarce digital asset, its value must relate directly to the utility of the platform it inhabits. The Bitcoin Blockchain has no moving parts without the limited number of bitcoins that course through it. It is a stale shell otherwise. Even other, more exotic blockchains must require some limited internal asset with which to perform operations. No blockchain exists without a unit of account. It stretches the imagination how one could even be built; conserved internal parts keep the system finite and protect against spam.

Others will claim that, while blockchains are interesting, bitcoins themselves are too flawed to serve as currency. The consensus mechanism is fine. But the currency unit is not. In their mind a blockchain representing a more traditional currency, such as digital dollars, would marry new and old more happily. This is also a very flawed conception.

A blockchain based on fiat money does not make sense; fiat money by its very nature contradicts the point of having a blockchain. IBM has suggested a blockchain representing major fiat currencies[xiii] to facilitate high-speed bank transactions. This proposal misses the point of blockchain technology. Their blockchain would not be permissionless; the government would maintain the same prerogatives it enjoys with traditional money. It could still print money at a whim. It could confiscate money. It could undo transactions that have already occurred. Such a system is not a network of peers. It is a centralized system. It enjoys all the flaws of fiat money, with none of the advantages of Bitcoin. It is not scarce the way Bitcoin is. It is not secure the way Bitcoin is.

Any system whose internal rules are subject to outside, human interference, not peers but members endowed with special privileges, cannot be truly decentralized. Are transactions to settle immediately or are they to be reversible? Who has the authority to interdict transactions? Can transactions be forbidden? Can funds be flagged or confiscated? Does a special party control all of these matters, including the most fundamental of all, the monetary supply? If the answer is anywhere in the affirmative, what one has is a centralized system, perhaps with additional technical pleasantries tacked on. No system built in mimicry of the Bitcoin Blockchain, but granting special privileges to special bodies, can equal Bitcoin. There are no special people with superior knowledge to whom such power can be safely relegated. The peer-to-peer nature of decentralized systems makes them far safer precisely because there is no special authority. Power stems instead from an equal opportunity democracy of hashing power.

Something peculiar is happening in the discourse on blockchains. To acknowledge the significance of blockchain-technology, but to denigrate Bitcoin the currency, is to have come most of the way to accepting Bitcoin, but turned back at the last second. Perhaps it is that, to many, Bitcoin as money must be rationalized as a failed project. The technology may be admired because it is fairly neutral. But the currency unit itself, bitcoin, must be discredited; it is too political, too threatening. A decentralized currency is such a provocative concept that, because it hits upon sensitive political issues on the role of government, must be denied. This is not how we normally judge new, unforeseen things. We give them a fair hearing. The plausibility of Bitcoin has been judged prematurely by many who should have adopted a more unbiased, wait-and-see attitude. It has been declared dead too hastily, not on technical grounds (which, if successful, would have carried far greater weight), but because it is perceived as infringing on governments' privilege.

The most dangerous of all statements (besides in a mathematical proof) is "That cannot be", for if it is, you become a laughingstock. "I don't know" is a much wiser answer. Most scientists practice this intellectual humility; they must to be taken seriously. We should practice it as well in social and economic fields in which the chances of *really* knowing something are much slimmer.

Blockchains are not separable from the fuel that runs them. Part of their core purpose was to create a digital scarcity that had hitherto never existed. The object that is scarce is the unit of account itself, i.e., bitcoins. As far as anyone can tell, a blockchain cannot be used without a unit of account. It cannot be secured via decentralized miners without one. Unsecured, it is unsafe, or worse, a de facto centralized database. Having conceded that blockchain technology is compelling, then the foremost blockchain, Bitcoin's, must have value. Its finite parts must also have value. That value stems not merely from secure data storage fees, but from its primary use as currency.

Those desiring to marry fiat money with blockchain technology are pursuing a contradiction. There must be a regime either of rigid, mathematical rules, verifiable on their own account by each peer, or a regime of men. The network will either be composed of peers or of unequal partners.

The desire to rationalize Bitcoin's unsuitability as currency most often stems from political preconceptions. But this is a deeply unscientific way to measure the plausibility of what is proposed. In pursuing this tortuous path, many are forced into a tenuous position: namely, that the Blockchain is worthwhile and bitcoins are not. In truth, they are two sides to the same coin.

Who is Satoshi Nakamoto?

Satoshi Nakamoto created Bitcoin. Beyond that, virtually nothing is known. His identity is an enduring, bitter mystery. He is a ghost. From the beginning, Satoshi took great measures to ensure his anonymity. So thorough was he that, despite widespread efforts to establish his identity, none succeeded.

We don't even know whether Satoshi was a man or woman, an individual or a hidden cabal. All that can be inferred stems from his writings, which are those of an articulate, native English speaker. He was very likely an American or an Englishman; this is all that can be reasonably guessed, and even that is merely strong conjecture.

Attempts to uncover his identity have floundered, sometimes disastrously. Newsweek claimed to have unravelled the mystery with Dorian Nakamoto, a befuddled

Japanese-American. The flimsiness of their account, relying completely on tenuously stretched circumstantial evidence, made them a laughingstock. The holes in their reporting were so cavernous that the story quickly sank. Still, the attention that their article attracted illustrated the deep interest in Satoshi's identity.

People are drawn to knowing who created Bitcoin. We want someone to speak to us through news cameras to answer for Bitcoin and all its implications. Who will take responsibility for the threat it poses to governments? Who should be held accountable for all the outcomes that stem from it? The public desperately wants to know, which face lies behind the enigmatic inhumanity of the Blockchain?

If we could find Satoshi, the thinking goes, we could interview him. We could grill him. We could ask him to defend Bitcoin. Let us see how he fares in a debate against all the experts. Satoshi the person would embody Bitcoin. To our senses, his human traits would become Bitcoin's. His personal failings would be Bitcoin's. Any misdeed or misstep of his would be inherited by his creation. We would like to think that the Bitcoin apple could not fall far from the human tree.

Imagine Satoshi himself appearing on a television interview. Perhaps he would stumble through questions. Perhaps he'd have a giant wart on his nose. Critics would jump at the chance to find something wrong with him, the better to tarnish Bitcoin. There is no deed he could accomplish that would not be turned around and used to render judgment on Bitcoin. There is no person who could pass such a test, in which human characteristics must meet the sublime standards of cryptographic proofs. Inevitably, Satoshi the man could never equal Satoshi, the creator of Bitcoin.

Stymied by the lack of a human face, pundits blame Bitcoin. Created by a mystery man, Bitcoin is tainted by Satoshi's unwillingness to show himself. As a defendant taking the Fifth is presumed guilty, Bitcoin must be insidious because its creator will not reveal himself. What does he have to hide anyway? Surely anything made by so pusillanimous a character could not be trustworthy. If we are to trust Bitcoin, let its creator come forth. As we trust the man, so too can we trust the algorithms. A faceless institution has no authority, so would they have you believe.

Such thinking is a relic from an era before cryptography, in which trust could only ever be as sound as human promises. Whether it was an individual, or an institution composed of individuals, trust always had a face. But judging Bitcoin in this way is deeply flawed. Meeting Satoshi is as necessary as meeting Euclid to confirm geometry. Newton's theories of motion had nothing to do with Newton the man; we could care less. Mathematics is subject only to proofs, which have no human component. Science is strictly based on repeatable experiments. These fields are composed of people with their own flaws. But over long enough time scales, human biases are washed out like so much random noise. In the Scientific Method, evidence and skepticism win out over any human authority. Bitcoin should be judged in a similar, strictly technical way, eschewing the qualities of its inventor. This is precisely the analysis many pundits would like to avoid. Because they can find no technical flaw, and being intent upon rationalizing Bitcoin's untrustworthiness, they must resort to old-fashioned mudslinging. Unsatisfyingly for them, there is no person to vilify.

Meeting Satoshi is surely unnecessary to verify the integrity of Bitcoin. As we have seen, all the code is open-source; the system has been intensively reviewed and stress-tested. And the protocol was designed in such a way that no one person, not even the creator himself, could manipulate it.

I suspect that meeting Satoshi would be deeply disappointing. Surely he would be a genius of the highest caliber. But invariably one would be underwhelmed by natural, human failings. The sublime workings of the Blockchain could not be mirrored by any person, no matter how brilliant or virtuous. Satoshi will remain much grander in anonymity than he could ever be in person.

Worse still, having a face to look to might undermine the very ethos of Bitcoin. The whole point is that a harmonious system exists with no trusted center. Even though Satoshi would hold no special place on a technical level, his continued presence would cast a long shadow over Bitcoin. We would find ourselves looking to him for guidance and for answers. He would ceaselessly be in the news. He would have the power, through public persuasion, to force through hard changes to the protocol. His celebrity status would give him undue sway over the protocol itself, rendering it his and not ours. The beauty of Bitcoin is that protocol changes must be wrestled over by the entire community. Although there are highly respected figures, such as Gavin Andreessen, no one can command the following of the network. Perhaps even Satoshi would fail in this today, had history unfolded differently. But surely, in there being no leader, Bitcoin is truer to its decentralized soul.

Satoshi's absence is an enduring gift to the legacy of Bitcoin and all that stems from it. A single person could have monopolized the spotlight, been the voice and face of a revolution. But the Bitcoin revolution is so much more powerful without a face. It is a system that is so open, so accessible, that even its creator is anonymous. There is no purer a beginning. It sends a message, that anyone may be involved, may contribute, fork it, or even attack it, regardless of the typical human qualities that distract us: title, nationality, gender, appearance, etc. Satoshi's imitators might be no-name hackers from a no-name country that introduce the Next-Big-Thing. Everything about Satoshi's work was flat, non-hierarchical, and utterly meritocratic. A peer-to-peer network that existentially threatens governments. A creator with no face. Code that anyone can see but none can crack. A naked idea, unsupported by even one person, so meritorious that it could catapult within years to unseen heights on raw strength alone. This is the stuff of legend. And we are living it.

Bitcoin's Weaknesses

The 51% Attack: Bitcoin's Achilles' Heel

By now I have extolled Bitcoin's virtues at length. But it is not all a ceaseless ticker-tape parade. Bitcoin has one core weakness. Just one. Everything I have described is contingent on that weakness not being exploited. This is the one fatal path that could lead to Bitcoin's undoing. It is Bitcoin's Achilles' Heel. It is a 51% attack.

As we have seen before, the central task for miners to agree upon, in the form of the Blockchain, is which transactions occurred in which order. It is essential to achieve this consensus to prevent double-spending. If one claims to send the same bitcoins to multiple different parties, who really received them? When only one of the broadcast transactions can be valid, which one should be said to have come first? Which transactions will be treated as legitimate, and which ones double-spends? This is the task of the Blockchain. It is an indelible record. But it is also a consensus mechanism for agreeing upon the order in which things occurred. This is the subject on which miners are endlessly voting.

Let us remember also the structure of the Blockchain. It consists of a long series of blocks, each one of which tracks transactions that occurred within a given time period. That time period averages around 10 minutes. So the history of all transactions is encompassed by a very long series of blocks. Together they describe the current state of the network in addition to its entire history. One need only analyze the blocks one at a time to reconstruct the current state of Bitcoin.

As blocks are discovered, they are appended as a descendant of a previous block. Every block, except the very first one, must claim to be the progeny of some parent block. Just as every person has a mother, every block, besides the genesis block, has a predecessor. But what if multiple, syntactically-valid blocks claim to have the same predecessor? The different blocks may describe a different series of Bitcoin transactions occurring within the same time period. They cannot exist together without being in contradiction. However each one might be valid in relation to every predecessor block. Which one is real?

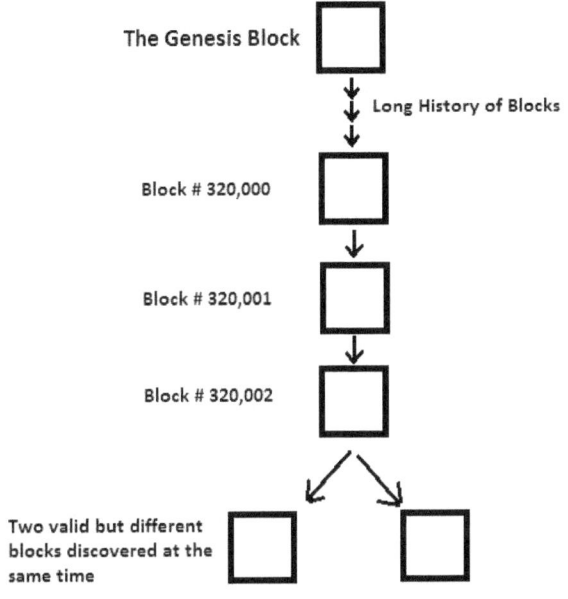

Which one of these valid solutions should be Block #320,003?

If multiple valid blocks are found, miners decide which block is valid. Miners choose which of the valid but disagreeing blocks to use as the predecessor for the *next* block. As miners stitch together blocks in series, they create branches in the Blockchain. Whichever branch is longest will have received consent from the greatest amount of hashing power. Even if two rival factions arose, vying to propagate different histories of the Blockchain, whichever branch solicits more miners will become the longest over sufficiently long time scales. In this way, the majority collection of hashing power always dominates in determining which branch of the Blockchain should be valid.

So far this process has worked well. Aberrant blocks are quickly left behind; no miner wants to work on the wrong Blockchain branch when it will never catch up to the main, consensus branch. A miner could theoretically work on his own branch in isolation at a slow rate. But that branch would soon fall hopelessly behind the pooled work of the main branch. No Bitcoin node would accept this other, minority branch, because nodes accept only the longest branch available. The minority branch will always lose out.

However consider a contrary scenario. What if a single miner controlled *more* mining power than all other miners combined? He could embark upon his own series of blocks. Although each block would be syntactically valid in Bitcoin, it would contain a different history from that of the main chain. A miner controlling 51% or more of the network could create a side branch that *could consistently beat* the main chain. Since this miner has more hashing power than everyone else combined, he can string together blocks at a faster rate, thereby creating a longer branch. Since the longest branch automatically becomes the legitimate one, such a miner can always create a new Bitcoin history. Thus a miner with 51% of the hashing power can always create a blockchain history that supersedes that of the other miners.

This is called the 51% attack. Able to consistently outpace the main Bitcoin Blockchain branch, such a miner can rewrite history unilaterally. Thus while transactions proceed normally on the main chain, an attacker could patiently work on *his own blocks* in secret, involving another set of transactions (or none at all, merely empty blocks). The attacker could make Bitcoin transactions on the normal main chain and receive goods or services when his Bitcoin payments are recognized. But then later he could nullify those transactions by introducing his alternate branch (which wins because it is longer). Then he would have purchased goods with evaporating money.

There are other sorts of things one could do in a 51% attack. One could censor transactions, allowing only those the attacker approves of. A government could censor *all* transactions by continually publishing empty blocks. The network could be brought to a standstill.

There are limits to what a 51% attack can accomplish. It cannot fake transactions. Your bitcoins can never be stolen, even during a 51% attack. Transactions signatures rely on elliptic curve cryptography, which predates Bitcoin. The internal syntax of transactions has nothing to do with mining or Blockchain branches.

While in theory an attacker with a majority of the hashing power could attempt to rewrite the transactional history of Bitcoin, it would be immediately obvious to the network. It would be detectable almost immediately. It would thus be quite simple to maintain the transactional history of Bitcoin *up to that point*. By merely recording the hash of the last block up to the moment of the 51% attack, the history of Bitcoin would be preserved. But having to resort to special-cases and hand-waving the rules is wholly contradictory to the Bitcoin ethos.

There has never been a 51% attack against Bitcoin. However certain mining pools have amassed large fractions of the hashing power. While a mining pool consists of many disparate miners, they collaborate in such a way that their mining power is wielded by the pool operator. Thus in theory a pool operator could use the miners in his pool in an attack that the miners themselves do not support. Presumably miners would quickly leave such a pool.

In fact, a mining pool called Ghash.io briefly possessed approximately 50% of the mining network. It did not execute an attack on the network. But the potential for foul play existed. Bitcoin should never have to rely on any party's good behavior to survive. Thankfully, their growth was noticed. A public outcry arose, urging miners to migrate to other mining pools. The threat subsided. Now the mining pools are more evenly distributed, with the largest pool currently controlling 21% of the hashing power.

No miner is *rationally incentivized* to attack Bitcoin because, in doing so, they will have undermined the value of their own mining capacity, which is useless without Bitcoin. The profit in perpetrating a fraud against the network can only pale in comparison to the massive investment necessary to amass a 51% stake of total mining power. Thus in attempting a 51% attack, one would only inflict massive financial losses on one's self with extremely limited up-side. One should not, however, rely exclusively on *rational* self-interest in forecasting human behavior.

While a mining operator would be committing financial suicide in conducting a 51% attack, governments could theoretically build up hashing power with the sole purpose of attacking Bitcoin, regardless of the cost. They could create a secret facility somewhere stowed with mining equipment on a colossal scale. They could then, in theory, paralyze Bitcoin via sustained and unrelenting 51% attacks. This would be very challenging to execute. The net hashing power worldwide is so vast that building a parallel hashing capability on such a scale would cost stupendous amounts. As Bitcoin grows, this figure will only increase. Moreover, it is highly unlikely that one entity could acquire mining equipment at such scale without tipping off the community; there are only a few manufacturers and such massive orders could not go unnoticed. Finally, even if attempted, it is dubious that any government could win an arms race against the vast, decentralized community of miners. Individuals could switch on countervailing miners from anywhere in the world to combat government's efforts. It would be a monumental effort of censorship with little chance of success and no pay-off. It would require enormous resources to build and sustain. The moment the power lapsed, or the government's efforts failed to grow at the same exponential rate as that of miners, the effort would be wholly undone.

There are some who claim that a 51% attack would not necessarily be the end of Bitcoin. Since the attack would be noticed immediately, the transactional history could be preserved. Countermeasures could be taken. And in the worst case, a fork could be made to Bitcoin, rebooting the mining algorithm from a historical 'safe point'. Such measures would be extreme; they are against the rules-based ethos of Bitcoin.

There is no doubt, however, that a 51% attack in any form would be a disaster for Bitcoin. Even if countermeasures were successfully taken, or other miners joined in to wrestle back control of the network, the damage to confidence would be incalculable. Even a momentary lapse would send shivers throughout the community. Having to impose a rushed hard fork on Bitcoin would be justly perceived as an act of desperation. We must plan now so there must never be such a moment.

The 51% attack is Bitcoin's most plausible weakness. Bitcoin's most publicized problems have been about perception, laws, and the inadequacies of 3rd party companies at the fringes of the network. But a 51% attack would be a blow to the very heart of Bitcoin.

We should be very concerned about the risk of a 51% attack. Bitcoin can survive the oscillations of the public mood, or governmental hostility, or market gyrations only if its technical soul remains pure. That technical core was built to be extraordinarily robust. As far as I can tell, the 51% attack is the only real threat to that. Thus it is something I think about intensely, far more than the more petty concerns surrounding Bitcoin.

Criticisms of Bitcoin too often focus on the human side: the political and economic implications or the perceived qualities of its users. Bitcoin has been labeled dead or doomed for so many lesser reasons that can never truly kill it. Bitcoin can only really die a technical death. Thus critics should center their attention on the technical underpinnings rather than the human distractions surrounding Bitcoin, such as who created it, or its purported libertarian or criminal connections. The problem is that too few critics are qualified to pass judgment on Bitcoin's technical merits, which are precisely the basis by which it should be judged.

For all the enthusiasm I have for Bitcoin and what it portends, the problem of the 51% attack will continue to give me pause. As we advance further in leveraging the potential of the Blockchain, let us keep our eye fixed on the mining pool distribution. There are grounds for cautious optimism, in the form of the continuing growth in global hashing power, to suggest that the dreaded 51% attack may never arise. But we should keep this Achilles' heel present in our minds at all times.

The Stability of Mining

Bitcoin Mining, as envisaged by Satoshi in the earliest days, consisted of everyday users turning on their Bitcoin clients on their personal computers. You could simply tell the client to start mining; if you personally discovered a block, you would be credited 50 Bitcoins. Most of the first bitcoins were created this way. It was so simple that anyone could do it.

In theory one can still mine using the original Bitcoin client. But it is so fruitless an endeavor that one would not attempt it. The client program mines at a laughably slow rate because it can only use the computer's processor. This is not optimized at all for the SHA-256 mining algorithm. In addition, mining alone presupposes that one will discover a block in isolation. One would then reap the full block reward, currently 25 BTC, alone.

Solitary mining has become a doomed effort. One has virtually no chance of discovering a block in this way. It would literally take billions of years, on average under current conditions, to discover a block alone with a CPU. In practice miners pool their efforts in organizations called mining pools. When a member of a pool discovers a block, the reward is split between all contributors. The winnings are split proportionately to the amount of work done by each individual. Because a certain amount of hashing power has a certain average time to discover a block, collaborating in a pool gives the same average payout, but with a drastically lower variance. Alone you could get lucky and find a block immediately, but more probably you'd die of old age first. In a pool, you can get a steady stream of income directly proportional to what you've put in. For this reason, mining pools are very popular.

Mining pools are run by a central operator whose responsibility it is to pay contributors and manage blocks. Managing blocks means making blockchain-related decisions on behalf of substituent miners. Mining is, after all, a voting scheme about the order of transactions. In a mining pool, actual miners simply turn their machines on, from anywhere in the world, and direct them to obey the mining pool operator. It is this operator who actually makes the decisions related to the voting function, such as which transactions occurred in which order. These decisions are the inputs for the hashing function, Bitcoin's mining algorithm, which is part of discovering new blocks.

Mining pools are entirely practical. Very few entities can expect to find blocks alone within reasonable time scales, so pooling one's efforts is quite logical. But in pooling efforts to achieve a lower payout variance, there exists a fundamental danger. A 51% attack becomes much easier to execute. Whereas if every miner mined in isolation, it would be necessary to co-opt many thousands of miners around the world to attack the Bitcoin network, it only takes a few mining pool operators in collusion to achieve the same results. Because they have many miners underneath them, almost at their command, mining pool operators can act and make decisions as if they were a single entity with enormous power. Thus it becomes easier to create a conspiracy with the requisite hashing power, because one would require fewer active participants.

Today the top 4-5 mining pools could collaborate and cause problems with the issuance of new blocks. They could censor new blocks and execute double spend attacks. This should be very worrisome.

Hash   Rate   Distribution,   6-28-2015

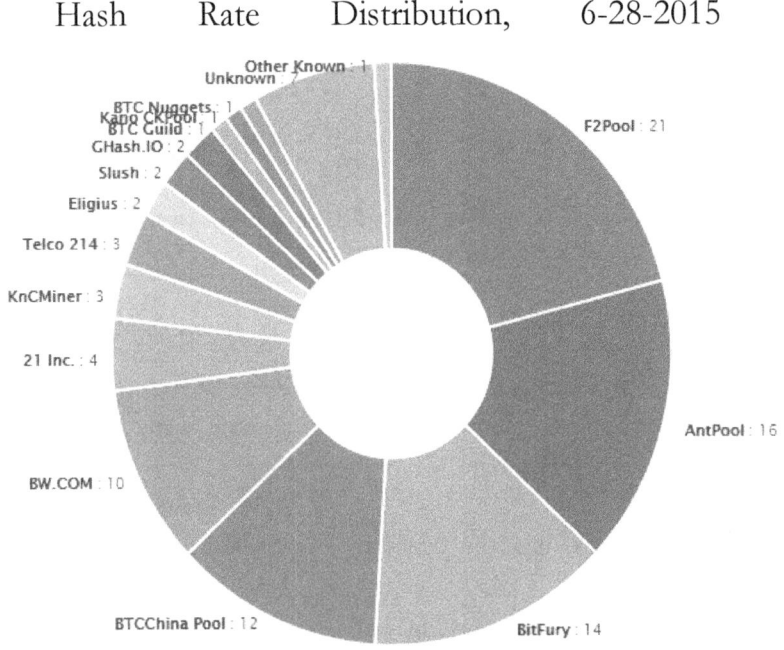

Source: Blockchain.info

Even a single mining pool operator, with less than 50% of total mining power, could *temporarily* disrupt the network. They would have a statistical likelihood of, over *short time scales*, solving many blocks in succession ahead of the main chain. This would be a rare, unsustainable occurrence. For example, a mining pool with 20% of the network could solve 5 blocks in a row, ahead of the rest of the miners, very rarely. But in such instances they could accomplish a double-spend attack lasting 5 blocks. Even this much more limited attack would be highly injurious to the network.

There seems to be no evidence of any such attack by mining pool operators. Of course, this should not be very reassuring; the whole point of Bitcoin is that it relies on no trusted party and no one's magnanimity. But it seems likely that such an attack would be of very limited effectiveness. Chiefly, it would be very easy to detect. If it became evident that an attack on the network were taking place, miners would *leave the perpetrating mining pool* almost immediately. No one wants to sink the ship they're on. Miners are completely free to change mining pools. If they sense that their pool operator is misusing his powers, they will quickly abandon him.

Thankfully this problem has been addressed with the creation of P2Pool, a decentralized mining network. Leaving the technical details aside, it is a trustless way for miners to collaborate and thereby lessen their payout variance. It empowers no single pool operator, vastly diminishing the probability of a conspiracy arising. While P2Pool usage is still quite small, it's a big step in the right direction.

Whatever happens, miners have a full financial stake in the continuance of the Bitcoin network. They cannot be expected to allow serious disruption. The most important concern, therefore, should be that miners are not co-opted to promote other sorts of agendas falling short of the downfall of Bitcoin. Censorship of transactions would be one such possibility. The existence of P2Pool, and similar systems, makes it much easier to prevent coalitions of pools from implementing heavy-handed measures.

ASIC Resistance

For Bitcoin mining to be safe, it should remain in the hands of as many players as possible. The larger the community of miners, the harder it will be to create a malevolent conspiracy designed to undermine the network. The converse, a world in which all mining power is held by a handful, is quite dangerous. We would revert to a trusted, centralized world, in which we must trust merely a few. This is not the Bitcoin way.

In the original conception of Bitcoin, there would be many miners. Each peer node would be a miner. Since the only miners were clients running on desktops, there were many participants wielding relatively equal hashing power. This status quo was fairly safe. But it was not to last.

Technology itself also had a centralizing effect on mining. As the profit motive to mine grew, people quickly began to compete for the limited 50 BTC block payout. Capacity surged. In the very beginning, mining occurred on CPU's. These general purpose processors were not particularly efficient at SHA-256, the mining algorithm.

A technological arms race began to compute SHA-256 more efficiently. The winner would reap a far greater share of the mining rewards. The gains were enormous. A PC graphics card can mine at least 50 times faster than a CPU. This off-the-shelf hardware was quickly co-opted for Bitcoin mining. As miners improved their technology, individuals mining the old way lost their share of the total hashing power. Sticking with CPU mining when everyone had switched to GPU graphics cards meant losing revenue by a factor of 10-100X.

Once graphics cards took over, still more efficient mining hardware was found. FPGA boards (Field Programmable Gated Array) are arrays of logic gates that may be programmed into any given configuration. Whereas your processor has a static arrangement of logic gates designed for a broad set of functions, an FPGA can be programmed and reprogrammed into many different combinations. Once FPGA's were designed to perform SHA-256, hashing rates increased by another order of magnitude. Anyone running a graphics card fell hopelessly behind; mining on a CPU became positively antediluvian.

Finally, modern Bitcoin miners use ASICS (Application-specific integrated circuits). These are highly optimized circuits built for only a single function. They are not reprogrammable like FPGAs. They can be engineered to the highest efficiency for one stated purpose. Manufactured en masse in factories in Asia, they are extremely cost effective. Once ASIC's were built for SHA-256, they came to dominate Bitcoin mining. The price of hashing power fell dramatically. Mining on anything less became a waste of electricity.

The advance of mining technology hasn't stopped. ASIC's are constantly evolving into more sophisticated forms. The latest in semiconductor technology has finely wrought features down to 14 nanometer length scales and offers even better performance. In the endless arms race of Bitcoin mining, no optimization can be left unexplored.

There's an important lesson to be learned from the explosion in Bitcoin mining. When you pay for something, the supply increases. When absolutely anyone can get involved, from anywhere, with no barriers to entry, the supply can become mind-bogglingly efficient. Satoshi Nakamoto didn't have to think about how mining would be implemented. Certainly no one uses the original peer client version he created; it's obsolete now. But that didn't matter. Once the incentives were properly aligned, it was left to other people to figure out how to optimize.

It's not just the technology that has improved. Bitcoin mining became a mass-scale business with extremely low profit margins. There are massive warehouses right now in China, in Scandinavia, in the Ukraine, etc., filled with racks of ASICS. Millions of dollars are spent on such facilities; they are often custom built factories specifically designed to handle demanding electricity and cooling requirements. Building-wide ventilation systems must be built to cool the vast expanses of custom-engineered mining gear. These facilities consume so much electricity that they have migrated to the parts of the world where electricity is cheapest.

Bitcoin mining is its own industry, and it has grown large. In pursuit of the arms-race to solve blocks first, miners have delivered staggering gains in hashing power. As we have seen, this serves the purposes of rendering the network more resistant to attack. However it also does something else, Bitcoin mining has become a *capital intensive business*.

To become a Bitcoin miner and actually make money, one now requires a huge capital investment. All the features that allow one to compete, the sophisticated hardware, the custom facilities, the ideal location, cost a lot of money. But as with many other industries, this has led to consolidation in market share. This is a natural phenomenon in many markets. The semiconductor industry is composed of only a few giant companies. They manufacture chips at incredible scale and efficiency, in massive, multi-billion dollar facilities. It requires a breathtaking amount of capital to compete in this space. One huge facility can dominate because the nature of the technology is capital intensive. We should be grateful because it means we all get dirt-cheap processors.

We've received *dirt cheap* hashing power. But this has come at the cost of the number of mining participants. While there are still enough participants at the present for Bitcoin mining to still be a rowdy democracy, the trend towards fewer substantial voters should be worrying. If one extrapolates the trend forward and consolidation continues, we could be left with only a handful of massive mining centers. This would leave Bitcoin much more open to attack. Governments could merely occupy a few such facilities, direct them in the right way, and lead a 51% attack on Bitcoin.

Thus the economics of Bitcoin mining have already spawned centralization of miners: precisely what the decentralized paradigm seeks to avoid. Many have sought to find an alternative mining algorithm, besides SHA-256, that has *different* economics that *don't* lend themselves to a few players. After all, many markets do not work this way. The trouble is, it has proven incredibly difficult.

Many altcoins use different mining algorithms. These are often designed to be *harder* to optimize. For instance Litecoin, a historically important altcoin, uses Scrypt, a mining algorithm that cannot be run on Bitcoin ASIC devices. It was thought that, as a more challenging algorithm to optimize (because it requires more RAM), Scrypt would allow Litecoin mining to be more diffuse than Bitcoin's. But with the profit incentive, others simply designed ASICS for Scrypt and the problem remains[xiv].

It seems odd to look for an algorithm for which one *cannot* improve the efficiency. It is very counterintuitive that this would ever be worthwhile. And yet people are working on it. Ethereum has been musing about such mining algorithms. Some of them appear quite sophisticated; maybe they will prove intractable to ASIC's. Others claim that any algorithm can be optimized with an ASIC if the price is right. No matter how many bells and whistles are attached, those bells and whistles can be optimized. It is beyond my expertise to know either way. But I suspect that the latter camp is correct and that any choice of algorithm will be optimizable. Nevertheless, the search for an ASIC-resistant algorithm, which would be run by a healthy democracy of millions, continues.

Long Term Incentives: Mining in 2050

As we have seen, the Bitcoin Blockchain is a democracy where computational power equals votes. The issue requiring consensus is the order in which transactions occur. Miners are incentivized to behave honestly and participate in the same blockchain-branch as other miners. Even malicious actors are channelled down a virtuous path by their own self-interest. One miner amassing too much hashing power, 51% or more, can cause major problems in the form of a '51% attack'. How is this to be prevented in the future? What will the game-theory landscape between honest and malicious miners look like in 20 years? Will the same tenets hold that coerce miners to behave virtuously? Will fees paid to miners suffice, in real terms, to dedicate enough hashing power to keep the network safe? In short, how does the maintenance of the network scale?

These are the deepest unanswered questions in Bitcoin. They revolve around the long-term avoidance of a 51% attack. Despite much discussion, no one knows for sure what the answers are. These scalability issues will likely determine the fate of the Bitcoin experiment, far more than the political or economic complaints that are often raised.

Let us first review the basic facts. Miners receive payment via the automatic block reward and transaction fees. At 25 BTC per block, the automatic reward presently constitutes *greater than 99% of their income*. Transaction fees compose a trifling amount of that received by miners. But in keeping with the fixed total supply of bitcoins, the automatic block reward is halved every 4 years. Just next year, in 2016, it will be halved to 12.5 BTC each block. By 2020, it will be 6.25 BTC. At this rate of exponential decline, it will eventually be a trivial amount.

Miners need to consume real world assets in order to mine. Due to intense competition, they already operate at razor thin profit margins. Although in the early days mining was a hobbyists' venture, now it is big business, with millions of dollars invested. For all of this to remain viable, it must be funded.

Over the long term, the Bitcoin network needs enough hashing power to make the cost of attack prohibitive. At any given time, there is a finite cost to executing a 51% attack. That cost should be as high as possible. If the miners' arms race keeps the network safe, that arms race should be as intense as possible. If it gets slack, for instance if the cost to execute an attack were small, its likelihood would dramatically rise.

Beyond raw hashing power, the *number* of miners must remain high. If too few miners control all the hashing power, even if it is a vast amount, the democratic element will have been lost. If Bitcoin mining becomes ever-more capital intensive, such that it is *proportionately* more viable for a few big players, the risk of too little diversity in miners grows. With only a few participants, it becomes easier to assemble a conspiracy for the execution of a 51% attack.

It is unclear whether this will occur. While Bitcoin mining has proven capital intensive, there may be limits to the consolidation of miners. There could even be a reverse-consolidation; if mining devices can operate as heaters in the winter, for instance, or in other disparate capacities, the hashing power could be better distributed.

Under any scenario, miners must still be paid. As the automatic block reward exponentially approaches zero, transaction fees must rise to compensate. No one really knows what the equilibrium state of this is.

The simplest way to consider transaction fees at equilibrium is to consider the real costs, in aggregate, of mining at the minimum required level. In the long run, those real costs must be borne by Bitcoin users as transaction fees. The burden this imposes depends heavily on the use of the network as a whole. If transactional volume is very high, then transaction fees summing to the necessary amount will impose a very low burden. If transactional volume is low, fees will probably not be adequate. This could conceivably lead to a death spiral, in which an insufficiently secure network could not attract enough volume in order to *become* secure. These forces may, indeed, only ever mean that one Blockchain will ever be truly safe. Currently, about $50 million is transacted each day over Bitcoin. And about $700,000 worth of bitcoins are paid to miners. This represents 1.4%, considerably higher than the nominal transaction fees of Bitcoin.

Miners are presently subsidized now by short-term inflation in the supply of bitcoins. However most of the foreordained inflation has already occurred; two thirds of all bitcoins ever to exist have already been created. This subsidy will wane, and the 1.4% figure should too. At least one of the following *must* happen: transactions fees will rise, volume will increase, or miners will receive less. Hence the only long-term scenario in which the network is both secure and cheap is one in which it incorporates a large volume.

Altruistic mining, in which people mine at a slight loss, is another possibility. It's not as far-fetched as it seems. If one could contribute to financial stability by plugging in an electric appliance, some people and institutions might do it. Or perhaps mining devices could be embedded in everyday items. I already alluded to the Bitcoin-miner doubling as a winter heater; why not generate heat and bitcoins at the same time? It's already being done by hobbyists.

The equilibrium state of the game-theory world of Bitcoin mining, in a future with trivial automatic block rewards, is the biggest open-ended question in Bitcoin. No one really knows what will happen. It's entirely plausible that Bitcoin mining will remain healthy, supported by small transaction fees stemming from a healthy transactional volume. Or maybe miners will dwindle and the network will become susceptible to 51% attacks. This could trigger a spiraling loss of confidence that destroys any incentive to mine and leaves the network vulnerable. But if the preservation of Bitcoin's trustlessness is a priority, these challenges must be solved. The indelible lesson is that trustlessness comes at a price. The unanswered question in the Bitcoin experiment is 'What long-term transactional cost is necessary to secure a trustless ledger?' Will people bear that cost ceaselessly over the long term? What happens in a crisis?

It is possible that over the long term the price of trustlessness can remain low under a single, consolidated standard. Other proof-of-work based schemes will experience the same challenges as Bitcoin, but they will be less well-endowed to deal with them. The scalability of mining may have a unifying effect across blockchains. Perhaps the resources exist to maintain just one trustless cryptocurrency. Maybe just one healthy, vibrant mining community will ever exist due to long-term economic factors.

Proposed alternatives abound. Some propound trusted consensus systems, in which 'permissioned' nodes cooperatively achieve consensus. Such a system can be basically free. But in sacrificing trustlessness, such a system endows itself with all the risks of human meddling endemic to fiat money. The threats posed by people are infinitely more intractable than those posed by mining.

Proof-of-Stake is another alternative consensus mechanism. It eschews mining in favor of endowing stakeholders, i.e. owners of tokens like bitcoins, with the right to vote on the order of events. There is still some debate on the stability and trustlessness of this approach. But it requires no costly diversion of resources to the miners' arms race. Thus it may be a viable alternative if mining suffers from excessive centralization.

Another answer is to embed permanent inflation in a cryptocurrency and to use it to pay miners. Personally, I find this to be a repellant solution; it violates the premise of a fixed monetary supply. But it does solve the problem of paying miners in perpetuity. It would still be far superior to fiat systems in that the inflation rate would be pre-programmed, fixed, and every bit as mechanical as Bitcoin's. In the absolute worst case, if Bitcoin mining collapses to a dangerously low level, such a model could be used. After all, even the supply of gold increases by 1-2% each year. But only the most devastating failures would justify such a step.

Currency should be expected to last a very long time. Dollars have failed to hold their value for the last hundred years. But gold has succeeded. Owning bitcoins should endow one with the same, time-insensitive confidence that gold owners possess. This is what the system should aspire to accomplish. As it is now, that system is exceptionally resilient. Satoshi himself believed that transaction fees would rise, and that the network would endure. But projecting the acts of others, decades in the future, is a hopeless game. A mechanism exists, in the form of transaction fees, to support Bitcoin miners. We must surely keep close watch on the health of that community. Preserving the alignment of incentives towards consensus, which has secured the network so well in the past, is paramount.

What We Don't Know We Don't Know

We've discussed the potential for a 51% attack: Bitcoin's one explicitly evident technical vulnerability. But Bitcoin uses many other nifty cryptographic features as well. What if one of these were to fail? What if breaking these systems were impossible until it simply... wasn't? Bitcoin is built on very powerful informational rules. But over what expanse of time have such rules really endured? Isn't human knowledge constantly overturned? How many historical certainties have been undone by clever successors in later generations?

It is a hard thing to address those things we don't know we don't know, the 'unknown unknowns' of Donald Rumsfeld. They are, by their very nature, almost impossible to deal with. Bitcoin in particular is highly susceptible to any great overturnings of knowledge. Since Bitcoin itself is pure information, leveraging purely mathematical rules, its security rests on certain assumptions. For example, Bitcoin's security requires that SHA-256 remains an NP-hard problem. If someone figures out a way to reverse SHA-256 hashes, solving a long-standing problem in mathematics, Bitcoin will be in serious trouble. Similarly, if someone figures out how to do division between points on Elliptic Curves, another variation of the discrete logarithm problem in mathematics, Bitcoin will be seriously broken. These problems don't even have to be solved outright, merely hastening the rate at which solutions are found (NP to P) would be equally disastrous.

A single failure in any of these assumptions could unwind the tightly bound informational system that is Bitcoin. There is no tolerance for failure. Because there is no higher authority to go to, the protocol must speak for itself. It must not lapse even once.

As a case in point, there's not much reason to fear the downfall of SHA-256 right now. There is no indication that anyone has come close to solving this problem. So many incredibly smart people have tried and failed to do so. It seems unlikely that anyone can now succeed. That may be comforting to you in the medium term. But certainly similar logic would have led one astray in the past. While none have solved these challenging mathematical problems, neither is there any proof that they *cannot be solved*! Amazingly, certain kinds of mathematical solutions have been proven *not to exist*! It *is* possible to prove that someone else *cannot* solve something. Mind-boggling. But sadly, the cryptographic functions upon which Bitcoin relies have no such assuring proofs. While, as a practical matter, virtually no one is worried about the integrity of Elliptic Curves or SHA-256, all it takes is one black-swan-like genius to overturn our assumptions.

In the event of a catastrophic unravelling of some core cryptographic function, there could in theory be a hard fork in Bitcoin to switch from compromised algorithms to safe ones. But as we've seen, a hard fork at this stage arising from a severe security lapse would be a massive blow to confidence. Moreover, even if we switch from one scheme to another, it is likely that the new scheme will suffer from the same fundamental problem as the old, namely, that unproven mathematical assumptions tend to break over long enough time periods.

Others might argue that this time is different. Perhaps the most intractable mathematical problems today will remain so. In other words, with *certain* problems we have hit an insurmountable wall. This may be the most realistic, albeit unsatisfying answer.

Even farther afield, there could be more off-the-radar threats to the Bitcoin status quo. It is said that quantum computers could break much of the cryptography Bitcoin relies upon. These super-advanced devices are the subject of intensive research; they promise to offer staggeringly superior computation such that they could solve cryptographic problems now considered to be unsolvable.

But almost like a natural riposte, quantum-resistant algorithms are also said to exist. So in theory, Bitcoin could be retrofitted with such algorithms in the unlikely event of an attack by quantum-computing attackers. The future is a frightening place indeed.

It should be of some comfort that, while these mathematical compromises would spell doom for Bitcoin in its present incarnation, they would cause mass havoc across the entire world, in almost every sphere. In the event of a break in one of Bitcoin's cryptographic algorithms, secure communications around the world would also be broken. The chaos in banking, identity theft, diplomatic relations, privacy, and so forth, would be massive. Thus many eggs have been placed in the cryptographic basket. Many minds are committed to ferreting out vulnerabilities before they can be exploited. An intensely competitive world of researchers scrutinizes their integrity on a daily basis. While this should perhaps not put you entirely at ease, it is probably as sure as we can be of anything short of mathematical proof. By using out-of-the-box cryptography generated from peer-reviewed circles, Bitcoin benefits from tools used across many global sectors.

Thus while the downfall of our mathematical assumptions is an incredibly remote possibility, if you think like I do, it should still make you just slightly nervous. Worse still are the unknown unknowns which future generations are sure to unleash on us. Bitcoin should be built to last, after all, not for five or ten years, but for hundreds of years. Such a long timespan requires worrying about the unknown unknowns, aliens equipped with quantum computers, and Satoshi Himself coming back from the dead. Only extraordinary technical paranoia can produce an informational system strong enough to outfox future generations, with all the wily Newton's, Einstein's, and Satoshi's yet to be born.

Scalability

The most pressing technical issue facing Bitcoin, aside from the threat of a 51% attack, is the scalability of the network. Bitcoin works very well now. However the demands imposed upon Bitcoin at the present pale in comparison to what may be expected in the future. Every good computer scientist knows to ask the question, "Yes it works, but does it scale?" This same question must be asked of Bitcoin.

Presently, the network records approximately 100,000 separate transactions per day. This is a historic high for Bitcoin, reflecting its increased use. It amounts to about one transaction per second on average. Compared to the early days of Bitcoin, this represents fantastic growth. In 2009 whole days, even weeks went by with scarcely any activity whatsoever. You can see the records for yourself in the Blockchain. However when considered in light of Bitcoin's aspirations as a global network, this is a pathetically low figure. By contrast Visa, the largest payment processor, handles 200 million transactions per day, or 2000 times more than Bitcoin. Even lesser, though still formidable rivals, such as PayPal, handle 100 times more transactions than Bitcoin does. While Bitcoin may be in greater use than ever before within its own history, the aggregate figures are frankly uncompetitive with incumbents.

The story actually gets worse. Not only does Bitcoin handle a paltry transactional volume, it is currently *structurally unable, even in the ideal case,* to handle more than 7 transactions a second. With the protocol as it is, the number of transactions could only increase by a factor of 7 before hitting a *strict* limit. This is hardly enough volume to shake the foundations of finance.

This limit, while presently in force, is not a permanent constraint on Bitcoin. It is self-imposed. It arises from the fact that each block in the Blockchain can only ever contain 1 MB. This limit was hard-coded in the early days of Bitcoin. Its purposes are manifold. The primary aim was to ensure the smooth propagation of blocks between peer nodes. Excessively large blocks, such as 1 GB blocks, could not reliably be transferred every 10 minutes among all nodes. Making the protocol friendly to ordinary, non-specialized computers was also a priority. Parsing blocks ought not to pose an undue computational burden for regular users. One gigabyte blocks, for instance, would mean that only expensive, specialized computers could operate as peer notes: hardly a network of equals.

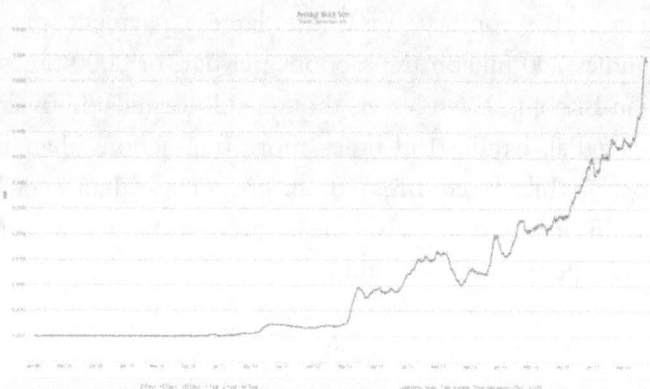

Average block size per month over Bitcoin's history:

current average is 0.55 mB   Source: Blockchain.info

The 1 MB block size limit was chosen arbitrarily and never with the intention of becoming permanent. It was a temporary measure before a more reasonable value could be established. It is this value that imposes the 7 transactions per second maximum throughput.

Raising the block size limit is a much discussed topic in Bitcoin technical circles these days. While the 1 MB limit has, thus far, never served as a noticeable bottleneck to transactions, there will likely come a time when it will. On the other hand, some worry that raising the ceiling on transactions will undermine the market price for transaction fees and thereby damage the strength of the mining community. It is thus hotly debated as to whether the limit should be raised, and to what value. This discussion encapsulates many of the conflicting ethoses found within the Bitcoin community.

Nevertheless, it appears probable that the blocksize limit will be raised to some degree. Gavin Andreessen, the former Lead Developer of Bitcoin, has demonstrated that blocks of 20 MB pose no discernible burden. It is likely that the limit could be raised still further without a significant effect on performance or accessibility. Gavin also proposed raising the limit programmatically, as part of the protocol. The block size limit would increase at a geometric rate, matching predicted improvements in digital storage capacity. Whatever the scheme, keeping Bitcoin accessible to normal users will remain a priority. Insofar as the block size limit can be raised without violating this requirement, it can and (probably) will be raised.

Even with an increase to the block size limit, this crucial parameter can only grow so far before compromising the peer-to-peer essence of Bitcoin. Remember that the Blockchain is something that anyone should be able to prove to one's self, without ever having to trust intermediaries. If the Blockchain becomes so gargantuan that normal computers cannot feasibly process it, then much of the original intent of Bitcoin will have been lost.

Even if the block size limit is raised to an ambitious 100 MB, this also only allows for a theoretical maximum of 700 transactions a second, still unequal to what VISA accomplishes. Of course, as a centralized system, VISA is superficially much easier to scale than Bitcoin.

So if the Bitcoin block size is raised to 100 MB, the network still cannot equal VISA's volume, though it does enter the same ballpark. How then does Bitcoin scale? Bitcoin is supposed to bank the unbanked. It is supposed to be the great financial liberator. Bitcoin can even be used to create new forms of economic activity involving programmatic money and micropayments. All this new behavior will itself require a large portion of the transactional throughput. Thus our benchmark should not even be VISA, the world's largest payment processor, but perhaps even another order of magnitude beyond that. If cars are to negotiate with parking meters for bitcoins, the network must be able to scale to an extraordinary extent.

Raising the blocksize limit alone will help. But it alone will not be sufficient to permit all the diverse uses to which Bitcoin may be employed. Special tactics must be created to stretch a finite amount of memory. There are various approaches available to maximize this limited resource.

The simplest way to get more mileage out of the Blockchain is to employ a centralized service that manages transactions 'off-chain'. This means that transactions occurring within the service exist only as rows on a proprietary database. They are not cryptographically secure, trustless Bitcoin transactions. Bitcoins may go in and out of such a black box as legitimate, verifiable Bitcoin transactions. But transactions managed 'within' the black box are not Bitcoin. They are merely denominated in bitcoins. Hence they do not meet the same security standards. In fact, centralized solutions built on Bitcoin share the same failings of the institutions they are designed to replace.

Coinbase, for example, is a large Bitcoin company which conducts off-chain transactions. I may transmit bitcoins from my Coinbase account to yours without actually triggering a bonafide Bitcoin transaction. Bitcoins are merely debited from my Coinbase account and credited to yours. Security here rests on their proprietary system: surely more fallible than the Bitcoin protocol itself. While the ultimate payout is denominated in bitcoins, this approach is endowed with none of the advantages of Bitcoin. But because it requires no transactions on the Blockchain, transacting 'off-chain' is cheaper and faster. The price is the loss of trustlessness. Unlike fiat money, that trustlessness may be restored at any time by simply withdrawing one's bitcoins from Coinbase.

You and I may transact many times 'off-chain', via Coinbase or other closed services, and 'settle-up' at the end by withdrawing actual bitcoins. At this final step, a legitimate Bitcoin transaction is published which actualizes and makes real all the off-chain transactions that occurred. Thus we may mitigate transaction fees and block-confirmation risk by surrendering trustlessness to a central party for a limited period. If transaction fees rise due to crowding of Bitcoin blocks, this trade-off might make more and more sense, particularly for micropayments most affected by transaction fees. Crucially, the risks of a trusted system are opt-in; only a small subset of one's funds need be subjected to centralized risk at any one time.

An excellent analogy, as ever with Bitcoin, would be gold. Transacting off-chain is like if you and I kept an informal ledger of transactions denominated in gold. Our gold ledger is not itself gold. It is more akin to paper money in its trusted, counterparty-dependent nature. However when settling outstanding debts, we would transact in physical gold. This physical gold transaction, which parallels the Bitcoin transaction actualizing off-chain activity, is infrequent compared to ledger transactions because it is more difficult. But because we may resort to the 'actualizing' transaction at any time, we can individually weigh trustlessness versus cost. In this example, you may similarly demand payment in physical gold for each and every transaction, if it is sufficiently important to you.

While perfect trustlessness should be the goal for any cryptocurrency system, a spectrum of risk is not a terrible outcome either. A centralized, off-chain system that exists as a layer on top of Bitcoin would still constitute an improvement over the current state of affairs. But is it possible to have our cake and eat it too? How can the Blockchain be scaled to handle transaction with the speed and cheapness of centralized, 'off-chain' transactions, but *without* having to resort to a trusted central party? Can seemingly intrinsic limits be defied to preserve the core ethos of Bitcoin: that each may trust none and yet still trust the outcome?

Payment Channels

It appears that, miraculously, the old limits *can* be defied while the trustless soul of Bitcoin is preserved. Payment channels are a clever technique that makes it possible to engage in high frequency transactions *trustlessly* without having to record them in the Bitcoin Blockchain. Thus these transactions would not take up space and impose computational burdens on the network. In fact, network participants would not even be aware of such transactions. Since they do not exist on the Blockchain, they cost no transaction fees and are instant. Payment channels occur at the same, stunning speed as those within any centralized service. Whereas Bitcoin transactions cost a fee and must be confirmed by peer nodes, transactions over payment channels are truly instantaneous.

There is a crucial difference between payment channels and 'off-chain' transactions. Payment channels remain trustless. Through the use of multisignature addresses and locktime transactions, a trustless relationship can be established between two parties. In essence, they exchange unpublished Bitcoin transactions to one another instantly, in such a way that they act as redeemable IOUs. It is as if you and I busily wrote and rewrote checks to one another, except with each micro-transaction, we varied the total amounts accordingly on the IOUs. In this way, through details I will avoid laboring over here, parties can engage in transactions as quickly and as often as they please. At any time, either party may exit the relationship. In doing so, each party redeems what it is owed in bitcoins from the unpublished transactions it has received from the other side. It is like if you and I, after writing a series of checks back and forth (only one set of which can be valid in the end), finally settled the net sum by cashing our checks. Crucially, neither party may defraud or steal from the other.

Payment channels are a truly brilliant innovation. They promise to vastly augment the scalability of Bitcoin. Because, in this scheme, the great majority of transactions may never be published on the Blockchain, a potentially huge number of microtransactions may occur for each 'settling' transaction actually published to the Blockchain.

Payment channels can be used to create 'hub and spoke' relationships in which payment processors facilitate transactions between anonymous parties. By establishing a payment channel with a single, well-capitalized entity, I may enjoy the convenience of a payment channel with anyone else who has also set up a payment channel with the same entity. It is even possible to arrange payment channels in a daisy chain, such that payments may occur instantly between disparate individuals across several iterations of payment processors. All this can occur without sacrificing trustlessness. These obligations are always redeemable back into bitcoins, without having to trust any institutions, not even the payment processors themselves.

The exact mechanics of the 'multiple hub and spoke' model of payment channels are too complex for our purposes here. But it has been demonstrated in theory that such relationships can be built while preserving the trustlessness of native Bitcoin. Such constructs promise to greatly expand the scope of microtransactions on the Bitcoin network because they impose a far lesser burden on the Blockchain. Under such a system, blockchain transactions become final enforcement mechanisms that occur rarely. They would only occur at the end of long, fruitful payment-channel relationships, or alternatively, as a guaranteed safeguard in the case of malicious counterparties. By relying on the Blockchain for enforcing fair play, rather than the day-to-day minutiae of regular microtransactions, payment channels vastly improve the prospects for Bitcoin's scalability.

Like everything else in the Bitcoin world, payment channels are exceedingly new. And at present, they are incomplete. Subtle issues with the Bitcoin protocol (transaction malleability) prevent a perfect execution of payment channels at present. A soft fork to the protocol is required to make payment channels truly robust. While forks to the protocol are never taken lightly, it is probable that we will see this particular issue addressed in the near future. Transaction malleability, the issue interfering with payment channels at the moment, is a well-known problem on the core developers' 'to do list'. Unlike many potential Bitcoin forks, the fixes necessary appear to be uncontroversial; we shall likely see the requisite changes far before Bitcoin scalability problems arise.

Payment channels are a beautiful example of a technology being built on top of Bitcoin above and beyond the expectations of its creator. Satoshi never foresaw payment channels. They are another layer of abstraction on top of Bitcoin and quite complex in their own right. But because Bitcoin is open source and permissionless, clever tinkerers can devise new functionality on top. The Bitcoin Blockchain is merely a foundation upon which more advanced features can be built, by anyone. This heralds great potential for the Blockchain. Its consensus power may be leveraged in new ways, solving todays problems without having to revise Bitcoin as a foundational layer, but instead, extending it.

The challenges posed by Bitcoin's scalability are serious. For Bitcoin to meet the high hopes placed upon it, it must scale orders of magnitude beyond its current capacity. Bitcoin in its original incarnation is unable to meet this goal. However clever extensions to the core protocol dramatically improve the prospects for handling greater transaction volume. Because the Blockchain remains an incredibly robust consensus tool, techniques such as payment channels can always resort to the Blockchain as an enforcement mechanism for microtransactions. In this way, a vast amount of traffic can occur trustlessly by the mere existence of the Blockchain.

Even with these promising solutions, the expanding computational burden of the Blockchain warrants continued attention. As Bitcoin grows, scalability will be something to keep your eye on.

A Better Bitcoin

Up to this point, I have consciously avoided discussing Bitcoin's cryptocurrency competitors. Much of what has been said about Bitcoin also pertains to altcoins. It is difficult to generalize because there are so many of them and they are so diverse. In the wide space of potential cryptocurrency implementations many features have been tried. From simple tweaks, to profound conceptual leaps, altcoins have already explored a vast space of concepts.

If Bitcoin does not founder on some internal technical fault, its greatest long term threat will be a Better Bitcoin. Perhaps something will arise that is so manifestly superior to Bitcoin that it can overcome its entrenched network effects. Indeed, Bitcoin itself attempts to defeat the network effects of fiat money. It is an incredibly steep slope to climb. And yet no human system is ever at perfect equilibrium. There are no stable points in history, no ultimate ends. Network effects may be powerful, and at certain times, insurmountable. But they cannot be relied upon to last indefinitely. What if, in the best case, Bitcoin survives to old age? What if it becomes venerable, respected, familiar, but dreadfully old-fashioned?

It is difficult to speculate in the arena of competing cryptocurrencies. There are so many promising ideas out there that have not been touched upon in this book. Ethereum is filled with heady ideas. Proof-of-Stake approaches could address the weaknesses of Bitcoin's long-term security, even as they introduce new concerns. For virtually every design facet of Bitcoin, a competitor has arisen to test its assumptions. Bitcoin the cryptocurrency standard is under constant attack from upstarts.

I don't believe anyone is qualified to *confidently* predict the future of cryptocurrencies. In such a turbulent field, there are no experts remotely well versed enough to know what technical solutions will work, how network effects will unfold, or how technology and society will collide. There are too many unpredictable forces in play. So I will venture into speculation.

I expect that Bitcoin's network effects will prove dominant over competitors for the foreseeable future. If the cryptocurrency space continues to grow, the overwhelming majority of growth will occur within Bitcoin and not within alternatives. The incentives for those building businesses and technology are overwhelming aligned with following the existing standard. The *lingua franca* gains disproportionately more adherents than the local tongues.

To me, the happiest long term outcome is a common standard of money that may be connected to alternative technical implementations. Sidechains seek to accomplish this marriage, preserving the scarcity of Bitcoin while permitting unfettered experimentation. As currencies go, stability should be paramount. A single enduring standard, in my mind, would be far superior to the oscillating fads of a small tech community. Money standards must last longer than the attention span of computer nerds. I would prefer a system of money that values stability over the knee-jerk inclusion of every feature.

Over the long run, Bitcoin will be subjected to serious technical stresses in the form of scalability and mining centralization. If these cannot be solved, an alternative implementation, better suited to such challenges, could conceivably take over. I sincerely hope that such is not the end. But if Bitcoin were to die, it could only be a technical death, not a political one. Thankfully, competing technical implementations, designed to address whatever felled Bitcoin, would take over. A replacement could quite easily even inherit the preceding Bitcoin balances. In this sense, the existence of so many competitors is a safeguard against failure. The demise of Bitcoin would not herald the end for cryptocurrencies. But rather, like an old tree toppled by a storm, would signal the emergence of a still-more resilient successor.

Finally, Bitcoin could thrive and grow and, thanks to a huge community of developers, overcome the long-term technical challenges. It could become a stubbornly enduring abstraction, conceivably lasting hundreds of years, or longer, so long as internet and computers last. But even then there remains the risk that a Better Bitcoin may be found. Perhaps some brilliant stroke of genius will reveal a better way to do things. Perhaps it cannot be retrofitted into existing Bitcoin, but would necessitate an entirely new system. While I cannot imagine it, it would be foolhardy to deny the possibility. Betting against the genius of future generations is a dangerous game.

But as I cannot imagine Bitcoin's fate 100 years hence, there may be still less certainty in dollars. Considering the vast revolution in money that occurred in the *preceding* 100 years, modern readers should soberly face the effect of time on sensibilities. No currency exists in a timeless status quo that can be assumed to persist for centuries: not even gold.

Even in the case of a successor to Bitcoin, would we really be at a lost? The transaction history of Bitcoin could be preserved and replicated in a successor system. Everyone's bitcoins could conceivably be reproduced, securely, as Bettercoins. Or perhaps there would be a period of chaos.

On the whole I see our options as quite bright. The trustless paradigm has been unleashed and it surely will not fail across all its incarnations. Its foremost exemplar, Bitcoin, shows no sign of weakness. Only in the clouded future are there risks, the game-theory environment of Bitcoin miners in 2050 or the invention of better systems down the road. These risks belong to another generation entirely. And even in the worst case, were there to be a disruption in Bitcoin, it would be a curative upheaval, making way for a still-more-robust successor. What is certain is that the trustless paradigm will endure. The spark of the idea lives in too many minds to be snuffed out.

On Risk

If this book suggested that Bitcoin is foreordained or that it is without risk, then I have misled you. There is, of course, some risk. Bitcoin is an experiment. A beautiful, miraculous, otherworldly experiment. The potential rewards are vast. The journey is long. When considering it, reflect on the *weighted average of outcomes by probability*. Then you will see that, if there is even a remote chance that Bitcoin could succeed, then it ought to be the chance of a lifetime.

Do not judge an uncertain event by what happened after the fact. Judge it by risk multiplied by reward across all possibilities as known at the moment of decision. In all the moments of life in which the future is unknown, crunching probabilities is the most rationale approach possible. It is in this sense that Bitcoin is a fantastic bet, albeit not a certain one. But measured against what it may accomplish, as a neutral, secure protocol for money, for cryptographic truth itself, the risks are tolerable. Consider that its feats of trustlessness, of a functioning global currency, already function on a massive scale. Bitcoin has, in fact, been extensively de-risked by the early pioneers. They paid a commensurately lower price for the vastly greater risks they took.

Bitcoin sheds risk every day. As it continues to survive and grow, it has impressed former skeptics by its durability. It has outlived so many prophecies of its death. It has been condemned as finished, doomed, and dead many times over. As the system endures, as it continues to serve its primary purpose as a medium for exchange, it cannot help but impress even rigid skeptics.

The Bitcoin codebase has also dramatically improved. From the amateurish state of the code in the beginning, to its much more refined form today, Bitcoin the open source software project is a carefully tended garden. The amount of focus and human capital it receives is tremendous. For such a complex system, it has run exceptionally smoothly and with few bugs.

Most importantly, the community and the infrastructure surrounding Bitcoin have grown by leaps and bounds. Until recently, most Bitcoin businesses practiced very amateurish standards in software, private key management, and product design. The polish and sophistication of modern Bitcoin companies vastly outmatch those of predecessors just a few years ago. A site such as MTGOX, famed for its poor execution would hardly acquire market share today.

So while Bitcoin cannot be said to lack risk, neither does it lack in opportunity. As an investment, it is a stake in a very high reward outcome. The potential importance of that outcome, namely, that Bitcoin heralds a new era of cryptographic finance, warrants the risks today. The potential for reward outstrips that of failure by a wide margin.

While the Bitcoin price has not always been upwards, the fundamentals of its use have been. It is still a burgeoning phenomenon. If its momentary attractiveness, as reflected in the market price, oscillates, its core metrics, such as the transactional volume and the number of accepting merchants, trend ever upwards. The health of the Bitcoin economy should first be judged by the utility it confers to users, and only second by its price.

The outcome for Bitcoin probably lies on a bimodal distribution of probabilities. Its fate shall either be greatness or total failure. Its place on the periphery of finance will not last. Buying bitcoins as an investment is a bet on a very big success. If you believe that there is even a small possibility of that success, the current price ought to be extremely attractive. The one thing you should not worry about is persistent mediocrity. Bitcoin will either succeed brilliantly, or fail loudly for a technical reason. There will be no middling stagnation.

What Everyone Thinks Bitcoin's Chances Are

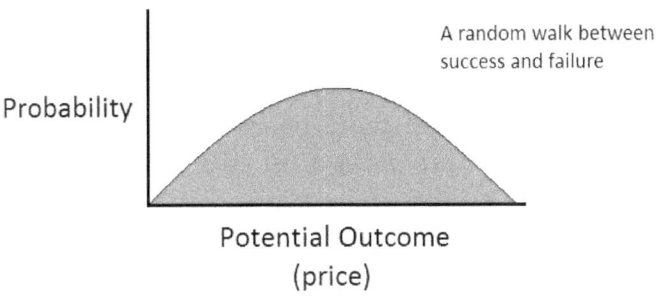

A random walk between
success and failure

Probability

**Potential Outcome
(price)**

People expect a random walk or a bell-curve distribution of
probabilities. Bitcoin's fate does not follow a Gaussian distribution.

What Bitcoin's Chances Really Are

Imagined Probability Graph for Long Term Bitcoin Outcomes

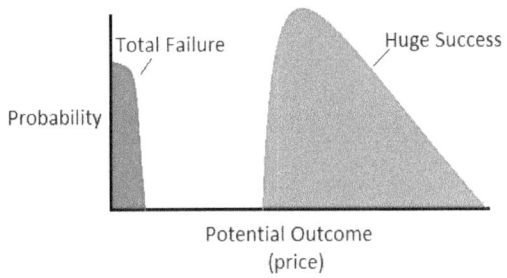

Total Failure

Huge Success

Probability

Potential Outcome
(price)

This probability distribution is **bimodal.**

Only a technical failure can break Bitcoin. This is precisely the test that Bitcoin has passed, with flying colors, for the past six years. It is precisely the dimension of Bitcoin least contested by critics. Such a failure could only ever be total. For this reason, as I see it, Bitcoin can only either succeed spectacularly, or fail cataclysmically. It cannot stagnate, nor can it be defeated by outside powers. If you accept this premise, the price of bitcoins looks awfully low. It is low, in fact, when you consider that companies trade today without earnings with market capitalizations individually of ten, twenty, or even more times the value of all bitcoins. Taking a sense of proportion of the numbers involved in the fiat system, the trillions of dollars of debt that have been monetized, the outsized valuations of tech startup, biotech stocks, and others, and the price of bitcoin should seem miniscule.

What May Be

The Significance of the Blockchain

Considering the Blockchain and what it accomplishes is really a staggering thing. We have said that it is a mechanism for establishing consensus. This fact has been amply demonstrated in the smooth operation of Bitcoin itself. There is an absolute certainty in its transactional history that is unequalled by any other historical record that we possess. That so-and-so paid so-and-so $1.50 for coffee on June 3rd, 2013, is an incontrovertible fact, beyond any power to subvert. Without exaggeration, it is written in stone such that no other earthly record can match it. We have never before known anything so well.

The Blockchain history is ironclad, and yet it is armed with no person's authority. It is a central point of truth, and yet there are no truthsayers. It boggles the mind. It defies our senses and our intuition. We cannot intuitively accept this fact. And yet it remains. The Blockchain is a source of truth that transcends humans. It is made by us, but it is not governed by us. Its rules are unbending. If it were a physical object we could crush it and remake it to our will. But as an abstraction, as data itself, the Blockchain is utterly beyond our grasp.

As it stands, the Blockchain is used to establish consensus over currency. We have seen that this itself is of great moment. Its currency function stands to transform quite a lot. And yet this is but one of the many functions to which the consensus-mechanism can be turned. The currency function is but one ray of light in a whole kaleidoscope of opportunity.

If you really stop to consider the full implications of the Blockchain, your reasoning may take you to distant, fantastical places. You will reach conclusions that surely cannot be. If knowledge is power, then what is authority in a world in which truth is decentralized and cryptographic? What role is there for governments when their chief function, as an arbiter, is obviated by cryptographic tools? What social functions, jobs, important personages, and customs now exist that are fundamentally doomed by the advent of a trustless consensus mechanism? If you truly ponder the implications of robust trustlessness, you will see that much that exists today need not exist tomorrow. Much of the paraphernalia of authority that we maintain at great expense is but a crude attempt to mimic what Bitcoin accomplishes so seamlessly. The pomp and ritual behind important offices and august institutions are window-dressing, seeking to impute a trustlessness that does not exist. This is true not just for financial matters, but for many human affairs.

In many ways, Bitcoin itself is far ahead of its time. We simple folk were not ready for such an advanced thing: not in this era. It was meant for a few centuries hence; perhaps those people would be better armed to cope with such an ingenious idea. And yet it is upon us. Understood or no, loved or hated, Blockchain technology is not going away. It's such a tenaciously good idea that it will infiltrate new areas hitherto occupied by the old priests of an earlier age. Many interests will be overturned by so powerful a paradigm. Many vested interests, downstream beneficiaries, and even merely the intellectually complacent, will decry the encroachment of the Blockchain in our everyday life. Much clever language will be conjured to argue it away. Precedents will be cited as to why it's impossible. Human emotions will be played upon as to why such a thing is not right. And yet it will be there, functioning with mechanical precision. As Bitcoin illustrates the lie of fiat money, the Blockchain tells the story of human incompetence.

The transformative nature of the Blockchain is so profound that the conclusions we may come to are unpalatable for most. We may question our government, our culture, and our norms. We may arrive at quite unpopular or uncomfortable conclusions. In fact, if you unleash real skepticism upon the world and all its facets, with which you are already so familiar, you will see that much that is need not be so. Much that we have grown accustomed to was not always so. And most of what is will not last. As the thoughts of our predecessors seem ludicrous to us, in hindsight, so too will our opinions be ridiculed by our successors. Such is the continuous overturning of history.

If you can shed the burden of your prior opinions and inspect the Blockchain for what it is, you will find that it is a marvelous thing. And if you can admit that, it is not much farther to perceive the full consequences to which it may be turned. Why aren't more areas of life subject to the same mathematical reliability as Bitcoin? If real world events can be tethered to a cryptographic entity, as they already are through Bitcoin, why aren't other human endeavors similarly managed? Why don't we vote for politicians cryptographically, from home? Why do notaries exist? Why does it cost so much money to transact a house when it could be transacted trustlessly on the Blockchain for pennies? How many other intermediaries exist to sell human trust who must soon be dangerously undercut?

Paradoxical as it may sound, it may be better to live in a world in which we must trust no one. Trust in loved ones may forever be sacred. But trust in reputable figures may be more a symptom of lack of options rather than an objectively superior source of truth. Already we have seen the virtues of trustlessness on the Internet which has so exposed divergent viewpoints. There was a time when Wikipedia was widely lambasted as lacking in authority. Authority it lacks. But it contains far fewer errors and far greater breadth than Encyclopedia Britannica could even begin to match.

We have become accustomed to looking up incredibly precise facts on the Internet. But this is far from the historical norm. Traditionally you had to merely ask a person nearby, someone you respected perhaps, for any particular factoid. I experienced this firsthand in my years in Africa. Without nearby libraries, without Internet, esoteric facts could not simply be 'looked up'. The best one could feasibly manage was to ask someone locally. Most questions cannot be answered this way with any accuracy. And yet this was (and is in some places) the reality for most people.

To a large extent, we abandoned tightly controlled sources of information and news with the explosion of the Internet. The breadth and quality of reporting is vastly superior to what it once was. Nor is it possible for a few actors to control the message; even in China, where a veritable army of censors is employed, information cannot be controlled. This progress is an immense social good.

And yet the task is incomplete. While the Internet may be replete with heterogeneous blogs, tweets, and articles, of practically every shade, no comparable diversity exists in other sectors. A house is owned by the say-so of government bureaucrats, in a central office with, I would imagine, truckloads of paperwork. Money itself has been taken over by the bureaucrats, who control its floodgates according to opaque rules, like Mandarins shuffling to unseen court politics. The heterogeneity and richness we find on the Internet is not equaled in other domains, particularly those in which an authority has positioned itself.

Technologies inspired by the Bitcoin Blockchain seek to expand what was accomplished on the Internet into other spheres. The diversity of thought online is contrasted by the monolithic centrality of other fields. The Internet put great power in the hands of disparate individuals because they could freely share information. Blockchains allow people to achieve a consensus between peers, without having to resort to the unfortunate expedient of empowering authorities. This is a new form of decentralized empowerment; it is no less profound than the Internet itself. But unlike the Internet, because it replaces authority figures with something mathematically much sounder, blockchain technology runs directly afoul of governments. The powerful will bitterly resist any decentralized system they cannot control.

The truth is that the full significance of the Blockchain is still not known. No one can say for sure to what ends it may be turned. But those ends are likely to be weighty, for if nothing else, blockchains unleash a fundamentally new capability. Trust, which had been so human, so precious, so expensive, and so faulty, has been replaced. It has been, to a certain extent, automated. It is an extension of the adage from Marc Andreessen that "Software is eating the world". Bitcoin's currency function already speaks to the high stakes roles that trustless systems may attain. Certainly other domains will be susceptible too to the ineluctable efficacy of algorithmic trust. If one revolution, the Bitcoin one, has just begun, what others remain yet to be fomented?

The Crypto Wars

The introduction of strong cryptography in civilian life in the early 90's was a harbinger of things to come. Strong encryption had been a tool happily used by the government and military. The government wanted to use modern cryptography because of its incredible strength. But that same strength inspired fear in the hands of other actors. No force on Earth could break such codes. It was such a double-edged sword that the government tried to jealously guard it for itself. It was classified as a munition and its export was restricted[xv]. Computer code and math itself were considered subject to censorship. It was a frightening imposition on free speech. It was also foolish hubris on the part of the government to think that math and ideas themselves could be controlled by fiat.

In 1991 PGP, the first encryption software built for individual use was released. It was both accessible and very strong. The government, feeling threatened, attempted to prosecute its creator, Phil Zimmerman. But the genie was out of the bottle; there was no going back. In 1996 export restrictions were relaxed. It appeared that the attempt to throttle free speech and free cryptography had ended.

As it turned out, it was naive to think that the government would not harbor a deep grudge against strong encryption. That tool it had enjoyed in isolation, when used everywhere by everyone, threatened the state's ability to eavesdrop. As we learned only recently from the Snowden disclosures, the NSA and other agencies have fought a long-running battle to undermine public encryption. Security companies were infiltrated by government spies. Whereas during the Cold War the government spied on foreign governments, in recent times they have spied on domestic companies. Companies such as Microsoft were strong-armed into adding security back-doors into their software. The NSA would have a magic key into every Windows machine. Subtle weaknesses were planted to expose encrypted ciphertext to NSA peeping. Codes that were thought safe turned out to have been compromised by the NSA. There was, and continues to be, a long campaign of subterfuge and sabotage against computer security. The list of abuse stretches on, and is far beyond the scope of this book. It should suffice to say that what were once paranoid delusions have become fact.

Even today, amazingly, the government continues the fight against true public encryption. Apple and other smartphone manufacturers have sought to encrypt their phones' data and communications across the board to protect user privacy. Recent breaches have brought security to the public's attention. However the FBI loudly complains of such standards, arguing that universal, strong encryption will allow 'the bad guys to get away'. This specious argument has attracted the attention of lawmakers; there is even talk of legislating the right to force companies to introduce backdoors for government consumption.

I highlight this brief history to make the point that the Crypto Wars, the struggle between authoritarian instincts and privacy concerns, are far from over. As evidenced by the Snowden leaks, the government has taken incredible steps to undermine Americans' privacy. On the other hand, the intrinsic power of modern encryption is so great that no human force can break it. Ultimately the fundamental advantage lies with technologically savvy privacy-seekers. The government must instead rely on subterfuge, intimidation, and legal maneuvers in its efforts to combat privacy generally.

Bitcoin is part of the Crypto Wars as well. It uses strong encryption, untainted by the NSA, and broadens the power of decentralized actors. As with cryptography, Bitcoin is internally consistent and mathematically unassailable. It empowers small actors, regular people, to accomplish what used to require large, well-connected players. Money itself has been brought under the crypto umbrella. Other pursuits are likely to follow.

In Bitcoin, a form of scarcity has been engineered with the same robustness as encryption itself. That scarcity is a cryptographic entity and thus is subject to no government control, just as encryption has not been. That Bitcoin exists to compete with currency is a direct challenge to governments, who have hitherto dominated it. As authorities decry the spread of encryption because it threatens their ability to surveil, officials will denounce Bitcoin because it threatens their control over money.

The power of the purse is perhaps the most powerful weapon of all. For it to be challenged should come as a severe shock to governments. It seems that this awareness has not fully dawned on many. But it may come to pass that Bitcoin will pose a direct threat to governments. Most of all, it would pose a threat to the US government. Enjoying hegemony as the issuer of the world's reserve currency, since at least 1944, the US has the most to lose from a currency challenger.

A war over money, fought through data rather than with tanks and guns, could loom. It comes at a fortuitous time, as the Dollar may be poised for unprecedented weakness. Had Bitcoin been invented in another era, it may not have posed nearly so much of a threat. Had it come about in the 80's or 90's, one could have said it was less necessary. The Dollar was rather stable after all. Or had Nixon never taken the world off the gold standard in 1971, and we had remained on it, Bitcoin would be much less of a threat. But at this time the potential for dollar weakness is nearly unprecedented. This is a momentous time for Bitcoin, the ultimate economic upstart. For what it lacks in authority or allies, resources or vested interests, Bitcoin makes up in simple integrity. And with the massive expansion of money-printing since 2008, monetary integrity is the scarcest, most valuable asset remaining.

Bitcoin exists within the wider context of cyber strife yet to come. Cyber war will occur, not just between nation-states, but between governments and their people. All sorts of lesser parties will be involved in battles over information. As everyday tasks are more and more abstracted as data, the strategic significance of controlling these data will grow. The imperative for governments to wage war in this field will be overwhelming. Encryption is one such battlefront. But another great question looms, "who will control the databases governing our money, our identities, and things all around us?" Will they be closed databases or open ones? Who will hold the keys? In this network architecture foreshadows society. The decentralized paradigm will contend with centralized competitors which are themselves underwritten by authoritarians. A broader conflict over personal liberty will be played out in the realm of technology.

The Economic Implications of Bitcoin

The decentralized paradigm long predates Bitcoin; it could even be argued as the human norm. When I lived in Africa, I observed first-hand how decentralized economics could solve problems no institution could address.

In Cameroon, where almost everyone is unbanked, cell phone time is paid for via 'credit' rather than subscriptions. This credit is issued by a large telecom. It is then sold to local distributors at a discount. These few sell it to still others. In practice, credit percolates throughout the entire country via a vast decentralized network of small, local vendors. Absolutely anyone can enter this business. In countries with horrible roads, virtually no infrastructure, with failing electricity and institutions, cell phone credit flows incredibly efficiently. Many remote villages, where no goods may arrive, have ample cell phone credit through this mechanism. Amid so much institutional failure, the transmission of credit is remarkably effective. It is only possible because the barrier to entry is so low. Countless entrepreneurs have arbitraged the profit to virtually zero. Very few things in Africa work this well.

Lowering the barrier to entry for suppliers is one of the principal aims of decentralized economics. We have already seen this occur in several industries. From Uber to AirBnB, and many other smaller players, it has been called the 'sharing economy'. It is more apt to call it decentralized exchange. As individuals own things like cars or spare bedrooms, it should have been obvious that these were underutilized resources. But previously it had been costly to transact them between small players. The transactional friction of letting out a spare room prohibited economic activity that would otherwise have made sense. Companies like Uber are merely connecting the dots of unexploited opportunities. This is a lesser form of disintermediation; it is more open to small players than traditional economics, even as it is supervised by a single company.

More purely decentralized forms of exchange could be devised using Bitcoin as their lifeblood. For instance, Uber could be replaced by a purely open market for drivers. Prices could fluctuate more freely than they do under the company's supervision. There could be bids and asks and even futures markets for drivers. What is now an opaque marketplace, controlled by a single company, could be entirely open.

An intermediary like Uber is necessary for the moment because managing payments trustlessly is too difficult. A taxi driver would prefer not to incur the risk incurred with credit cards; he gladly passes it on to Uber or a taxi company. But paid in bitcoins, he would not have to worry. A decentralized Uber, with no center, might be cheaper and more efficient. Uber has surge pricing, whereby prices fluctuate according to demand. But who determines this formula? Who is in a position to arbitrage it away? No one. It is closed. Open markets are so efficient because they transmit information to economic players. Closed markets, on the other hand, involve asymmetry of information; the informed party is in a position to extract asymmetric profits.

The beauty of decentralized economics, demonstrated imperfectly by Uber, is that small players get to participate in markets at a micro level. An Uber driver can drive as little as an hour a week, or even less. In the tumult of markets, this is a form of latent supply that had been untapped. In aggregate these small players can create huge efficiency gains.

Bitcoin equips small economic actors with a heavyweight payments system right out of the box. Because it is invariant to size, there is no disproportionate advantage to large companies over individuals. And because Bitcoin supports cheap microtransactions, amounting even to mere pennies, it enables small scale transactions that would otherwise not have merited the costs.

Certainly not *all* economic activity ought to be decentralized. The importance of economies of scale will not diminish in many industries. Semiconductor plants, to take one example, will remain multibillion dollar investments that cannot be decentralized. But for those activities in which small players have been edged out, by virtue of transactional and informational costs, technology may create more niches. The decentralized economy will likely grow as it ferrets out unexploited nuggets of opportunity. Such a model, in which many small players deliver small services, en masse at unprecedented levels of efficiency, will need a currency to match.

The future may well entail transacting with a huge number of peers for hyper-efficient deals. In some cases, economies of scale will win out, centralizing supply. In others, a vast array of providers may dominate because they are cheaper and more responsive to demand. Users could run open source software that interacts with open markets; the price of even mundane things may fluctuate with the nuances of local supply and demand. An environment in which everything may be arbitraged is one in which profit margins are driven relentlessly downwards. Bitcoin is once again a model, because its exchanges are totally open, and it is built on open-source software. As a guy in a basement in Thailand can today arbitrage bitcoin prices across international exchanges, perhaps arbitrageurs of the future will smooth out prices for everyday services. Bitcoin is both an inspiration and a potential medium for decentralized economics.

Paying Taxes

Many have worried whether governments will be able to collect taxes on Bitcoin activity, either at present, or in a world more fully dominated by cryptocurrencies. The cryptographic, permissionless nature of Bitcoin makes it virtually impossible to confiscate funds, except perhaps through arresting the owner and torturing him for his private key. Unlike bank accounts, bitcoins cannot merely be debited by government fiat. Many worry whether, in such an environment, the government will be equipped with the necessary tools to collect tax revenue.

Leaving aside the question of the legitimacy of taxation, I am not as pessimistic as some in government's ability to collect. It seems quite likely that the government will succeed in collecting taxes, even if direct confiscation of bitcoins remains infeasible. The government has many tools at its disposal to facilitate collection.

Monitoring Money

Consider the parallel with physical cash. I could, in theory, be paid wholly in cash by my employer and then neglect to report my earnings. The government has few *direct* tools to prevent this, just as they have no direct tools to interdict bitcoins. I could bury my cash somewhere secret, and the government could not confiscate it by fiat. It would have to physically find the buried money: a virtually impossible task. And yet, in light of the supposed ease of such a strategy, tax fraud of this kind is extremely rare. Virtually no one, save perhaps the most fringe criminals, attempts to launder money this way. Why not?

Large payments in cash can be tracked, not in the cash itself, but in the entry and exit points, where it is earned and spent. One can ask, where did this money go? Or, where did it come from? If suitable answers cannot be found, a deeper investigation will commence. The cash will either be discovered directly, or inferred with a high degree of accuracy. The perpetrator can be prosecuted on this basis alone. If the cash is not physically found, it can usually be extracted in other ways.

We all know that the government is capable of such monitoring with great ease. Thus the risk-reward balance is too heavily skewed towards risk to justify such efforts. The same logic goes for Bitcoin. How was something bought? Where did this revenue come from? The same questions that complicate laundering of money through cash make Bitcoin a difficult vehicle for money laundering.

Bitcoin is much more traceable than cash. Whereas cash transactions leave no record, Bitcoin transactions are permanent. A complex web of identities can be constructed, as we discussed earlier, making it possible to detect 'undeclared bitcoins'. Via the Blockchain, the entire process of monitoring becomes much more efficient. In this sense, the Blockchain is a tragically double-edged sword; its very immutability may make it easy for the IRS to review our transactions. The same technology that makes Bitcoin's transactional history so transparent also leaves ample records for investigators.

Obfuscatory services will remain to hide the origin of bitcoins. It seems likely that these services will stay one step ahead of those seeking to deanonymize the network. But against this the government still has options. It can discredit, or even criminalize, the intentional mixing of coins for the purposes of defeating detection techniques. It can consider as 'valid' only coins that have never been subject to such mixing services, thereby lowering the value of laundered bitcoins. It is debatable how efficacious such efforts would be. But the government can surely impose pressure to forestall technical countermeasures to surveillance. Even if such pressure fails against a substantial minority of cases, the government's purpose will have been accomplished. The same legal apparatus that makes laundering fiat money a risky affair will similarly make Bitcoin laundering very dangerous. While in a pure, technical sense, the ownership of coins may be robustly hidden, the government has a wide and proven array of tools to discourage evasion among the majority.

Central Players are Points of Weakness for Tax Evaders

In theory I could mail you a block of gold, or physical cash, in exchange for services, without the IRS detecting it directly. But virtually no payments actually happen this way. Central parties are vital in clearing transactions. Visa, MasterCard, and many others facilitate vast numbers of fiat transactions. As large corporate entities, they are scrupulously accountable to tax reporting laws.

While Bitcoin in its purest form is antithetical to the rise of powerful, central players, it is probably inevitable that at least some central actors will arise. Coinbase and BitPay are already major players. My relationship with Coinbase is not peer-to-peer, it is between client and patron. And though one may philosophically prefer decentralized systems, in practice there will be some place for central parties. At the very least, central parties may facilitate activities that remain trustless. The payment channel processors described earlier are one such example; they are not trusted with bitcoins, and yet they are vital intermediaries with exceptional access to information. Any large company that deals with large numbers of Bitcoin customers could become a weak spot for investigators. The susceptibility of large corporations to governmental snooping is amply demonstrated by recent history.

These central players will be points of weakness to those trying to hide their bitcoins from tax authorities. Interacting with regulatory-conscious organizations would compromise an evader's anonymity. Just as I may choose to deal solely in gold bullion, or physical cash, I may use pure Bitcoin totally independent of any service. But in practice losing the convenience of central services, for all the utility they provide, may not be worth the anonymity. This is for individual users to decide; fortunately they may choose how to live on a spectrum of privacy. But the risks of tax evasion, coupled with the necessity of avoiding *all* regulatory-compliant intermediaries, mean that very few will seek to skirt taxes. As with cash, the vast majority of users will be tax-compliant.

Bitcoin may even offer unforeseen advantages to governments. There are technical schemes one could do to identify transactions as compliant or not. Perhaps transactions could include a 'sales tax' output pointing at the government's wallet. It would become mathematically provable to demonstrate that one had paid one's taxes. If taxes must be had, let compliance at least be easier. Since Bitcoin is programmatic money, it could be possible to prove algorithmically and in seconds that one's taxes are correct. W-2 forms would be unnecessary; it's all in the Blockchain. One could receive a tax refund instantly. Deductions such as charity donations would not be vague declarations, they too could be immediately provable (a transaction to a known charity address). Or perhaps if I owed the IRS money, I could simply send bitcoin to their public address. That would save everyone time and expense. Altogether tax compliance costs a vast amount in resources in the US. Including administrative costs, tax prep fees, and the sum value of the man hours spent doing taxes, the costs amount to hundreds of billions of dollars a year. We could actually colonize space with that much money. Making taxation algorithmic could save huge sums and divert skilled manpower to more productive sectors.

There could be entirely new ways for the government to extract money from people (not that this gives me much joy). Auto drivers could be forced to put up a deposit which is algorithmically deducted for parking fines or traffic infractions. The police wouldn't bother pulling you over; your ticket would immediately *self-execute* on your DMV safety deposit. This could be a highly efficient way to incentivize lawful behavior. Multisignature wallets could be used in arbitration or inheritance proceedings with the government holding one set of keys out of many. Smart contracts and multisig wallets could be used to create self-enforcing terms to simplify legal arrangements; feuding parties could be *incentivized* to reach a compromise by the threat that their funds would be vacated if they fail to come to an agreement. All sorts of legal tools could be created that greatly simplify the functions of government.

In pursuit of transparency, auditing, and regulatory compliance too, algorithmic money could help immeasurably. Algorithmic bitcoin auditing could become a facile way for the government to audit companies, measure financial health, and monitory regulatory compliance. A minute-by-minute picture of a bank's solvency, for instance, could be extremely useful. Consumer protection services could save time and energy by resorting to cryptographically robust record-keeping. In many of the tasks of government, which to a great extent involve monitoring money, permissions, signatures, and their rectitude, cryptographic money could help regulatory agencies deliver high quality service.

The bigger risk to government revenue than tax evasion would be their inability to perpetrate negative interest rates on savers. As money that can be independently held, outside banks, bitcoins cannot be forced to undergo negative interest rates. We have also seen that it cannot be inflated away. As of this writing, savers in Europe should be jealous; they are now effectively hostages to negative bond rates. Over $5 trillion dollars' worth is currently held in negative interest rate bonds. Government's explicit means of raising revenue through taxation is probably unaffected by Bitcoin. But its *indirect* and *immoral* means of extracting value, namely inflation and negative bond rates, *are* impaired by Bitcoin.

While Bitcoin may threaten governments in other ways, there is no reason to believe that it can prevent government from collecting taxes. If there is one certainty in life, it is that government will receive its cut. This should not surprise us. The historical norm has been of government's effectiveness in extracting value. When money was physical gold, governments still managed to extract taxes, even though that gold could be hidden. The same goes for paper cash. The obstacle has never been the physical security of money or the practical difficulty of confiscating it. Whether physical, fiat, electronic, or cryptographic, the real obstacle for governments has always been the citizens' willingness to go along with taxation. Pushback from the populace is the only real limiting factor for governmental confiscation, not the technical ease of actually performing it. As long as money is held by people and not machines, authorities will be able to coerce individuals into acceding to some level of confiscation, regardless of the technical security underlying the money.

The Backbone of Universal Decentralization

Cryptography as Identity

We already have identities on the Internet. They're called Facebook, Twitter, and Gmail. We must log into each of these separately. Users don't really own their own identities; they lease them from their true owners: big companies that profit from their data. My online identity is not a single discrete entity that I control. It is a series of weakly held appendages, different from one another, ill-fitting, redundant, and tedious. It's like medieval times when nobles had overlapping feudal obligations to multiple lords. It doesn't make a lot of sense. I must remember a vast slew of different passwords. I have so many profiles to maintain; it has become laborious. It's like tending not one ornate Japanese garden, but three. And the sheer number of Terms of Service I have agreed to surely guarantees me some special place in legal hell.

Digital identity would be much more elegant as a single, consistent entity across all domains. It would have to be controlled independently by the user, apart from the grasp of any one company. It would interface with various 3rd party services, but always in a non-obligatory way, the way my car is not obliged to any one car wash. I could log into websites with it. I could write messages that were undeniably mine with it. I could even perform legal functions using it. I could sign important contracts, move money, post tweets, log into websites, and almost anything with a single digital identity. It would be so convenient. But what form could such a tool possibly take?

A digital entity so dear to my person that it can sign contracts on my behalf should not be controlled by any one company. It cannot exist on a proprietary database. Then it would not really be mine. And it goes without saying that, with all the log-in and signing actions I will do with my identity, it must be cryptographic by nature. Virtually all my interactions with my digital self and the outside world should be cryptographically provable, non-forgeable statements. Cryptography must reside at the very heart of such a scheme.

But if my digital identity were a cryptographic entity, administered by no outside party, and controlled solely through cryptographic keys, then it would be wholly suited to exist on a blockchain. If consensus must be had on certain facts, such as the name of such-and-such identity, what more neutral arbiter is there than a blockchain? Whether built directly on Bitcoin, an altcoin, a sidechain, or some clever variation, a digital entity imbued with such vast powers should exist trustlessly. I should not have to trust any corporation with my Ipassport, my Icitizenship, or my Google-Power-of-Attorney. It should exist apart from any one physical device and it should be subject to no 3rd party control. My identity should be truly mine. It should be both non-corporeal and inviolable. There is no better place for this than a blockchain.

It makes quite a lot of sense for identity and cryptography to become synonymous. My public key could be my outward facing self in every respect. Everyone interacting with me, sending messages, identifying my profiles, sending money, etc., would identify me by my public key. The private key counterpart would be my password, my treasured soul, my innermost sanctum. Hackers have known this for many years. Sophisticated computer users routinely sign messages with public keys proving their origin. Satoshi himself did this. While it may seem esoteric for ordinary people to sign everything they do with elaborate math, it really makes a lot of sense. A digital signature is an elegant, platform-neutral way of proving one's identity, surpassing any handwritten signature, government stamp, or witness testimony. Despite the apparent complexity, computers render the marginal cost of such services to be nil.

Logging into the plethora of websites one meets every day could become dramatically simpler if identity were purely cryptographic. Rather than giving each website a password and rendering it vulnerable to whatever security flaws that website may have, I can offer it a signed message that in no ways helps malefactors uncover my private key. By contrast, under the current system I am supposed to manage a vast inventory of separate passwords for each site I access. To be secure, passwords must not overlap. And they must each meet a sufficient level of complexity. Actually meeting this standard across a wide range of platforms is extremely difficult in practice.

Just as credit cards, by exposing sensitive data to counterparties, make the entire system as weak as the weakest member, the labyrinthine status quo of passwords and identities makes them all as weak as the weakest website. Humans rarely practice the diligence upon which the security of these systems is premised. A single pair of keys that never change, and whose private element is never exposed, could be much easier, robust, and consistent.

The question remains as to what to do if a user loses his private key. If this private key commands such vast powers that it can sign contracts in his name, or change his DMV registration, or move his money, or access his websites, it could be potentially disastrous to lose. Of course, being hacked today is already fairly disastrous. But this remains an open-ended question. Some good solutions may exist, such as waiting periods for especially sensitive decisions like signing contracts. Or one could select trusted family members ahead of time as guarantors of one's identity. For instance, if my private key were lost, a cryptographic vote-of-confidence from my mother and father, signing with their own keys, could create a new key pair to supersede the old one. Certainly other such solutions may exist.

A cryptographic identity would not just utilize pure cryptography. It would need to reside on a blockchain. Certain questions about that identity would need a universal, neutral consensus mechanism. What is the name of this identity? Are there any cosigners to verify its authenticity? Perhaps a baby, upon being born, may be assigned a provably random private-public key pair. Perhaps the doctor who bore that baby signs a birth certificate, cryptographically, and publishes it to a blockchain. A signing operation links the doctor's cryptographic signature with the baby's new identity. The mother, father, and witnesses sign as well with their keys. Now there is a preponderance of cryptographic proof that the key pair belongs to the stated individual. Since all these records are in a blockchain, perhaps even in the Bitcoin Blockchain[2], they are impossible to erase. The full record of evidence, ranging from the signatures of all the cosigners, to the people who cosigned them, to all the other things they have signed, and whether those things have been legitimate, can be surveyed algorithmically. A vast pile of evidence, created by people, but linked inextricably by mathematics, becomes instantly available.

If my identity becomes cryptographic, it becomes untethered from any one place, any one set of documents, or any one nation. I could cross borders effortlessly, while still retaining full command over every aspect of my life. I could disenfranchise countless gatekeepers, whose petty powers would be neutered. I could render obsolete a vast array of jobs premised on shuffling paperwork: the permissions, official documents, and licenses that stifle us. Never go to

---

[2] *Such as via a Merkle root that is published in the Blockchain. One may provably timestamp an arbitrarily large amount of data this way without hitting Bitcoin's scalability limits.*

the DMV again, you need not go in person anyway. A broad swathe of wasteful activity could be slashed out and replaced by purely digital, cryptographic tools.

Cryptographic signatures could be recognized by courts and in legal contracts. Notaries could become extinct, gone the way of ice-cutters, milkmen, and switchboard-operators. Signing a contract could become incredibly simple, effortless, and unbounded. You could sign a contract from Tahiti with your cell phone and it would be undisputable. Contracts could be written, signed, and published algorithmically, all without any doubt of their veracity. If contracts became so cheap to use, a greater portion of economic activity could be encompassed by them. Things that are handled informally now, things too small to justify the transactional costs of a legal contract, could be handled by cryptographic contracts. If, as they say, property rights and the enforcement of contracts are the basis for any capitalistic society, then those rights can only be augmented by making contracts algorithmic. The prosperity that could ensue in providing legal protections for trifling forms of economic activity could be enormous. If the rule of law itself acquires a low transactional overhead, the consequences for society could be profound.

The technology for cryptographic identity and contracts largely exists already. Its implementation is a matter of changing social norms. More faith should be placed in cryptographic mechanisms as they are applied towards new social uses. We shall have to see how and if society adapts.

Cryptographic Finance

We have thus far largely discussed Bitcoin's role as a currency tool. This is what Bitcoin was built for and what it succeeds in doing today. Money, however, is not the only financial instrument that may come of Bitcoin. There is a very exciting prospect of abstracting other kinds of financial instruments on top of the Bitcoin Blockchain. In such a world, any kind of asset that would ordinarily be managed through intermediaries, such are brokerages or title management services, could be represented more powerfully using the Blockchain.

The Blockchain is a consensus mechanism which records the comings and goings of bitcoins. However, it has been known for a long time that other kinds of entities may be abstracted at a layer above bitcoins themselves. There are many ways of approaching this technically, coming under a variety of names: various incarnations of colored coins, sidechains, and other 'meta-protocols'. Ethereum seeks to abstract arbitrary assets in an entirely separate blockchain. This may be ill-advised because it enjoys none of the network effects of a common standard. But whatever the technical implementation, assets may be depicted as digital tokens akin to bitcoins themselves.

A digital asset shares the properties of Bitcoin itself. It is instantly transferrable, cheap, and efficient, the same way bitcoins are. Digital assets are programmable. Their settlement is nearly instantaneous and absolute. As with Bitcoin, transactions cannot be reversed. Asset schemes directly linked to the Bitcoin Blockchain enjoy further advantages. Colored Coins and Bitcoin 'meta-protocols' such as Counterparty inherit the security of the Bitcoin Blockchain: a marked advantage over other implementations.

A digital asset could represent shares of a publically traded company. A bitcoin address can hold digital tokens which are known to represent particular shares. I could create tokens from a unique address inscribed on top of Bitcoin. I could then publicly proclaim these tokens, say 10,000,000, to be shares of Exxon. If Exxon controlled these tokens and promised to honor their shareholder rights, they could then be transacted between Bitcoin addresses. Ownership of these tokens would then be directly equivalent to owning shares of Exxon.

Any kind of paper property, title, or claim, could be represented in this way. Currently, if I own a house it means some county office somewhere has stamped and hand-signed paperwork corroborating that fact. If I own shares of Apple, it is because some brokerage company says I do. These systems involve central, trusted parties. They come with inevitable inefficiencies and trust issues. Consider the transactional expense of buying or selling a home. Lawyers are needed, not to mention forms, stamps, and clerks, to corroborate an informationally very simple transaction. One must even buy title insurance to protect against errors or liability in the transfer of ownership itself. This is a ludicrous waste of resources. It is as if each check or each share transaction required third party insurance to protect against the bank making a clerical error! It is appalling that such things still exist in the 21st century. These are precisely the sorts of industries that may be wholly obviated by blockchain technologies. The maintenance of sound records is not an activity that should require insurance, or indeed any third parties, in the modern era.

Even when you think you own something, you don't really control your paper property. You own it at the sufferance of the law. The control one has over one's bitcoins is unmatched in finance. I cannot truly control my shares of a company except insofar as an elaborate legal framework permits me to. While this may work most of the time, consider the costs. How many well-paid professionals arbitrate full-time, in a legal system renowned for its overloaded complexity, over ownership disputes that ought to be simple? What is the hidden cost for all the people involved in certifying, authenticating, and adjudicating what I own and what I don't own?

Up until now systems of men were necessary to administer ownership; there was simply no other way. But with blockchain-technology, consensus can be arbitrated according to mathematically clear rules. While in some cases we may not be able to formulate objective legal rules, able to be parsed by a computer, in many other cases we certainly can. The house that is transacted need not be accompanied by so many hangers-on, extracting value at each step. Who owns what, be it shares, titles, deeds, and others, could be arbitrated algorithmically according to mutually agreed upon rules with considerable advantages in speed, cost, and fairness.

A system could be constructed whereby stocks were held by Bitcoin addresses and controlled by the underlying private keys. At any time one could ascertain all the addresses owning each share of the company. Dividends could be disbursed to those addresses in bitcoins extremely easily. Why not distribute dividends every week or even every day? The old transactional costs would have prohibited such frequent, precise payments. Bitcoin makes it unnecessary to deliver payments as infrequent lump sums. We should be free of the necessities imposed by old ways.

There will be other advantages to distributed, cryptographic shareholder ownership. Shareholders can prove, by signing a cryptographic message, that they are owners. They may even participate in distributed shareholder votes. Each owner could sign a ballot, to hire a new CEO for example, with the private key controlling his shares. Votes could be collected this way. Pure data itself authenticates each shareholder, his vote, and his share of the company.

If stocks, bonds, and titles become digital assets they will enjoy the unique advantages of Bitcoin. The low transactional costs will mean it could be feasible to publically trade a much broader range of assets than is currently traded. Relatively illiquid assets, such as real estate, which suffers from high transactional costs, could become much more fluidly traded. Greater transparency in markets, even for small items, could deliver markedly greater value to consumers.

Among the other benefits of residing on a blockchain, financial instruments could be self-enforcing. Via various proposed mechanisms, such as multisignature approaches, or other, more advanced techniques, it is possible to construct financial agreements that enforce themselves. There need be no recourse to trusted parties, or even to legal authorities to enforce contracts. Self-enforcing contracts obviate the entire legal apparatus in business disputes. When rules are mathematically foreordained, there is no need for courts. Just think of the productive pursuits to which our excess lawyers could be employed!

With the simplicity of self-enforcing contracts, the risk from legal uncertainty may be avoided. More importantly, the diminution pf legal and transactional risks opens up the possibility of engaging in transactions with a much broader array of people and circumstances. Individuals who previously would have been too untrustworthy to do business with, even under the adjudication of the judicial system, can become safe partners through self-enforcing contracts. By designing agreements such that parties **cannot** steal from one another, regardless of what they think about each other, the number of nodes in the trade web grows dramatically. If I can transact with someone in Bangladesh trustlessly, or even better, enter into a futures contract with him trustlessly, the scope of possible transactions will have grown by leaps and bounds. Greater economic activity must surely result.

These schemes may be coupled with each other in totally unprecedented ways. A house trader may sell a house, which he owns as a digital token, to someone else in a single transaction. That transaction includes the Bitcoin payment for the house; both sides of the trade have been settled in one, trustless move without intermediaries. Perhaps the buyer is a corporation headquartered in Malaysia, the seller in Canada. The house could be resold within seconds, the way hedge funds trade stocks in microseconds. Or perhaps the house is rented out; the proceeds constitute income for the company owning the house. These proceeds are paid out as dividends to the company's shareholders later that day. The dividends are paid proportionately to every Bitcoin address holding that company's shares. It can all be done automatically, simply by running computer code. While landlords exist, and long distance transactions exist, and shareholders exist, these steps cannot all occur quickly, over such long distances, in a way so invariant with the people and nations involved. What economic opportunities would exist but for these missing powers?

Beyond Us

Distributed Autonomous Entities

If the Blockchain is the first entity set adrift with its own logic, others may follow. What if people could be united in purely cryptographic organizations? What if code itself could be set off on its own to pursue its own destiny? Via the Blockchain, parties may be united in a common purpose that knows no boundaries. The normal rules for membership in organizations, whether they be clubs, or companies, or nations, could perhaps be radically stretched. If contracts are self-enforcing, what other mechanisms are needed to coordinate large, disparate groups across great distances? The communities we inhabit, with which we identify ourselves, could themselves be subsumed by cryptographically-driven systems of law.

A Distributed Autonomous Community (DAC) is a community bound only within a cryptographically self-enforcing, trustless system. It uses smart contracts to enforce agreements programmatically. With money and digital assets falling under the purview of algorithms, adjudication can become a programmatic affair. If one's contract is itself computer code, what one has agreed to can be a self-enforcing mechanism, outside any courts or contrived legal structures. Under such a regime, voluntary associations could be formed across incredible distances. The challenges of running any organization, contractual feuding between members, agreement on rules, the handling of money, could be run seamlessly within a cryptographic society.

We already have Google groups, online memberships, and countless siloed web communities. These already exist. But they live within proprietary systems. Perhaps their impact has hit an upper limit; their legitimacy is capped by their authority. What meaning does a Google Group have if it is subject to Google? If an online society had sufficiently grand ambitions, would it be content to live under Google's roof? A cryptographic society could exist independent of any provider.

For example, a simple society could be established on the Bitcoin Blockchain. One of the 'Bitcoin 2.0' protocols (Colored Coins, Counterparty, etc.) could be used to denominate digital membership tokens. Perhaps a multisignature address would be the sole issuer of these tokens. In that case, votes could be held, and encrypted messages transmitted, solely between members. They could send each other money, and even potentially enter into contracts with one another. Some of this could be accomplished without recourse to a blockchain. But by putting it on Bitcoin, no authority could snuff out the society. Perhaps dissidents in China could use such an organization to coordinate, outside the power of their government to intervene or even to erase. Bitcoin could be the ultimate free speech platform.

There could be other kinds of distributed entities too. Distributed websites could exist that have no central location but are *reconstructed* from publically available information on a blockchain. A distributed website might be impossible to censor or shut down. It could leverage the consensus power of the Blockchain to create an uncensorable instruction manual for how to create almost anything: a website, a community, one's own encrypted data, and who knows what else.

The principle of digital scarcity introduced by Bitcoin could be turned towards all sorts of different ends. If people can own something solely by virtue of a private key, that paradigm could conceivably be turned towards all sorts of uses, from membership in a website, to owning data itself, to one's own identity. It's not just the economic principles of Bitcoin that are so inspirational, it is a paradigm in which matters are settled transparently and according to clear rules. It is about empowering people through cryptography to own what they use, to control their own little slice of the Internet. The blockchain will continue to inspire distributed entities that are completely unrelated to bitcoin-as-money. That journey has scarcely begun.

When Machines Own Other Machines

Thus far, we have discussed Bitcoin as currency for the only sphere we know: our own. Human economic purposes appear to be the only economics purposes. No entity has ever controlled money that was not a person, or a collection of them. At all times a human hand has held the lever on every financial decision. So questions of finance, economics, and trade pertained only to us. It would be natural to assume that this was inevitable. But maybe we've been tainted by the short scope of our experiences. What happens if the paradigm is changed? What happens if machines have money? What if machines didn't just interact with money, but actually controlled it themselves? What kinds of economic decisions would a machine make anyway? Let us venture into speculation, for nothing like this has ever happened before.

A vending machine is a very simple case of a machine executing a particular logic to participate in economic decisions. This may seem like a tenuous stretch; by all accounts vending machines are imbeciles making the same idiotic trades, often faultily. But in a sense it is true, a vending machine has been programmed to sell items at particular prices. One could imagine a vending machine that possessed a more subtle logic. Perhaps it changes the price of soda based on its latest observations of the futures market for sugarcane, or inflation, or consumer sentiment, questions it could easily answer on the Internet. Perhaps it images the buyer, matches his demographic with an expected price elasticity, and charges accordingly. This would be a step towards something quite a lot more interesting.

At the other end of the spectrum, high frequency trading bots can be staggeringly complex. These are programs making trading decisions on Wall Street, often run by hedge funds, dealing with serious money. It's no joke; billions of dollars are won and lost on the relative efficiencies of completing algorithms. These bots are highly sophisticated, interacting in a crowded, competitive space. They have been designed for almost anything, it seems. There are trading bots that read Twitter in milliseconds and buy or sell accordingly. The fastest bots compete on timeframes measured in *millionths of a second*. Bots compete with each other, in a wildly complex dance of machines, tricking one another, fooling each other, extracting information, and running wildly complex strategies. All this deeply competitive behavior occurs on time scales that are imperceptible to humans.

If you have doubted the message of this book, that algorithmic solutions can supersede traditional, human ones, you have only to look at modern day finance, where the triumph of algorithms is total.

While vending machines and Wall Street trading bots may be interesting examples, in neither case do these machines actually *have* money. The vending machine may store physical dollars, but it is hopelessly unable to repurpose them without a human hand. The trading bot, though endowed with a complex trading logic, can only make trades on internal databases. While trades are executed on such platforms, dollars are not *actualized* on them at the speed of the bots. Dollars are withdrawn and deposited lazily into human bank accounts. The trading bot only controls money within the confines of a narrow space, a trading platform, in which the ultimate keys are held by people.

Machines cannot truly control fiat money. Because governments insist that fiat transactions be supervised, machines cannot simply execute a transaction and assume that it will be completed. If transactions are reversible, as fiat proponents insist they must be, then machines cannot rely upon them. A system in which machines need to ascertain whether their transactions have been approved by people would be hopelessly cumbersome. Software ought to be able to know absolutely what it owns without having to parse legalisms. If fiat money is subject to fickle things like laws, regulations, or the judgments of people, no machine will be able to manage it independently.

Bitcoin lends itself to machines over any fiat scheme. The latter, no matter how seamless the user interface, must inevitably pass through a bank-clearance layer where it may be subject to intervention, reversal, and scrutiny from authorities. Because Bitcoin transactions need no such human approval, and have no risk of reversal, a machine may always rest assured that its bitcoins are truly its own. Whereas fiat transactions are condoned by people, Bitcoin transactions have the same self-executing finality as the laws of nature.

As money for machines, Bitcoin makes genuinely new forms of economic activity possible. It was meant to be used by machines most of all. While people may enjoy the properties of Bitcoin, they are underutilized in our relatively clumsy hands. Since Bitcoin is composed of data, it may move as fast as the Internet itself. Bitcoin transactions are purely algorithmic affairs at heart. Machines that run *billions of operations a second* deserve a currency to match. It is a natural marriage. By contrast, the timescales of humans are laughably slow. You should ask yourself, what feature of money, apart from its technical obsolescence, necessitates that everyday transactions occur at a human pace? Why aren't everyday economic decisions optimized algorithmically, the same way other activities are smoothed by computer programs?

To a limited extent, computers have already smoothed out pricing irregularities in our everyday lives. If a shop is overcharging for an item, I can quickly lookup its price elsewhere on my smartphone. As a result of the Internet, it is much harder to perpetrate misinformation on consumers. Amazon and other websites allow us to be hyper aware of price discrepancies. Through our everyday, rational consumer choices, we effectively arbitrage prices across an ever-broader expanse of vendors. This has an immense social value, clarifying the price signal as a carrier of information.

People tend to perform price arbitrage very efficiently within the scope of their daily lives. Even the most economically illiterate people, virtually all of us, have a natural affinity for smelling out a good deal. Yet perhaps there are forms of arbitrage not well covered, either in global markets, or by individuals? What sorts of trades exist out there that have insufficient liquidity for technical reasons? What sorts of trades *would* occur but for barriers imposed by transactional costs, insecurity, and slowness? While many markets have been optimized-to-death, rendering them extraordinarily liquid (the stock market), are there any others that are not, but could be?

Commoditizing Bytes

A market for information could arise that prices data at floating rates and with extreme granularity. Information is already bought and sold today en masse. Corporate giants, such as Google and Facebook, in addition to a slew of smaller players, exist to monetize user data. Information has clear financial value. But that data is traded inefficiently. Large players may exchange data easily, in such a way as to make transaction fees meaningless. But how does an individual sell data worth ten cents? Why is data not sold peer-to-peer? When a human must ordain each and every transaction, the fees, the *transactional friction*, is too great. Micropayments for information are unviable, not because they are uneconomical, but because of transaction costs.

This paradigm, in which central intermediaries such as Google capture nearly all of the value from monetizing data, is ripe for disruption. Allowing for the monetization of peer-to-peer activities is a great way to loosen the power of intermediaries.

Mesh networks, in which many small parties cooperate to produce a decentralized graph of connected devices, provide unique advantages. When internet access is shut down, or scarce, mesh networks exchanging bandwidth peer-to-peer may fill the gap. Thus far they have not been well monetized. Whereas peers in a mesh network provide a service worth money, it has not been possible to attach a price. The low value of any one contribution disallows traditional transaction channels. But in aggregate the large number of contributors could produce something far greater than the sum of its parts. The trouble is providing a medium for fast, trustless transactions.

Bitcoin is well suited to address many of these problems. Because it is a currency for machines, data may be bought and sold at the same speed at which it is sent. As devices communicate with one another, they can continuously negotiate and renegotiate prices on a *per packet basis*. Bitcoins could change hands in infinitesimal amounts as services are provided. Lump sums would not be necessary; all payments would be precise down to the last byte. Instead of actually writing and publishing Bitcoin transactions to the Blockchain, devices could use payment channels. As we have seen, these promise to be instantaneous, trustless, and virtually free. Thus they would support the granular, high speed, low trust transactions needed by machines.

So for instance, your phone could constantly search for other phones selling extra bandwidth. Instead of having only one or two providers available with static payment plans, the competitive space of providers would be massive. Your phone could pay the market rate for bandwidth on a per gigabyte basis. Everything in the cost would reflect local scarcity, demand, and the amount of bandwidth used. In an environment without barriers to entry, in which prices may fluctuate freely, consumers will receive the greatest value.

Conversely, a phone with extra bandwidth could sell it, instead of wasting it. It would be likely that individuals would begin to specialize, finding areas of greatest bandwidth scarcity and arbitraging the difference with dedicated devices. The fast responsiveness of many small players will be a huge advantage over the sluggish, entrenched competition.

Data could be bought and sold in many other ways as well. Machines could be paid simply to relay the data they have available. Smartphones could become a remote sensing network in which, perhaps, video from a certain place is paid for seamlessly from somewhere else. Why should Google Street View be static? What if I could pay 2 cents to see a certain street corner in Prague *right now*? Would someone take my offer and stream the video live? Google Street View is only so static, so old, so boring, because it has not been possible to pay people to maintain active feeds. Different market rates would determine the coverage of different areas. Perhaps Timbuktu is trending right now, while Archangelsk is not. Incentives would work magically to create supply in one but not the other. The only reason such systems do not exist at present is not that they would not be valuable, but because there is no technical mechanism to arrange low-value, international transactions.

A Bike Handling its own Safety Deposit

Devices able to control their own money can execute their own logic according to their own purpose. A bicycle could be rented out with a safety deposit. The money could go directly to the bicycle. When it senses that it has been returned back to a proper location, it could refund the deposit minus rental charges. Everything would be precise to the smallest detail; you'd pay the exact amount for the exact number of seconds, or the exact number of miles ridden, or any criteria. A large and unwieldy bike-rental-management system could be entirely bypassed if bikes themselves could handle money. Consider what this accomplishes. It allows software, which has no marginal cost and is infinitely extensible, to replace real world infrastructure.

Everyday devices could have payment terms of superior complexity and less overhead. Because the infrastructure of payments and subscriptions need not be built, small items could be more effectively monetized. There are already many things we own that we only occasionally use. What good is a car that lies idle 95% of the day?

A new model of ownership could arise in which we rent more and own less. The overriding principle would be that things should lay idle as little as possible. And for every use, no matter how small, there should be a precise micropayment. In such a world, I buy only the things I use intensively or absolutely cannot trust to someone else. But everything else, I only pay per use. Such a system would be more efficient in aggregate. We have already seen this with ride-sharing services like Uber. When everyday items can be monetized by everyday people, supply is allocated more efficiently, prices decline, and new forms of economic activity arise.

Blockchains in the Real World

Blockchains can transmit ownership even in corporeal forms outside the realm of currency. A device could use the Blockchain to answer the question, "who owns me?" Access rights could be represented as digital tokens on the Blockchain, whether as colored coins, through sidechains, or other Bitcoin 2.0-type technologies. These tokens would inherit the properties of Bitcoin, such as its security and transmissibility, while denoting *some other* asset class. Just as bonds and equities may be captured as cryptographic, scarce entities on a blockchain, a token for pretty much anything can be created.

A device monitoring the Blockchain could be aware of the current state of any 'ownership token'. An internet-connected, blockchain-aware device could track the movement of the unique token that represents it. As it is passed between addresses, each new address is recognized as the device's owner. Only the owner may encrypt a message, via his Bitcoin address public key, which the device will obey. When a token is transferred to another address, the device ceases obeying the messages of its previous master. In this way, a blockchain-aware machine may respect property rights, even as they are transmitted and transacted at high speed. It also endows that device with ownership rules that are akin to those of bitcoins; mathematical self-evidence is akin to the "laws of nature" whereas fiat instruments must resort to the "laws of man".

Such a scheme, dubbed 'Smart Property', is well within the Bitcoin community's technical capabilities. It would enable two parties to sell ownership of some physical device, such as a car, from anywhere in the world. It is a way of reliably surrendering the rights to something. Because it inhabits the Bitcoin Blockchain, it inherits its protection against double-spending, the primary obstacle to such exchange currently.

Digital property could be abstracted even more easily through the use of smart property cryptotokens. Membership to a website, for example, could become a *tradable commodity*. Consider that almost every personal service we must pay for is inherently an illiquid asset. If cryptotokens were used, all manner of property, whether digital or physical, would become seamlessly tradable. The point-to-point nature of these trades obviates the need for intermediaries and enhances the value captured by consumers.

Digital property could even obey contractual commands, in a meta-protocol abstracted above the Bitcoin

Blockchain or a sidechain. A distinct protocol language could easily be devised governing contractual agreements inscribed in a blockchain. Thus for example, the owner of a car, denoted by a cryptotoken, could agree to a rental agreement with another user. In exchange for bitcoins, an ineffaceable statement is written in the Blockchain detailing the contract's terms, such as access rights for the next 7 days. The car, being blockchain-aware, observes this contract, and gives the renter 'guest access rights' for the next 7 days. Besides the binary nature of ownership, subtler contractual terms may also be enforced via blockchain-aware devices. Rentals, leases, and even arbitrary scripting logic involving other signatures or other data sources, could all be expressed and traded on blockchains. Such contracts would enjoy the same benefits as Bitcoin itself, transparency, trustlessness, and the disenfranchisement of intermediaries.

An API for my House

If devices become blockchain-aware, I could veritably turn my house, the door, and even the dishwasher inside into API servers. Blockchain-awareness could allow for the *monetization* of virtually all devices. This is what has been missing from much of the discussion of the Internet of Things (IoT). Devices shouldn't just be on the internet, they should be living financial organisms, capable of holding money, transacting according to their own logic, being themselves traded, and become easily monetizable for transient use.

In our daily lives, we do not need to own many of the expensive things we occasionally use. I don't need to own the plane I fly on in coach. I don't need to own the expensive machinery I would work with in a factory. We often enjoy contractual, mutually beneficial relationships with capital intensive items that fall short of outright ownership. Why don't we maintain similarly structured financial relationships with other types of assets? Do I need to own my own car, or can I transiently rent a self-driving car, accurately down to the last mile? Perhaps a wide variety of things may be commoditized and actively traded with microtransactions. The number of things one must own in daily life may shrink as we increasingly rent them. This could be a far more efficient financial arrangement.

I want my house to have an API. I want opening the front door to be a cryptographically secure process. My house should be blockchain-aware, such that when I sell it, perhaps while on vacation in Indonesia, a digital token is transferred. In minutes, the house observes this transaction in a provable fashion. Obeying a meta-protocol, it reads a specific Bitcoin transaction as a change in its own ownership state. Anyone trying to spoof such a transaction could not succeed for the same reason that I cannot spoof Bitcoin transactions. As the house detects the change in its ownership, it stops obeying my commands and respects those of the new owner. When he clicks a button to open the front door, an encrypted message is written from his Bitcoin public key owning the corresponding cryptotoken. The message simply states "Open the door". And it opens. Any other such message, even one from its previous owner, would be unheeded. It is, in essence, a key that can be transferred digitally but not be copied.

Machine-Machine Capitalism

If machines can be trained to respect property rights in a truly robust way, then the space of possibilities grows enormously. What then is to stop a machine from owning *another machine*? If ownership is just a cryptotoken, it may be held by anyone who can purchase it. Thus even software itself could own a house! The marriage of blockchains with physical devices allows the mathematical rectitude of the crypto-world to infiltrate into the real one.

Not only could I own my car via a private key, but my car could in turn own a parking garage. I would not own the garage, the car would. The car could write an encrypted message ordering the garage to open. But I could not! Perhaps while the car may be bought and sold between owners, the garage itself remains the property of the car. Because these are cryptographic tokens, even the car's owner would not be able to steal ownership of the garage.

Once my car can own a parking garage, it may then transact it with other cars according to its own internal logic. Perhaps cars will trade parking algorithmically with one another. Who knows what could ensue? Once machines can execute their own financial logic, not just with money but with *each other*, the space of possibilities blows up exponentially.

If ownership becomes purely cryptographic and informational, the role of financial intermediaries could itself be taken up by software. As trading algorithms dominate parts of Wall Street today, perhaps software could trade everyday items. Software could arbitrage away the many little inefficiencies left in typical markets. Tiny price differences, too small to justify the human effort, could continuously be rectified by ceaseless, property-wielding algorithms. For them the marginal cost of any transaction is zero; no profit is too insignificant to justify an algorithm's attention. While price discrepancies are already at an unprecedented, historic low software dealing directly in assets could bring them even lower. In such a world, one could hardly overpay for anything, as anything tractable to software would be arbitraged to death.

In such a world, in which owning anything is merely equivalent to possessing a private key string, the dizzying array of possibilities is hard to fathom. The amazing thing is that what has been described is entirely possible. Bitcoin itself proves that this is so. Extending the benefits of cryptographic ownership to physical items could extend the trustless, algorithmic paradigm much further.

AI Swarms Bound By Blockchain

The future won't just have robots, it will have huge swarms of them. They'll be small, probably non-specialized, and they'll work together to accomplish larger goals. Think about ants. Ants individually are so much simpler than what they accomplish together. There is a logic to their behavior that transcends an individual's programming. We should build machines to behave the same way.

Robots could move in huge, mutually-reinforcing swarms. Sophisticated capabilities that would require a large, expensive robot may be distributed among many, replaceable lesser ones. This lends the swarm far more redundancy. As individual units fail, new ones take their place. Since there are so many of them and they are built to be non-specialized, they can be mass-produced with staggering efficiency.

A robot swarm could be more than the sum of its parts. For example, by sharing sensor data, they could achieve an accuracy far superior to that which could be acquired individually. Consider how your ear works. Individual hairs of different lengths resonate at different frequencies. Only with many hairs, at different lengths, can you integrate their numerous signals to achieve sophisticated hearing. The individual units, the hairs, don't have to be effective at all frequencies, merely one. Indeed, the point goes further; certain capabilities such as interferometric techniques are only possible with large networks of discrete elements. Masses of simple robots can accomplish what highly-engineered individuals cannot.

Consider the parallel with multicellularity in nature. If you stop to think about it, multicellularity is deeply bizarre. If it had not already happened, an unbiased observed would judge it phenomenally unlikely. What began as loosely collaborating colonies of plankton became tightly bound and highly specialized organizations, such as mammals, where only a small subset of cells were destined to reproduce at all. It is staggering to consider that the overwhelming majority of cells in your body are meant to die, are ready to die, in the service of the germ cells (sperm and eggs). Our bodies are collections of celibate specialists who have foresworn any hope of reproduction themselves. Their sole aim, through the most circuitous means, is the propagation of the germ cells. For this they must cooperate in exceptionally choreographed harmony. The maintenance of that harmony is one of the central challenges of multicellularity.

Robotics may take yet another page from biology. The future may contain fleets of drones, building our structures, excavating, performing grand projects, miscellaneous heavy lifting, finding people lost in the wilderness, helping to form mesh networks, deliveries, and much more. We must carefully consider the network architecture underlying so many AI elements. It may not make sense for numerous little robots to obey a central server somewhere else. What should the command and control hierarchy look like? Already the US military chafes against the limitations inherent to controlling drones with human operators from thousands of miles away. Delegating responsibility to local AI will become essential as the number and scope of drones grow. But how to delegate without focusing too much responsibility on trusted 'master' nodes? What happens when master nodes fail? What happens when malicious actors try to spoof commands? What is true and what is untrue in the world of peer-to-peer networks? Who has access? *What happens when the drones start lying to each other?*

Here I believe the Bitcoin Blockchain (or another blockchain built from its principles) may offer some potential. It is a universal consensus ledger: a place to provably and irrevocably write things. Drones may use that to achieve consensus on *other* topics, such as those that pertain to their swarm.

The Blockchain resolves a crucial failing in multicellularity. What happens when cells go rogue? When cells stop heeding the interests of the organism, when the celibate specialists reject their place and pursue their own aggrandizement, we call it cancer. It is a problem that is basically intrinsic to multicellularity. A cell is always only a finite number of mutations away from total rebellion. Mutations accumulate through the progression of time. A fraction of cells will become rebellious due to stochastic forces. When this occurs, as statistics dictate it eventually must, the interests of the individual and the collection diverge. Havoc ensues. This is a fundamental design flaw with, to my knowledge, no ultimate cure.

A similar question should be posed for robotic swarms. How can one prevent the equivalent of cancer between nodes? No matter how many safeguards are installed, a trajectory of devolution will exist that leads to 'robotic cancer'.

Perhaps if robots were designed to obey instructions according to rules posted on the Blockchain, the system of obedience keeping them in check would be vastly stronger than any biological equivalent. Cells slide down a slippery slope; as mutations accumulate, a cell's risk for cancer grows steadily. It is the viability of precancerous states that makes the final cancer orders of magnitude more likely. A mutated cell, halfway to full rebellion, can survive and continue to accumulate the last few necessary mutations. But if fitness had a steeper cut-off, in which the first trace of mutation met with full retribution from the other cells, the pathway to cancer would become almost impossible.

Consider the contrast with deciphering strong encryption; the results are always binary, total success or total failure. In combinatorically difficult problems, there is no steady progress, no slow, upward path to success. Robots could not mutate their way outside of constraints imposed from the Blockchain along a gentle and gradual evolutionary fitness landscape. They would fall off a fitness cliff, from 1 to 0. It would be immediately obvious whenever a robot had gone rogue if subjected to a cryptographic test.

Just as alterations to Bitcoin constitute hard forks that are immediately identifiable, rogue or aberrant drones could be identified from the very first instant. Perhaps honest robots could mathematically prove their own 'loyalty' to the common governing protocol. A Blockchain ledger could ensure honesty between drones, even as they consist of large assemblies of peers with no trusted center.

Discrete math arms us with powers our multicellular bodies will never have. The enforceability of strong encryption and the consensus power of blockchain mean that truths can be mathematically self-evident. This could be used to curtail the divergence of AI robot swarms in a way our bodies cannot do chemically to cancerous cells.

Homomorphic Organisms Inhabiting Blockchains

Homomorphic encryption is an area of cryptographic research experiencing extraordinary breakthroughs. It allows for the most amazing things. I may give you ciphertext to which I alone hold the deciphering key. Neither you nor anyone else will ever be able to decode it. You may then perform boring, repetitive operations on that ciphertext. Do a bunch of mechanical things on it without understanding why. After cranking through operations that are standardized and uninformative, you produce a *different* piece of ciphertext. The results of all this work are as meaningless as what you received. But to me, the possessor of the private key, you have just done computational work. Perhaps you just did 3 + 5 = 8. You not only can't decipher the numbers, you don't even know you performed addition. Only I know.

Homomorphic encryption allows you to perform computations on data *that you cannot actually decipher.* These computations can be arbitrary, meaning that *any* computational task can be performed in this way. Anything a computer does can be ultimately boiled down into simple arithmetic operations. Using this technology, I could assign computational work to an untrusted third party without compromising the security of my data. This offers a whole new world of trustless cloud computing.

If these capabilities feel magical to you, they absolutely should. This is an area of unfolding research and very recent developments. Some of the smartest people in the world are wrestling with such things. In Bitcoin, homomorphic encryption allows for tantalizing possibilities.

What if there were an organism that was purely digital? Imagine a computer program that could sign its own bitcoin transactions in such a way that *whatever computer it exists on cannot steal the bitcoins*. What if a computer program existed, like a virus, but with its own logic on how to write Bitcoin transactions? It could become a financial entity, earning and losing money, that is decentralized and nowhere.

I can already write a script that executes a particular logic, such as executing API calls on other websites and writing Bitcoin transactions. Software can already command money through Bitcoin. But to ever write a transaction, a Bitcoin private key must be exposed in the act of signing. The mathematical steps involved with signing a transaction require that the private key be visible. Thus my script, which spends and earns money, controls money, and writes transactions, could never be executed on an insecure platform. Running somewhere unsafe, its private key could be stolen at any time. With that the script potentially loses control of its money to *every* machine that runs it.

Homomorphic encryption could change the game. It could be possible to sign a Bitcoin transaction using a ciphertext version of *someone else's* private key in such a way that, while the resulting Bitcoin transaction is valid, the computer doing the signing could never have stolen the private key. I could be tasked with executing some particular logic, that I am not even aware of, that inexorably results in me writing only the Bitcoin transactions that the program intended. Any other transactions, such as those I may write to steal its funds, could never be written. Homomorphic encryption converts me from a clever clerk, fully able to read the documents he's working on (and steal their contents), into a totally blind automaton, unable to peek, but still unfailing in execution.

A symbiotic computer virus could exist that *pays* its hosts to run it. What if you ran a script of sheer ciphertext, knowing nothing of its activities, but you received bitcoins regularly in return? What if that script *had no human master?* What if it were encoded with an original logic, and then released into the wild? Its private key destroyed forever, but the logic left running! Funds could be permanently granted to a program such that they could not be redeemed, save through the agency of the program's logic. And yet we humans would be impelled by our own profit motive to run the program. Perhaps some such entities could even earn money on the Internet and thus perpetuate themselves. Consider what that would mean: abstract money held by abstract logic, shielded entirely by cryptography, yet active nonetheless. It's a sort of self-replicating financial organism.

If machines can own money, that is a powerful thing. But if *software* can command money in such a way that not even the hardware it's running on can steal it, then that is altogether different. It is no less than financial logic detached wholly from any physical grounding. To my knowledge such a thing has never before been proposed. I call it a homomorphic digital organism. As far as I can tell such a thing is entirely possible: an amorphous, distributed organism that controls money and performs arbitrary logic, and yet is mathematically inviolable.

How We Get There

Drop in Block Reward

The supply of bitcoins has been growing at a rapid rate since Bitcoin's inception. As we have seen, the number of coins grew dramatically at first, but will asymptotically approach a finite total of 21 million coins. All of the increases, and decreases, of the Bitcoin price occurred in the context of a massive and rapid growth in the total supply. Although Bitcoin is not an inflationary currency, in the sense that its total supply is limited over the long term, the *actual* supply in existence has experienced extreme inflation. This is set to change dramatically.

Next year, in 2016, the automatic block reward will decline by a factor of 2, from 25 BTC created each block, to 12.5 BTC. Thus the growth of the monetary supply will fall dramatically. This will likely have a large impact on price. Currently, miners sell virtually all of the coins they earn, 25 BTC per 10 minutes, or approximately 3,600 BTC per day, on the open market. They convert BTC to fiat money to maintain their mining businesses which operate at razor thin margins. Whereas previously, Bitcoin miners operated with much higher profits, and thus could afford to retain many of their bitcoins, modern miners must constantly sell them.

Unlike most commodities, the supply of bitcoins is totally unresponsive to price signals. If demand were to increase, the supply cannot be expanded, as it is in virtually every other economic arena. At best, coinholders can be coaxed into selling. The decrease in the supply growth of bitcoins could drive the price much higher as fewer coins are sold on the open market. Simply put, because the bitcoin supply is price inelastic, a modest increase in demand can send prices skywards. Similarly, the twofold decrease in the supply growth coming next year could dramatically alter the price dynamics.

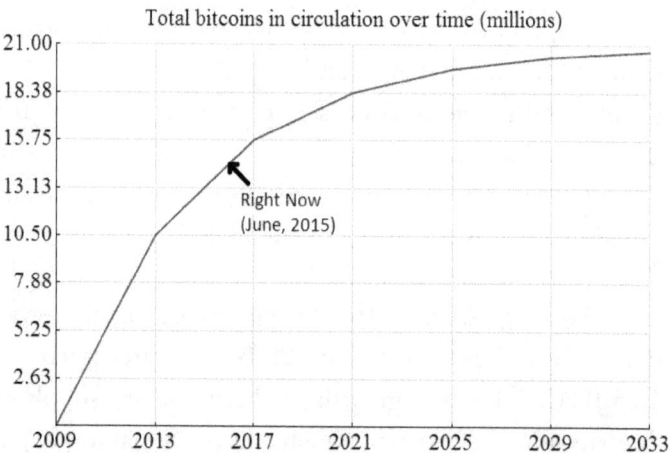

Total bitcoins in circulation over time (millions)

Seen in another light, Bitcoin is a non-inflationary currency. But that fact has been masked by the rapid *short term* growth in its supply. The benefits of owning non-inflationary currency will manifest themselves with the next block reward halving.

The Next Currency Crisis

It's only a matter of time until the next currency crisis. Generally this statement is always true; the world is pretty much always on the brink of a currency crisis *somewhere*. But today crises loom on an unprecedented scale.

A currency crisis could erupt in many places within the near future. The most obvious example is Greece. There they are on the brink of currency failure. First capital controls would be instituted. It would become illegal to withdraw too much money as cash or to have it leave the country. Assets like gold would be interdicted because they provide an exit strategy. At all costs, the government would close the exits.

If Greece left the Eurozone, for example, there could be a series of events that profoundly shake people's faith in fiat money. Such a cataclysm would drive people to Bitcoin in droves. They won't be technophile libertarians, but simply panicked savers looking for a store of wealth that cannot be undermined. It could happen very easily.

Sooner or later, Greece will default. It has to. Barring massive and permanent subsidies from surplus countries like Germany, many of the other weak European countries will default as well. Italy, Spain, and France aren't that much better. They're *all* in bad financial shape. None of them can pay their debts honestly. There could very plausibly be a financial panic on a massive scale.

Bonds that currently trade at 1-2% interest in countries like Italy and France, who should never merit such creditworthiness, could plummet like a stone during a crisis. Under such circumstances, the ECB would have little choice but to print money in massive amounts. And if it isn't the ECB, it will be the Japanese Central bank, which is in even worse fiscal shape, or any of the world's major central banks. For there are virtually no currency stalwarts left around the world.

In an inflationary catastrophe, in whichever country, savers would be crushed. They would flock to safe-haven assets. Anything tangible or offering a yield would rise dramatically in value. Alternative currencies, such as gold, would rise dramatically. But in an environment in which paper money has failed, the biggest winner will be cryptocurrency competitors, namely, Bitcoin.

The Bail-In

It is also quite plausible that, in addition to inflating away the value of money, governments could directly confiscate it in a 'bail-in'. This was already done in Cyprus in 2013. Certain depositors who had nothing to do with the government's debt received a "haircut" on their savings deposits. Basically their money was taken from them by fiat. As electronic money on a centrally administered database, it was incredibly easy to confiscate.

Bail-ins could increasingly become the norm for stricken governments. Greece could easily enact mandatory fees on all deposits to raise money. This is a much more direct form of confiscation than inflation, where one must at least bother to create additional money. Bail-ins are naked grabs of cash from the financial equivalent of innocent bystanders.

Negative Rates

Trillions of dollars' worth of European bonds presently offer *negative nominal* interest rates. As of this writing, you must actually *pay* the German government to borrow from you. This stands common sense on its head. It was previously believed to be impossible. And yet it is reality today.

Negative rates have been imposed through the actions of the European Central Bank. It has driven down yields by buying bonds with printed money, effectively crowding out savers. The foregone interest is another disincentive to holding cash. After all, we are often told that the advantage of fiat money over gold is that the latter does not offer yield. But if there is no yield to be had in paper money, there is very little cost to holding non-inflatable assets like gold and bitcoins.

The Destruction of Cash

With the arrival of negative interest rates, it has become economically rational to hold physical cash instead of keeping it in a bank deposit. It is a sorry state of affairs when cash under the mattress is actually safer than in a bank. But with negative rates, fees, and the risk of confiscation, it can actually make sense to hoard physical money. Financial instruments are being devised today that do exactly this; store physical money in vaults, the way gold is stored. It is ludicrous that such a thing should ever be necessary: another indicator of today's financial insanity.

With the hoarding of physical cash, it is possible for savers to exit negative interest rates, albeit at great inconvenience. Inflation can still sap value, but perhaps less immediately as confiscatory interest rates. The existence of this exit means that rates cannot go *too far negative*. Central banks would love to impose even greater negative nominal interest rates. According to their logic, this would encourage spending and demand. It would also lessen the debt burden on grossly insolvent governments. But it is not possible to set interest rates too low because savers would increasingly opt out of banks.

It is already astonishing that interest rates could be so low as they are today. For them to actually be negative is insanity. And to think that rates should be even more grossly negative because they will increase demand is downright sadistic. It is saying essentially that saving should be so penalized that people don't do it. The resulting spending, really a flight from confiscation, is supposed to boost the economy.

In the pursuit of forcing this involuntary flight-demand, some economists complain that the existence of physical cash is an impediment to the strongly negative interest rates they prefer. Some have offered that *cash itself should be phased out*[xvi]. As a refuge from confiscation, cash is not a team player. All the financial exits must be closed. Keynesian economists are actually starting to suggest that governments end physical cash. It would be unbelievable if it were not actually true.

Governments, particularly those in Europe where rates are lowest, have already started clamping down on cash. France just instituted a law that requires one to show an official identity card to engage in cash transactions exceeding 1000 Euros[xvii]. Denmark has taken steps to phase out physical cash altogether[xviii]. In the US, possessing large amounts of cash is taken as suspicious behavior. It is not possible to opt out of banking without running afoul of the law. One is forced to live under a severely confiscatory and invasive regime. **Our money is not our own.**

The clampdown on cash is often excused for other reasons. In France and the US, impositions come in the name of anti-terrorist or anti-crime measures. This is naked authoritarianism. It is an awful coincidence that the most indebted countries in the world would impose such restrictions on their citizens. The link between terrorist activities and physical cash seems extremely tenuous. The real agenda is an imposition on one's right to possess property independent of central authority. We are to only own anything by their leave and at their sufferance.

If these forces accelerate, there will be an inevitable backlash from regular people. If cash cannot be had, alternatives will be found. There are limits on governments' power to subdue the rational economic behavior of millions of people. Confiscatory policies cannot be imposed without limit; individuals will find a way to opt out. They will buy hard assets. They will seek out alternatives. And it just so happens that a ready-made, censorship and confiscation-resistance alternative already exists. It's a perfect tool for those who want to opt out while still retaining the advantages of currency. Gold is bulky and difficult. Real estate is only owned by the leave of local authorities. There is only one medium that cannot be broken by outsiders, but still has international value. It possesses the fluidity of conventional money, the integrity of gold, and the lightness of a password. Bitcoin will be the ultimate alternative, the ultimate safe-haven asset when fiat currencies fail.

The world isn't used to currency alternatives. Previously when fiat failed, as it has many times throughout history, the alternative was *another* fiat currency or, at best, gold. These were easily interdicted. Now a plausible alternative exists that cannot be stopped. Bitcoin offers a historically unprecedented escape valve for the next currency crisis. Rational self-preservation by individuals, and the misdeeds of governments, will propel Bitcoin. In this, technology will satisfy a long-denied human want: truly sound money.

Bibliography

[i] *Jameson, J.F., Narratives of New Netherland, 1609-1664, p 176*

[ii] *Indian Money as a Factor in New England Civilization, William Babcock Weeden, p. 396*

[iii] *Lynch, John, Spain During the Price Revolution*

[iv] *Cooper, J.P., The New Cambridge Modern History: Volume 4, The Decline of Spain and the Thirty Years' War, p.442*

[v] *Braudel, Fernand, Civilization and Capitalism, 15th-18th Century: The wheels of commerce. P .171*

[vi] *A Method for Obtaining Digital Signatures and Public-Key Cryptosystems, Rivest, Shamir, Adleman, Communications of the ACM, Feb. 1978*

[vii] *https://blockchain.info/charts/tx-trade-ratio*

[viii] *Argentina's official peso weakens to record low of 9 per US dollar, Reuters, June 2, 2015*

[ix] *A TALE OF TWO 'GLOBALIZATIONS': CAPITAL FLOWS FROM RICH TO POOR IN TWO ERAS OF GLOBAL FINANCE, MORITZ SCHULARICK, International Journal of Finance and Economics, 2006*

[x] *See the IMF website for reserves by country, http://www.imf.org/external/np/sta/ir/IRProcessWeb/colist.aspx*

[xi] *Deflation and Depression: Is There an Empirical Link?, Andrew Atkeson, Federal Reserve Bank of Minneapolis*

[xii] *http://coinmarketcap.com/*

[xiii] *http://www.reuters.com/article/us-bitcoin-ibm-idUSKBN0M82KB20150312*

[xiv] *Alpha Technology Takes Pre-Orders for Litecoin ASIC Miners, Coindesk.com, http://www.coindesk.com/alpha-technology-pre-orders-litecoin-asic-miners*

[xv] *Department of State – International Traffic in Arms Regulations, April1, 1992, Sec 121.1*

[xvi] *Costs and benefits to phasing out paper currency, Kenneth Rogoff, NBER Macroeconomics Annual Conference*

[xvii] *France steps up monitoring of cash payments to fight 'low-cost terrorism', Reuters, 3-18-2015*

[xviii] *Denmark proposes cash-free shops to cut retail costs, Reuters, 5-6-2015*